PUBLIC TELEVISION
AMERICA'S FIRST STATION
AN INTIMATE ACCOUNT BY WILLIAM HAWES

SUNSTONE
PRESS

SANTA FE

Sunstone books may be purchased for edcational, business, or sales promotional use. For information please write: Special Markets Department, Sunstone Press, P.O. Box 2321, Santa Fe, New Mexico 87504-2321.

First Edition

Printed and bound in the United States of America

10 9 8 7 6 5 4 3 2 1

Library of Congress Cataloging in Publication Data:

Hawes, William, 1931-
    Public television: America's first station: an intimate account
    /by William Hawes.—1st ed.
        p. cm.
    Includes bibliographical references (p.137-157) and index.
        ISBN: 0-86534-245-8 (case)
1. KUHT-TV (Television station: Houston, Texas—History.
2. Public television—United States—History. I. Title.
HE8700.79 U6H38   1996
384. 55' 06' 57641411—dc20   96-14798
                                                CIP

Published by   SUNSTONE PRESS
                  Post Office Box 2321
                  Santa Fe, NM 87504-2321 / USA
                  (505) 988-4418 / orders only (800) 243-5644
                  FAX (505) 988-1025

To the pioneers

of what is now called public broadcasting,

this book is affectionately dedicated.

CONTENTS

PREFACE

The venture was speculative, risky and expensive, the kind of action some Texans go for, like bringing in an oil well. But at five o'clock in the afternoon on 25 May 1953, the first public television station went on the air: KUHT-TV, Channel 8, Houston, Texas. In those early days it was referred to as an "educational," not a "public," television station and the main reason for its existence was to educate a growing university community.

This project was serious business, the culmination of efforts by many people from all over the country: one tenacious woman believed in an alternative television service, a pragmatic university president needed an effective way to instruct a surge of new students, a wealthy philanthropist with little education himself wanted to help working men and women, a dynamic politician and showman was able to inspire a dedicated staff and many volunteers, and finally a federal bureaucrat helped to give educators an opportunity to articulate their perspectives. Meanwhile, Texans, never hesitant about letting the world know of their achievements, have not lost sight of the fact that KUHT-TV was born during the presidency of one Texan—Dwight D. Eisenhower—and the Corporation for Public Broadcasting came into existence during the presidency of another—Lyndon B. Johnson.

In any case, prior to KUHT-TV no one had put all of the elements together to create a noncommercial educational television station. The odds against a fledgling private university, on its own a mere eight years, bringing a successful television station into existence were high. But no one at the university thought it would fail, and it didn't. The station was on the air for about seven months before the next successful station entered the marketplace.[1]

KUHT-TV is mainly important for its primacy, some early innovations, and its tenacious struggle to remain on the air. Channel 8 defined what an alternative television service could accomplish. By experimenting in credit and noncredit courses for universities, junior colleges and public schools, KUHT-TV demonstrated the potential for an instructional television (ITV) service. By introducing a variety of low-cost enrichment programs, it suggested a range of subjects a select audience would enjoy and appreciate. By filming some early programs, it hinted at the level of quality more money and sophistication would eventually produce. Educational television revealed human experience to a select population, often consisting of intelligent adults, children, and others not well served by commercial broadcasting. The KUHT film unit proved that enrichment programs well conceived and executed could compete with all other kinds of programs, and would enjoy longevity. In fact, a few films made in Channel 8's initial years are still in world circulation. And, to its credit, KUHT-TV got on the air without financial assistance from the federal government or foundations.

After the passage of the Public Broadcasting Act of 1967, KUHT-TV became a founding member of the Public Broadcasting Service (PBS). PBS brought stimulating, imaginative, insightful information and entertainment programs to viewers. Consequently, over the next 15 years Channel 8 gradually relinquished its prime time hours to PBS and its daytime schedule to the Houston Independent School District (HISD). Channel 8's role then became that of an exhibitor of programs mainly produced outside the station. But with the introduction of cable television to Houston during the 1970s, competition for viewers intensified. By the time HISD programs were largely terminated in the mid-1980s, Channel 8's heyday of providing local programs relevant to the Houston area was long past. Thus, as the station approached its 40th anniversary in 1993, seeking more money from fewer funding sources and new facilities for sustaining its PBS exhibitorship, the question being asked was, "Why?" Why should the Houston public in the 1990s support Channel 8, or for that matter PBS, when a plethora of available cable channels provide the alternative services Channel 8 once offered exclusively?

Channel 8 has always fought for survival, and it has continually been snatched from disaster due largely to its devoted employees, student interns, community volunteers, viewers, underwriters, commercial broadcasters, critics, and regents who believe that Houston Public Television is contributing a unique service to the region. So long as Channel 8 involved its viewers with issues of local interest and allowed them to participate or provided alternative television services, KUHT has had public support. Perhaps that loyalty will continue. Indeed, of the many theatrical venues, museums, libraries, and institutions of culture and learning in the greater Gulf area seeking support, none serves a larger or more diversified population every day than does Channel 8.

While visiting the Broadcast Pioneers Library in Washington, D.C., I realized that one aspect of television history that has not been well preserved or documented is the history of this first public station, located on my own campus. Director Catharine Heinz suggested that an interview with the Hon. Rosel H. Hyde, who was FCC chairman when KUHT-TV went on the air, would be a positive start. I have known nearly everyone who has worked at Channel 8, especially those responsible for major decisions. I first visited the station in 1960 and joined the radio-television faculty in 1965. I created the University of Houston's student laboratory series, currently titled *Video Workshop*, and thereby, Channel 8's first local colorcast, in 1967. I produced briefly KUHT's *The Arts in Houston* and narrated commencement exercises from 1967-72. I was station manager of KUHF-FM from 1965 to 1969, and therefore, am familiar with the relationships of radio and the academic department to KUHT, and with the dedicated service of those who have participated in its benchmark historical accomplishment.

Where possible, I let the participants tell their own story, for I have had interviews and conversations with many of them, including those recently deceased: Walter Kemmerer, Paul Owen, and John Schwarzwalder. Noteworthy printed sources are the university's only history, *In Time: An Anecdotal History of the First Fifty Years of the University of Houston* by Patrick J. Nicholson, the minutes of the UHS/UH Board of Governors/Regents from 1945 to 1994, *The Daily Cougar*, and the columns of *Houston Chronicle* TV Editor/Critic Ann Hodges. Specialists helping to find information sources were Jill Pickett, communications director, KUHT-TV, Peggy Cervenka, executive administrator, University of Houston System, and Patricia Bozeman, head, Special Collections, University of Houston Libraries. Photographs are primarily courtesy of KUHT-TV and Special Collections, UH Libraries. Recent KUHT photographs are the work of David Dale.

My appreciation goes to James Clois Smith, Jr., for recognizing the importance of this history and to his fine staff at Sunstone Press on their 25th anniversary year. And my gratitude, as always extends to my family—Ella, Kent, and Robert—and to Michael Cloud for their unwavering love and support.

—William Hawes
Houston, Texas

1

ORIGINS OF BROADCASTING

After World War I, as radio stations sprang up across the nation, some form of federal regulation for this broadcast medium seemed necessary. That matter came to a head when in 1926 the courts ruled that licensing by the Secretary of Commerce under the Radio Act of 1912 was unconstitutional.[1] A series of conferences resulted in the Radio Act of 1927, which established the Federal Radio Commission (FRC).[2] The FRC was to determine engineering standards, assign frequencies for operation, and then presumably, dissolve. Radio stations were licensed according to specific engineering requirements in regard to use of the amplitude modulation (AM) portion of the spectrum. Agreements were reached nationally and internationally. "Finally it became apparent that the dynamic realm of radio communication would continually raise difficult administrative problems, and the FRC was made a permanent body on December 18, 1929."[3]

FEDERAL REGULATION AND NON-PROFIT GROUPS

Authors of the Radio Act and others were concerned about the encroachment of advertising and the tendency toward monopoly by wealthy companies. To protect the interests of non-represented or non-profit groups, Congress passed the Davis Amendment in 1928 requiring the FRC to make reallocation of the spectrum. "It was the resulting reallocation, which was mandated by the FRC in late 1928 in the form of General Order 40 and a number of following directives, that established the framework for modern U.S. broadcasting." [4] The reallocation, however, resulted in stronger networks, increased growth in advertising, fewer frequencies, and the near demise of non-profit broadcasting.[5]

During the reign of the FRC, lobbying on behalf of education proved futile; no legislation was forthcoming. The FRC took the position that whatever needed to be done for special interest groups, including educators, could be accomplished by commercial broadcasters and that government should not reserve a major role for itself or provide direct funding for broadcasting.[6]

By 1933, commercial broadcasters were looking for permanent legislation. This time was the depth of the Depression, and President Franklin D. Roosevelt faced numerous problems concerning the economy. To expedite communications legislation, he had Secretary of Commerce Daniel Roper appoint a committee to make recommendations. Without discussing radio, the Roper Committee took a position that favored the commercial broadcasters. In early 1934, at the request of Secretary Roper, an independent committee was asked to study the radio question; but within two months Senator C.C. Dill, Democrat of Washington and author of the 1927 legislation, and House Representative Sam Rayburn, Democrat from Texas, had convinced FDR to cancel it, thus squelching further discussion of non-profit broadcast allocations.[7] Rayburn was aware that a few Texas radio stations had been licensed since 1920, and were owned by some of the most powerful men in the state; especially Governor William P. Hobby and multi-millionaire Jesse H. Jones.[8] As the non-profit broadcast issue faded, Father B. Harney, a Catholic priest, rallied impressive popular and labor support for an amendment requiring the new FCC to set aside 25 per cent of the channels for non-profit stations.[9] Again, Senator Dill managed a compromise that would ensure passage of the bill without the amendment's constraints.

Based largely on the Radio Act of 1927, Congress rewrote the legislation as the Communications Act of 1934.[10] Although it has been amended frequently, it provides the substance of federal jurisdiction over interstate communications and replaced the FRC with the Federal Communications Commission (FCC). In section 307(c), however, the non-profit matter persisted, for the Act says: "The Commission shall study the proposal that Congress by statute allocate fixed percentages of radio broadcasting facilities to particular types or kinds of non-profit radio programs or to persons identified with particular types or kinds of non-profit activities, and shall report to Congress, not later than February 1, 1935, its recommendations together with the reasons for the same."[11]

The FCC conducted hearings while the educational AM radio stations dwindled from 171 to only 38 operating stations by 1937."[12] I attended the hearings," Rosel Hyde said reflecting on his many years in government. "Then the Commission made a report to Congress. It was a very brief one. It determined that there wasn't enough spectrum space to allocate specific amounts for specific subject matter. It wasn't necessary to do this, because a licensee of a radio station has the duty under the Act [to serve] the public interest, convenience and necessity, [and] to serve all elements of the public interest in its community."[13] The government held this position regarding educational broadcasting until after World War II.

When the war ended in 1945, the prospects for noncommercial educational broadcasting were considerably brighter. One reason was the new frequency modulation (FM) radio service. Though technically superior to AM, FM was not looked upon as having any great commercial value, yet both commercial and educational broadcasters were encouraged to use it. Even so, the proliferation of FM radio stations on campuses and the emergence of an educational network lagged. Educators were wary of investing limited financial resources in radio, when signs of returning servicemen flooding the campuses required expenditures elsewhere. Then too, television, which had been delayed in its development because of the war, was beginning to appear and its potential for education seemed even greater than radio. Nevertheless, in 1948, to ease the cost of educational FM stations and to encourage them on campuses, the FCC allowed licensees to reduce the usual 250-watt minimum to a mere ten watts, enough power to reach a two to five-mile radius from a transmitter that would more than cover most campuses. The number of educational FM stations increased from six in 1946 to 92 in 1952, more than one-third of which were 10-watt operations.[14]

Even educators who were enthusiastic about FM and television recognized the immense problems associated with these media; yet, interest in broadcasting remained high. Experiments and classes using rudimentary teaching tools quietly proceeded. By the mid-1940s, the FCC was being asked to allocate certain television channels exclusively for educational use. Meanwhile, commercial stations held to the notion that they could meet the needs of education without comprehending the scope and the depth of programming some educators had in mind. As commercial television gained momentum, educators began to work together to convince their school boards that educational broadcasting had a unique role to serve and would greatly benefit the multitudes of new students.

FCC COMMISSIONERS AND EDUCATIONAL TELEVISION

The FCC consisted of seven members appointed by the President and confirmed by the Senate. A brief sketch of the FCC membership will suggest the delicate political nature of the commission, as well as its leanings. Of FDR's original seven appointees, five of them served more than ten years. The agency, therefore, was relatively stable. The key figure was the FCC chairman designated by the President. President Harry S. Truman's criteria contained three components: "First, it was essential to have an energetic chairman who has strong sympathies with broad administration objectives and the political ability to carry them out. Second, since the chairman could not operate effectively without a majority in the commission, commissioners were selected who could be counted on to be generally cooperative, which meant the agency chairman was consulted on the decision. Finally, while partisanship was allowed to dominate the selection of the chairman, President Truman deemphasized this faction in his selection of a majority of the commission; that, in itself, was an adroit political move which furthered the President's objectives without antagonizing the Republican leadership.[15]

From 1947 to 1952, Truman's key figure at the FCC was Chairman Wayne Coy. He was generally supported by four commissioners who had lengthy careers in communications regulation. These experts included the elderly Paul

Atlee Walker, who was originally appointed by FDR in 1934. He had seen radio and television come of age. While studying for his law degree at George Washington University, Rosel H. Hyde was hired as disbursing officer at the FRC in 1928. An avid radio technician since he built his first receiver in 1908, George Sterling was largely self-taught. From serving in the Army Signal Corps during World War I to becoming chief engineer for the FCC, Sterling was a very knowledgeable practitioner. A naval officer appointee, Commodore Edward M. Webster, was highly recommended by then-Chairman Charles R. Denny. Webster graduated from the U.S. Coast Guard Academy in 1912 and became a recognized expert on maritime communications. After retirement from the Coast Guard, he too joined the FCC as an engineer.[16]

In the 1948 presidential election year, Truman appointed Webster, an independent, and Sterling, a Republican. At the time the Republican-controlled Senate believed that Truman would not be elected once he had completed his term after the death of Roosevelt. Within the year another FCC vacancy occurred, and the Senate was in no mood to let a Democrat President appoint someone for a seven-year term to the FCC. This time President Truman nominated an active Jewish Democrat, Frieda B. Hennock (1904-60). Miss Hennock was the only female associate of Choate, Mitchell and Ely, a 140-year-old New York law firm, Hennock's appointment took some powerful maneuvering by her friend, Julius Klein, who was national commander of the Jewish War Veterans. Klein obtained an interview for her with Republican Leader of the Senate, Robert A. Taft, who later said, "It is fair to say that her confirmation grew out of that interview."[17]

During her confirmation hearing Frieda Hennock assuaged all doubts concerning her ability to be independent. Television was not mentioned. Once confirmed however, she took an aggressive, outspoken and hard-working position, especially toward educational television, a cause she would champion. "She became impatient for the day when television would become an electronic blackboard, 'a classroom of the air,' serving American students as the proscenium from which culture was to enter the living room of every home."[18] Commissioner Hyde recalled that Commissioner Hennock was a very talented person particularly in press relations. "She apparently felt that a commissioner ought to have a cause to make themselves known. She took a considerable interest in educational television. She sort of envisioned herself as carrying on a crusade."[19] In contrast to Oveta Culp Hobby, a staunch member of the Republican party and the establishment, who was the World War II commanding officer of the Women's Army Corp (WAC), Frieda Hennock, "a Democrat, radiated the confident glamour of a woman who had been a stunning beauty in her earlier years. Decked out in modishly tailored black dresses and a well-cut blonde coiffure, she was still winning the battle against the ravages of many state dinners and Washington cocktail parties. She always attracted attention at public events, arriving late and swishing up to the dais in a floor-length ermine wrap."[20] On 30 September 1948, three months after Hennock joined the Commission, the FCC temporarily suspended action on all new permits. The 108 television stations with allocations or construction permits were not affected. The Freeze, as it came to be known, lasted for 43 months (1948-52). It allowed Commissioner Hennock and educators time to mobilize. Hennock fashioned a unique stance in regard to her role on the Commission. "Not content with a passive regulatory role, it was Hennock who organized the FCC's first consumer constituency around the issue of reserving channels for educational use."[21] Rather than letting the commercial broadcasters' old argument prevail, she pushed her position that television was the "electronic blackboard of the future"; and consequently, organized a campaign, unlike anything the FCC had seen before, that aroused support in the academic community.

Hesitant educators notwithstanding, by spring 1948, at least five universities were active in educational television. "The University of Iowa had applied for a station, Iowa State University had received a construction permit, the University of Michigan was providing educational programs over a Detroit station, American University was doing the same on a Washington, D.C. network outlet, and Kansas State University was continuing experimentation. In February 1950 Iowa State's WOI-TV at Ames, Iowa, became the first nonexperimental educationally owned television. Taking some programs from the networks and selling advertising, the station was able to support a variety of educational programming without expense to the university."[22]

Legitimate concerns surfaced and were presented to the FCC. They centered on these issues: First, if educators had specially designated station allocations would they have the money, the production capability, and adequate facilities to attract sufficient audiences so that the precious frequencies would not be wasted? Second, if educators were limited to allocations in the UHF range only, would they be denied potentially large audiences especially in urban areas, where most of the viewers were unable to tune in the UHF frequencies during these years long before the all-channel selector was required (30 April 1964) on television receivers? Third, if, as expected, commercial stations gained popularity mainly as purveyors of news, entertainment, and commercials, wouldn't educational programming be relegated increasingly to less attractive time periods? The answer to these questions was "yes."

Encouraged by Commissioner Hennock, numerous educators appeared before the FCC. While the FCC's Freeze remained in place and vigorous debate concerning allocations, color and other matters raged, the value of a television channel became increasingly apparent. "Television's revenues increased spectacularly between 1950 and 1960, rising from about $106 million in 1950 to over $1.25 billion in 1960."[23] This rise prompted more zealous lobbying by commercial broadcasters against reservations for educational television.[24] Simultaneously, Commissioner Hennock and numerous educators had several months to build a convincing case for an alternative to commercial broadcasting.

UNIVERSITY OF HOUSTON BROADCASTING

In 1950 the University of Houston joined the venture into FM radio with extraordinary enthusiasm. Grand FM facilities were built. These facilities would provide the home for educational television within three years, but no one imagined that at the time. The university was little more than an experiment itself. About 20 years before (1924), the Board of Education for the Houston Independent School District (HISD) had hired as its superintendent of schools Dr. Edison Ellsworth Oberholtzer (1880-1954). Dr. Oberholtzer was born into a large family in 1880 and spent much of his early life being educated in and teaching in Indiana rural schools. With a great deal of perseverance he gradually obtained his teaching credentials while rising up the ladder of public school administration, culminating in a doctorate from Columbia University and as head of Houston public schools. Within a few years of his arrival, Dr. Oberholtzer and the Board of Education recognized that its graduates, many of whom worked while going to school, needed to further their education by attending advanced classes at an institution within the Houston area. Although Rice Institute, later renamed Rice University, existed, it was unable to meet the broader educational needs of the community.

So, the Board of Education added to its responsibilities the development of a junior college. On 5 June 1927 summer classes began at the newly formed Houston Junior College (HJC). Dr. Oberholtzer was given the leadership role for both the HISD and HJC. In 1929, to assist him with his complex duties, Dr. Oberholtzer, who was always reluctant to delegate authority, hired a bright young graduate whom he had met at Columbia University, Dr. Walter William Kemmerer (1903-1994). It was Kemmerer, a staunch, sometimes stubborn, hardworking liberal administrator who grasp the idea that instruction could be delivered to students economically by way of television.

Dr. Kemmerer became director of curriculum for the HISD, and subsequently, the HJC. Besides, his administrative skills, he introduced a key concept to Houston Junior College—vocational studies. The HJC offered many traditional courses, but it catered largely to career oriented adults. An early survey indicated that among HJC 19-year-olds, radio, which was just emerging nationally as a mass medium in part because receivers were still costly, ranked seventh on a list of favorite subjects.[25] To technical radio courses already offered in electrical engineering, Kemmerer added a non-technical radio course in speech as his first expansion of the HJC curriculum.[26]

The workload for Oberholtzer and Kemmerer was staggering. In fact, Dr. Oberholtzer did not carry the burden for running the HISD alone. His co-equal, in what was admitted to be a weak administrative structure, was H. L. Mills, business manager and a vocal Oberholtzer rival. The opening of the HJC, its good enrollments and fairly sound financial start, together with the rivalry, aided the rather swift upgrading and separation of HJC from the HISD. After a great deal of maneuvering, Dr. Oberholtzer accepted the charter establishing the University of Houston as a four-year institution on 9 June 1934, the same month the U.S. Congress passed the Communications Act establishing the FCC. Formal classes for the university began on 19 September 1934, with Dr. Oberholtzer as its president and Dr. Kemmerer as vice president. They would continue to build the university for the next 16 years.

Everything about the first decade of higher education was temporary. For a while the HJC/UH was housed at San Jacinto High School and then very briefly in the Second Baptist Church. Some HISD faculty served part-time in the junior college, until a permanent core of faculty was hired for the University of Houston. An immediate search for a suitable location eventually located donors and purchases of land from the J.J. Settegast estate, Ben Taub, Monroe D. Anderson, and Hugh Roy Cullen. Of these distinguished city fathers, H.R. Cullen took a personal interest in the university. Soon the campus consisted of 250 acres of swampy mosquito land shaded by numerous native trees and occupied by some snakes.

"I remember our first visit to Mr. Cullen's office," Dr. Kemmerer recalled. "Dr. Oberholtzer and I went down to see him about getting a possible gift for the university. At the time he was always involved in politics. He was trying to defeat somebody or get somebody in. He said he had more money than time, so we were glad to help him get rid of some of it. I prepared a bulletin on the University of Houston. I had it off-set printed, hand-lettered, not set in type. The center spread of that bulletin showed the typical night school student getting up in the morning, having breakfast, going to work, going home, having supper, and going to the university. Then I gave it to Mr. Cullen. That was the one thing that appealed to him. That sold him."[27]

Hugh Roy Cullen (1881-1957) was born 3 July 1881, in Denton County near Dallas. He spent his youth in San Antonio after his parents separated. At age 12, without completing the fifth grade, he quit school and went to work in a candy factory for three dollars a week. Tenacious and hard working, at 17 he had gained experience in the cotton business and opened a real estate office in Houston, buying oil leases. In 1918 he hit it big in the oil fields of West Texas, where other companies had drilled and failed. His Quintana Petroleum Company amassed a fortune. In 1938, the death of his only son, Roy, redirected his philanthropic efforts toward the fledgling University of Houston, and the idea of young adults working while attending school.[28] At the dedication of the first building on the new university campus—the Roy Gustav Cullen Building—on 4 June 1939, the Reverend Dr. F.B. Thorn, pastor of the Second Baptist Church where the university's first day classes were temporarily held, reminded the assembly of

Cullen's objective: "I have only one condition in making this gift. The University of Houston must always be a college for working men and women and their sons and daughters. If it were to be another rich man's college, I wouldn't be interested."[29] So long as administrators followed Cullen's sage advice, it served a unique role in the Houston community.

Throughout World War II the frugal, much admired and highly respected Oberholtzer pursued a steady, cautious path through periods of low enrollment, and consequently, low revenue. Simultaneously, Kemmerer kept track of enrollment trends that proved to be generally accurate. "From a student body of 2,700 in 1941, Houston grew to 8,500 in 1947 and has 14,000 this year [1951]."[30] The GI Bill aided returning veterans eager to resume civilian life, resulting in a campus alive with thousands of young men and women wanting a college education, while they supported themselves by working in the city. How could the university provide enough faculty and enough classrooms? Where could it find enough money to meet the demand?

A modest cluster of permanent buildings were being constructed around a central quadrangle. There was the Roy Cullen Building, a science building, and nearby, a half-stone, half-wood building for technology, the Recreation Building, commonly referred to as the "Cougar Den," and a lot of holes and trenches for sewers in preparation for a second major building, the Ezekiel W. Cullen Building. A bustling community of "shacks," temporary quarters provided by the government, sprang up as classrooms for radio, band, orchestra, and dramatics. Shacks also provided significant low-cost housing for veterans whom Kemmerer encouraged by means of innovative "refresher" courses.

On 12 March 1945, a few months before the second world war ended, the University of Houston was separated from the Houston Independent School District by action of the Texas Legislature, Senate Bill 207. The University of Houston Board of Regents was immediately organized, and Dr. Oberholtzer was offered the presidency of the University of Houston and its branches, which included the Houston College for Negroes.[31] He readily accepted the position for the sum of $15,000. Dr.Kemmerer, who had different titles over the years but served in the same basic capacity, was now assistant to the president. At last the University of Houston was established as a private, non-tax supported four-year institution.

As enrollment increased, the curriculum expanded. Reflecting change and greater diversity during the late forties, colleges were renamed "schools." Their internal structures illustrated uncertainty and revision. The School of Arts and Sciences had three divisions: sciences, social sciences, and cultural arts. The Division of Cultural Arts consisted of fine arts, languages, journalism, and speech. Such administrative divisions were typical. The Division of Cultural Arts would provide most of the faculty, student labor and enthusiasm for educational television.

EDUCATIONAL TELEVISION'S PREREQUISITE: RADIO

Before an educational television station emerged, an important interim step took place: the construction of an exceptionally fine FM radio station. The radio station was the brainchild of Dr. Wilton W. Cook, coordinator of Speech, Radio, and Drama. The 50-year-old Cook had spent 15 years as dialogue director for David O. Selznick International Pictures, working with Freddie Bartholomew, Deanna Durbin, Jane Withers, and Bobby Breen in films and network radio. Claiming a doctorate in education, he was hired as an associate professor in Radio Production at a salary of $5,220, including $200 to be division chairman. Well liked and insightful, he urged that the inadequate radio facility in the Cougar Den be upgraded. By fall 1948, Cook and Kemmerer had won approval from the regents for university architect, Alfred C. Finn, to plan and construct an FM radio tower.[32]

Promoted to full professor, Cook immediately sought young faculty that had at least a master's degree and commercial experience.[33] "Miss" Lillian Thorson was hired as assistant professor of Radio Production at a salary of $375 a month for nine months or 12 months, if needed. She had a master's degree from the University of Michigan in radio, drama, and speech. She wrote a history of Chicago theater, plays, and scripts for radio. She spoke eight languages and was an expert in voice and diction. Wendle Randolph Quick's master's degree was from Baylor, and he got his commercial radio experience at Texas stations. He was an instructor in Radio Production.

Foremost among the new faculty of 1948 was a vocalist and choral director who had two master's degrees from the University of Michigan, one in music, another in speech. John C. Schwarzwalder (1917-1992) had Hollywood credits at Republic Pictures, including the choral direction for Nelson Eddy's last picture *Northwest Outpost* (1947). Good looking though balding, with a rich voice, and plenty of self confidence, the 30-year-old Schwarzwalder zealously supported Kemmerer's liberal innovations and was encouraged by Cook to divide his services between the Radio and Music departments, where he would teach a new course, "Music in Radio." He also assisted in production projects from radio studios in the Cougar Den.[34]

Schwarzwalder's contributions to the university were immediate successes: he co-directed with Marguerite Lenert, a theater instructor, the dramatic portions of *Song of Norway* on 16-17 March 1949. This was a joint project of the departments of Music and Radio. The "magnificent production" drew an opening night crowd to the Music Hall that had the university administrators hosting members of the Norwegian and Danish diplomatic corps. The Cullens, the Hobbys, and other Houston dignitaries attended the event. On 23 June 1949, the "world premiere" of Schwarzwalder's *Abelard*, a twelfth century classic romance between a philosopher-teacher and his pupil was, according to *Houston Chronicle* Fine Arts editor Ann Holmes, "retold with a renewed force and vigor in an original dramatization on the stage of the San Jacinto High School."[35] Playwright Schwarzwalder headed a cast of the Houston Players' Guild, a newly formed faculty group. Even more prophetic was Schwarzwalder's Impromptu Theater that debuted on 9 December 1949 as "the first local drama offering on television."[36] The program, shown on KLEE-TV, Houston's only television station, was directed by Gene Lewis. It was promoted as the beginning of a bi-weekly, half-hour series of experiments attempted by Schwarzwalder, local professional actors and students. It even warranted a live discussion and reviews by critics.[37]

By summer 1950, under Cook's auspices, Miss Thorson sponsored an open house at the Cougar Den with live radio productions, maps and newsreels of the Korean conflict, television receivers, photographs of television celebrities, and a chart of how television was transmitted. This open house forecast what was to come. As the Ezekiel Cullen Building was being constructed, Kemmerer, Cook, and Schwarzwalder realized that there would be room on the fifth floor of the center tower for a radio station. "Somehow Kemmerer got this one past Oberholtzer," Schwarzwalder recalled, "and that's how KUHF came into being. It was not cheap."[38] It cost $400,000. Interviewed many years later, Dr. Kemmerer did not recall that the installation of the radio station was anything other than an administrative decision that "just followed the general philosophy of the university. It would be a practical service to the institution. That was just one outlet. There were many."[39]

After giving the building in memory of his son, Cullen funded the university's main administration building and named it in honor of his grandfather, Ezekiel Wimberly Cullen.[40] As a throng of spectators cheered wildly, William P. Hobby, president of *The Houston Post*, delivered the main address for the laying of the cornerstone of the Ezekiel W. Cullen Building. "This is a cornerstone of peace and understanding," Hobby noted, as he praised H.R. and Lillie Cullen. "Students know better than anyone else the Cullens' generosity. Their acts will live not only of this century but for the centuries to come."[41] During the ensuing year observers applauded the construction of the building, and of equal significance, the retirement of the university's first president, Dr. E.E. Oberholtzer. At age 70, Oberholtzer left the university amidst a shower of well earned accolades for steady conservative progress.

Appointing a successor was up to Cullen, as regents chairman, and board members. Uncertainty about selecting Dr. Kemmerer was apparent, but at the dedication of the Ezekiel W. Cullen Building on 31 October 1950, Cullen told *The Houston Press*: "We're not figuring on a new president, except for the man now serving as acting president, as far as I'm concerned. We've never discussed any-

The original site of KUHF/KUHT was on the fifth floor of the center tower in the Ezekiel W. Cullen Building, 1950.

body else. We're not hunting at all. The regents are trying to give Dr. Kemmerer a chance to see what he can do out there." Then he added, "I'd hate to see any New Dealers or Fair Dealers associated with the University of Houston, or with anything else I'm hooked up with."[42]

The $5.5 million building with an exterior of Austin Shell Stone and an interior of imported and domestic marble and wood was an elegant monument to Cullen's grandfather, whom he referred to as the "Father of Education in Texas."[43] The first four floors of the main part of the building easily accommodated luxurious offices for administrators, a boardroom for the regents, and 46 classrooms. The east wing of the T-shaped floorplan was a 1,680-seat auditorium, a key element in the utilization of the building. The auditorium was to be used for musical and dramatic productions of the kind that had been so successfully staged at the Music Hall downtown. The vacant fifth and sixth floors, located in the central tower and reached by an elevator became radio classrooms and ideal space for an educational FM radio station. Dr. Cook formulated the three main purposes for radio programming: "To provide vocational training for the students, enabling them when they leave the campus to find and hold jobs in professional radio; to serve as a public relations medium for the university; and to give programming to the community which it might not otherwise receive."[44] A nationally recognized expert on acoustics and on the University of Texas faculty, Dr. C.P. Bonner, was asked to design the KUHF-FM studios, including a 120-seat audience participation studio called the Ezekiel W. Cullen Theater.[45] "I was the junior member of this," Schwarzwalder once remarked. "Kemmerer was sold on the idea by Dr. Cook, and I was to implement the job." Anticipating television, Schwarzwalder wanted temporary seats in the large studio. "They overruled me totally. They put in solid, plush seats. They were eventually taken out."[46]

KUHF-FM was to go on the air five days after the dedication. Program tests were scheduled with FCC approval, but a frequency meter failed. General Electric flew in a new meter from Schenectady, which was installed while eager students practiced the planned schedule over a public address system. KUHF-FM went on the air on 10 November 1950, transmitting on a frequency of 91.3 megacycles or channel 217 on the FM broadcast band. Transmitting hours were from 12 noon to 6 p.m., Monday through Friday. Selected programs were rebroadcast over KTRH via leased telephone lines.[47]

H.R. Cullen presented the station to Acting President Kemmerer and the university: "This university is here to help men and women to get training necessary to get jobs and get ahead in the world," he reiterated. "Naturally I hope that the graduates will help provide radio with good entertainment for the citizens and at the same time find ways and means of using radio to help keep all people informed about the truth and our way of life and also about the forces at work in the world trying to destroy these things. I am sure," he went on, "that you will do all in your power to use this station to keep before the people of Houston the best of talent and show the way of preserving and defending our democratic way of life."[48] Soon these words would seem oddly contradictory to Dr. Kemmerer.

"These are the finest radio facilities in the country, commercial or otherwise," FCC Commissioner Paul Walker declared.[49] The radio station, occupying the entire fifth floor of the Ezekiel Cullen tower, had three studios resembling those at Rockefeller Center. A fourth small studio was in the main auditorium. In fact, all of the equipment was from the Radio Corporation of America (RCA) at an itemized cost of $20,000. Massive walls with three-inch sound-absorbing panels were free floating in that they were connected to the main structure by felt hangers and layers of felt cushioning between the floors and the metal girders. Large glass windows separated the control rooms from the studio performing space.[50] United Press installed wire machines in KUHF and in the journalism laboratory, still located in the Recreation Building.

Faculty hired for radio would take key responsibilities for television. Patrick E. Welch, who had a master's degree from Tulsa University, conducted auditions for announcers.[51] Radio news was expected to be demanding. Richard M. Uray, with a master's from Kent State University and 12 years radio experience, planned to dramatize the news in a weekly "March of Time of the Air." "The news service will operate in much the same manner as downtown studios," he told the *Houston Chronicle*, "in that we will have reporters covering police, fire, social, business, church, agricultural and general news events."[52] Eventually, some 16 university departments contributed more than 40 of the 60 weekly programs presented on the FM station that offered mainly an information format.[53]

Of course, none of the programming was possible without keen engineers. Like others on the staff the engineers were trained, in part, while in the service. William T. (Bill) Davis was the chief engineer. "In February of 1950, I answered an ad in *Broadcasting* magazine for a director of engineering for an educational FM station. I came down and interviewed with Wilton W. Cook. They hired me on the spot with the agreement that not only would I be their chief engineer, but I would be allowed to go to school here."[54] He had trained in radio while serving in the Coast Guard, furthered his education at a Port Arthur vocational school, and had installed transmitters for two commercial stations in Texas. Robert Franklin was the studio engineer, having been in radio with the Army in the Pacific. The transmitter operator was Clement LaFond. He was a Navy radar specialist who studied radio at a technical school in Hollywood. All of the engineers held the FCC required First Telephone Operator's License.

The first transmitter site was located on the northeast edge of the campus. "He [Cullen] had built and given to the university an oil derrick," Davis recalled, "to put the FM transmitter and antenna in. The company that built oil derricks built the tower, and it looked like a big 250-foot [actually 285-foot] oil derrick. A line went from the fifth floor to the northeast side of the campus. It was next door to the trailers. Right in the base between the legs of this tower was where they built this transmitter building, and it had the same beautiful stone that the Cullen building had. I believe it was a five kilowatt transmitter with a two-bay antenna. We had call-ins a good 25 to 30 miles away."[55] The FM transmitter remained there for about two and a half years, then it was reinstalled on the new television tower.

From 1950 to 1953, KUHF-FM flourished. But when the administration turned its attention to educational television, it took over everything on the fifth and sixth floors except a modest studio for radio. A six-line notice in *The Cougar* said KUHF-FM would be back on the air on 27 April 1953, its schedule having been interrupted for the conversion to television.[56] Eclipsed by educational television, however, radio continued in a free-fall decline for the next 12 years.

2

INNOVATIONS

KUHT-TV's chief claim to fame, perhaps its only one, is that it was the first noncommercial educational television station on the air, and that it has survived. An odd mixture of timing, alleged academic need, and politics made this event possible. Inside and outside the university and the City of Houston forces moved swiftly and unexpectedly. On the national scene President Truman was soon to be replaced by General Dwight D. Eisenhower; the political climate was changing. In Houston, H.R. Cullen virtually controlled the University of Houston and established a permanent memorial and legacy on behalf of his family. His gifts to the university had coincided with academic objectives of the revered President Oberholtzer. But after Oberholtzer retired in 1950, the time had come for Dr. Kemmerer as acting president to make a statement of his own.

In early 1951, Dr. Kemmerer made an "uneventful" trip to Washington, D.C., where he watched the televised hearings on organized crime conducted by Senator Estes Kefauver, a Democrat from Tennessee (1950-51).[1] On campus, he announced his enthusiasm for television and was immediately supported by Cook and Schwarzwalder.[2] Schwarzwalder had become something of a local celebrity because of stage and radio appearances and his budding friendship with Mayor Roy Hofheinz, "The Boy Wonder of Houston Politics," a Democrat.[3] Hofheinz later wrote Schwarzwalder: "Few people have understood—as you have—that the past three years has [sic] been one continuous campaign. The political machine which has dominated Houston politics for 30 years, with powerful spokesmen outside City Hall and with control of the city council, and much of the administrative machinery of government, has attempted to dictate policies throughout my stay in office. The only choice we have had from the beginning has been to fight those who attempted to dictate city policy, or to surrender to them."[4] Like Hofheinz, Schwarzwalder and Kemmerer enjoyed a good fight. This spirit would seal their fate at the University of Houston as a conservative mood swept the country. Before their time had past, KUHT-TV, an innovation that required lots of "push," would materialize.

On 1 April 1951, the Joint Committee (later Council) on Educational Television (JCET) was formed by seven national educational organizations, and a meeting under its auspices was held at Pennsylvania State College, where its president, Dr. Milton S. Eisenhower, expounded on the future possibilities of educational television. After attending this meeting, Kemmerer was more convinced than ever about its values.[5] The JCET got more than 800 representatives of educational institutions to testify before the FCC on behalf of educational television reservations. It provided information to the public, for the public would have to support it. This function was taken over by the National Citizens Committee for Educational Television (NCCET).[6]

The National Association of Educational Broadcasters (NAEB) gathered useful data by conducting a series of investigations into the content of programming in New York and other cities. An analysis of commercial station programs found almost none devoted to education. During the year, however, "fifty-six colleges and universities, four medical schools, nineteen local public school systems and two public libraries have rendered public services via television. Almost all of this telecasting has been through commercial stations. The educational organizations have resources in their libraries, laboratories, [and] staffs which a commercial operation would have great difficulty duplicating if it could be done at all; and if it were done, it would be at almost prohibitive expense," declared Dr. Franklin Dunham, chief of radio, U.S. Office of Education.[7]

Dr. Kemmerer was convinced of the justification and necessity of an educational television station to be operated by the university.[8] "It was explained [to the regents] that television was expected to be the greatest educational media [sic] of all time and that the University should express its interest in establishing such a station at the University."[9] And so, on 17 April 1951, an application for a television permit was authorized and forwarded to the FCC. The motion for this initial step was made by Colonel W.B. Bates, vice chairman of the board of regents, a prominent attorney who came from Nacogdoches, and close associate of H.R. Cullen. Bates was KUHT's key advocate. This time, however, the application was rejected with the understanding that it should be refiled in conjunction with other educational institutions so that maximum use could be made of the allocation.[10] A month later the board authorized Acting President Kemmerer to offer participation to other educational institutions in the city: the HISD, Rice Institute, and the newly chartered St. Thomas College.[11] In October an understanding was reached with the HISD that a joint application would be filed. By December 1951, American Telephone and Telegraph had linked the East and West coasts, and for Christmas, Dr. Kemmerer bought his first television set.

As the year began, Kemmerer became deeply involved in educational television by attending conferences on a potential network discussed in St. Louis and on instructional television research at Pennsylvania State College. On 14 April 1952, the FCC adopted its *Sixth Report and Order*, a bulky, monumental document and administrative tool that ended the Freeze. An attorney quipped to Chairman Hyde, "You could kill a man with that."[12] The *Report*, among other things, authorized 252 channels dedicated to educational television. Many broadcasters lamented the "exorbitant" number of channel reservations for education, of which 80 were VHF. *Broadcasting* magazine called it a "sell out to the educators, who were hardly aware of TV's existence in 1948."[13] In Houston, commercial television broadcasters supported an educational station, in part because its presence reduced further competition. "It has been the freeze, its interminable delay and the work of Frieda Hennock which permitted and created the rise of consciousness on the part of educators. Although only 11.8 percent of the total, it was a clear victory for Hennock and thousands of citizens who had campaigned for educational reservation."[14] "Strong support for the final reservation of this channel was filed with the Commission by the University of Houston, this city's Independent School District and others, all under the leadership of your own Dr. Kemmerer. The needs and desires of the educational, cultural and civic organizations in this entire area were investigated and were thereafter correlated in a complete and forceful presentation to the Commission," Frieda Hennock declared. "In view of it, it is no wonder that the FCC on April 14, 1952, finally reserved Channel 8 in Houston, as well as 241 others throughout the country, for educational purposes."[15]

UH President W.W. Kemmerer (l) provided the vision and Regents Chair Hugh Roy Cullen the funds for the radio and television stations, 1953.

The day after the FCC granted the license, the University of Houston Board of Regents was prepared to act. After serving as Acting President for nearly three years, the board promoted Dr. Kemmerer to the full presidency. His popularity was at an all-time high. Then, the board took the next step toward becoming a station licensee by approving a resolution for joint application with the Board of Education of HISD for a construction permit:

> WHEREAS, the Board of Education of the Houston Independent School District and the Board of Regents of the University of Houston have submitted sworn statements to the Federal Communications Commission in behalf of educational television and indicated therein their intention for joint construction and operation of an educational television station in Houston, and
>
> WHEREAS, the Federal Communications Commission has reserved Channel 8 in Houston for educational purposes, and
>
> WHEREAS, in accordance with directions from the Federal Communications Commission, if more than one educational institution seeks this channel, that such institutions shall voluntarily work out mutually agreeable arrangements for the operation and use of the channel, and
>
> THEREFORE BE IT RESOLVED, that the Board of Regents authorizes its President, W.W. Kemmerer, to make joint application with the Houston Independent School District for Channel 8 and for the necessary construction permit, with the Houston Independent School District and the University of Houston as joint operating partners, each bearing 50% of the capital cost and 50% of the technical operating cost. W.W. Kemmerer is also authorized to sign any other necessary documents in connection with this application and construction permit.[16]

Dr. Kemmerer's vision extended beyond a single television station. He suggested the possibility of a Texas Television Center on the campus. This center was to serve all commercial and non-commercial stations in Houston. He said space could be leased to other stations, and they perhaps could use the same transmitter tower. This idea suggested a money-making enterprise that appealed to the regents. On 20 May 1952 a Joint Advisory Board [Committee] on Television was appointed. This committee consisted of Colonel Bates, co-chair, President

Kemmerer, and Vice President and Business Manager C.F. McElhinney representing the university and their counterparts—Holger Jeppesen, co-chair, Superintendent Dr. W.E. Moreland, and H.L. Mills representing the HISD. From the beginning the sides could not agree. One HISD board member said the station might cost one million dollars to construct. Holger Jeppesen thought the sum would be exorbitant and that it would be cheaper to buy time on the station.[17] With this split in the board, Superintendent Moreland decided not to attend the Pennsylvania State conference, so President Kemmerer went without him, saying that, if necessary, the University of Houston would apply alone. But after several meetings and disagreements, mainly with Holger Jeppesen who was "doing that just to be ornery," Kemmerer thought, "they said go ahead and get the application in. So I got busy. I took it to Washington. I prepared it myself, and took it in, carried it in physically myself. I wouldn't have done it, I couldn't have done it, if I hadn't had the release from the school district."[18] This consent suggested that there was agreement as to benefits from granting the license. In addition to instruction, Kemmerer told a reporter there are "too many detective stories and not enough programs devoted to important social problems."[19] He cited a rare study of horticulture, the wonders of New York's Museum of Natural History, and the U.S. Constitution as possible content for programs.

In the fall, the Joint Committee on Television was asked to study and recommend: (1) the location of the station, (2) an architect-engineer, (3) an authority to advertise for bids for equipment, and (4) legal documents to establish a working agreement between the UH and the HISD. Again, unanimously, the University of Houston Board of Regents recommended that $300,000 be appropriated by each board for a capital fund account. As a private school, the University of Houston could authorize its money "from oil working proceeds" immediately, but the matching amount from the HISD was never forthcoming.[20] The parties could not agree on the location, either. Governor and Mrs. Hobby offered to donate the KPRC studios located on Post Oak Road, just south of where the Galleria is today, because Channel 2 was moving to new facilities. The University of Houston believed it would be more economical and more accessible to faculty and students to have the studios on campus. Engineers said "that the university's [radio] tower would be more effective than the 500-foot tower on the Post Oak Road."[21] The ground was higher and more centrally located.

By spring, the Joint Committee on Television had reworked its operating plan. Colonel Bates reported to the regents that under the revised plan "the University of Houston will be the operating agent and will furnish all the money but that the Houston Independent School District will have the right to lease time they need or will have the right to purchase one-half the transmission facilities at any time in the next ten years."[22] The University of Houston and the Houston Independent School District remained licensees. The Joint Committee became the Permanent Advisory Committee on Television. Bates was praised for his efforts, and the regents remained enthusiastic. Equipment already authorized was purchased, and a target date for actually going on the air was set at not later than 20 April 1953.

THE CONVERSION FROM RADIO TO TELEVISION

Optimism was high at the beginning of 1953, but to comply with the regents' expectations several internal areas of the university had to be mobilized. Foremost was the administrative merger of KUHF-FM and KUHT-TV as units under the supervision of John Schwarzwalder. Second was the utilization of resources and personnel from the broadcast-related academic departments under Dr. Wilton Cook, especially Radio Production with its faculty— Schwarzwalder, Patrick Welch, Lillian Thorson, Wendle Quick—and the multitude of students studying broadcasting and, to a lesser extent, the four and one-half radio faculty members in the College of Technology. Many on the KUHF/KUHT staff held academic rank and taught at least one course. Third, faculty participants from various departments served as television teachers and research specialists. Fourth, other faculty expertise was applied temporarily to specific problems the station faced.

The physical changes required redesigning studio space, improving lighting, increasing ventilation, installing a transmitter, and remodeling for a film unit. A local designer and instructor in the School of Architecture, Edward Furley, redesigned the KUHF studio and control room space into a studio suitable for television. It resembled an NBC radio-to-television conversion. The rebuilding mainly involved KUHF's elegant large audience participation studio, the E.W. Cullen Theater, referred to as "Studio C." As already mentioned, the red plush permanent seats, doomed from the start, were removed.[23]

The overhead steel grid and lighting were installed by Safway Scaffold Company. Lighting equipment included three 2,000-watt spots, eight 1,000-watt floods and two 500-watt floods for general illumination. Fifteen 1,000-watt spots were for backlighting and fifteen 750-watt spots for modeling. Four 1,200-watt striplights were dedicated to background and sky effects cast on a huge, tightly hung seamless drape called a "cyclorama." The lights were centrally controlled by a dimmer board and switching panel designed by Art Director George Collins. Numerous floor stands and four small lights installed on top of cameras allowed for some lighting mobility and added illumination for close-ups. "The theory now is to use strong floodlights for a base or overall illumination, and to add a modeling light to give depth to the face, a fill-in light to soften shadows caused by the base lights, and a concentrated backlight to separate people from the

John C. Schwarzwalder, director, Radio-Television-Film Center, put KUHT-TV on the air, 25 May 1953.

background," *The Cougar* reported in its special television section.[24] A key light was added to accent the hair. A big blue translucent screen used for rear screen projection was hung against the back wall.

Ventillation was a noticeable problem, especially in the sixth floor attic where the scenery was assembled in cramped quarters. Large student crews made six basic sets and 20 flats that were carried down to the fifth floor studio.[25]

The KUHT-TV studio as seen from the control room, 1953.

Initially, the transmitter was crowded on to one side of the stage in Studio C, and the antennae were installed on the 285-foot "oil derrick" tower at the northeast end of the campus.[26] Video power was 15,000 watts. Chief Engineer W.T. (Bill) Davis expected the A-signal, the best coverage area, to have a radius of 21 miles, and the B-signal to have a 40-mile radius. Along with Davis, Arvil Cochran, Clement LaFond from KUHF, and Alfred L. Haubold from a commercial station brought valuable engineering expertise.

A film unit including a library and modest film production facilities fell to the skills of another new faculty member, Dr. John W. Meaney. Meaney's background will be discussed later, when he is appointed Channel 8's second station manager. He was hired to head up Film Operations, an important task in these pre-videotape days.

The conversion required $129,500 for studio facilities and $116,500 for transmitter equipment.[27]

THE OPERATION

Schwarzwalder organized his television production staff into two teams. Production Team "A" was headed by George Arms and Team "B" by Paul Owen. George Arms had a master's degree from Ohio State University (1941) and four years in commercial radio as a production director in Columbus. He held reserve rank as a lieutenant colonel. Prior to his arrival in Houston, he was director of radio at Kansas State College (1949-52). Arms was eager to try on-air instructional courses and dramas. Paul H. Owen was a soloist and musical director in Los Angeles. His B-Team dealt with music, variety, and women's shows. Each team had a writer, assistant producer, and a student staff. Cora Lewis, a graduate of Mississippi State College for Women, and Roy Barthold, a University of Houston graduate, were writers. Arms and Owen divided 13.5 hours a week of live programming. Patrick E. Welch, hired two years earlier in Radio Production, became assistant station manager and instructed students in the use of microphones and cameras.[28] George Collins, technical director for the Attic theater, assumed responsibility for staging, lighting, and art work. He summarized the

Art Director George Collins (center) and crew built scenery, 1953.

schedule: 1. Thirty days in advance of each new production, the staff met with the director to determine the nature of the show. 2. Two weeks later a complete Routine Sheet listing all of the audio and visual requirements was prepared. Then a floor plan was worked out. 3. One week before the program went on the air, a live rehearsal was set up, for the settings were now finished. 4. A final dress rehearsal was held before air time on the day of the production. Dramatic shows were given extra late night rehearsals.[29] Eight or nine programs were produced each night.[30] News Director Richard M. Uray had to face the challenges of television. He predicted that the 24-member student staff would bring viewers "the best in television news production."[31] KUHT used The Associated Press wire service and AP photographic materials that the *Houston Chronicle* had donated to FM radio. The news schedule projected two 15-minute programs daily, two 5-minute summaries daily, and two 15-minute sportscasts weekly. Outside producers also prepared programs. The HISD formed a three-person production group. Its Audio-visual Education Director, Dr. Harold E. Wigren, planned three programs. *The Art Cart* was a series that taught creative art to upper elementary children, and *It Doesn't Just Happen* was an aid to parents and teachers about understanding the behavior of children and adolescents. These programs were to appear weekly from 7:00 to 7:30 p.m. Another program targeted for the summer was *Five O'Clock Whistle*. It was devoted to pre-school and kindergarten children, stressing activity in art, music, story telling, and handicrafts. Dr. Wigren had earned his doctorate from Columbia University by writing on the topic, "Planning for the Development of Educational Television in Houston." Holding a bachelor's degree from the University of North Carolina, Mrs. Dorothy Sinclair had taught school, was a newspaper reporter, radio program producer, and former advertising director. The third person, Producer Charles Gray, was previously in professional theater, radio acting, and engineering in Nebraska, South Dakota, and Louisiana.[32]

By mid-April 1953, everything seemed ready for launching this first ever educational television station. Mayor Hofheinz proclaimed the week of 20-27 April "Educational Television Week." "All Houstonians are urged to take appropriate interest in this new wonder of the educational world and to visit the Texas Television Center on the campus of the University of Houston, and especially to attend the dedication ceremonies which will be held at the Center on May 4th, 1953."[33] But the mayor's message was premature. At the last minute "someone in Massachusetts left the coaxial cable of the station's antenna exposed to the rain," causing a delay until it dried out.[34] Anticipation in Houston and the academic world heightened. But behind this bright scene, the view was darker. Kemmerer was forced to resign. Probings into alleged Communist activities in American life, especially in government, entertainment, and communication, conducted by Senator Joseph McCarthy, a Republican from Wisconsin, cast a pall over the country that enabled certain conservative groups to carry out purges of their own. One such group was the ultra-conservative Minute Women, headed by Mrs. Ross Biggers. "They were against everything except themselves," Kemmerer believed. "They succeeded in ousting a number of people. Three of them had come to see me, their big breasts sticking out. They wanted to get a teacher to apologize to them [for something she was supposed to have said in class.] I told them I'd talk to her about it and I'd see. I wouldn't promise anything. I don't like that kind of confrontation, and I don't usually run from it either."[35] Dr. Kemmerer was known to be outspoken.

He felt secure so long as H.R. Cullen maintained his public stance of "preserving and defending our democratic way of life." But early on the morning of 17 April 1953, Kemmerer was called to a secret meeting in Cullen's office. Colonel Bates was with him. Cullen said most members of the board no longer supported Kemmerer and he had gotten so many letters from the Minute Women that he was sick of the pressure. "At least, this was the reason he gave. I don't know the real reason, I never will."[36] Cullen offered Kemmerer a year's salary; they agreed on two years' salary—$21,000. Press speculation suggested that some regents were unhappy because the television station had cost more than they thought it would, and that Regent Corbin J. Robertson felt Kemmerer did not budget enough money for athletics. Robertson was Cullen's son-in-law.[37] Kemmerer accepted his termination without remorse. The campus, on the other hand, was shocked.[38] Students threatened to strike; but Kemmerer appearing in casual Western wear at the 1953 Frontier Fiesta, a major annual week-long fund-raising event, told the students: "Concentrate your energies and wisdom to the advancement of this school, for the honor and credit of the University of Houston."[39] Instead of striking, they set up a fund to buy the President a new Cadillac. Kemmerer presided over the highly praised benchmark in education and television history and gave the summer commencement address. His resignation became effective on 31 August 1953.

Finally, KUHT-TV began operation on 25 May 1953. Two weeks later, on 8 June, the station televised its official dedication ceremonies. The transmitter, which had been working perfectly, developed trouble with the modulator output and went out for two hours. Frustrated, Bill Davis gave it a kick and it came back on the air. Smoke caused technicians to think the cable was "hot," instead it was a cigarette burning a cleansing tissue in an ashtray. The clergyman who was to say the opening prayer was late. Dave Garroway's opening congratulatory film broke. "Frieda Hennock, the FCC member who was to dedicate the station, was terribly upset," Houston Press TV Editor Millie Budd reported, "about the absence of a make-up artist."[40] Although scores of individuals had contributed to the development of KUHT-TV, its formal dedication must have been particularly rewarding for Commissioner Hennock. During dinner she kicked off her shoes, and then could not find them when it was time for the petite "hard boiled honey," as Roy Barthold once referred to her, to give her speech.[41] At the podium she threw away much of her six-page address to extemporize. "John Crosby, the great television critic, told me, 'When you say educational TV, I don't know what you are talking about until you get it on the air.' Well, it's on the air. This is what it means. We're showing the scoffers—We're showing the world."[42]

KUHT-TV's dedication ceremony featured (l to r) W.W. Kemmerer, Frieda Hennock, H.R. Cullen, 8 June 1953.

"For here in Houston begins the practical realization of the tremendous benefits that television holds out to education. With TV, the walls of the classroom disappear, every set within viewing range of the signal is a potential classroom. With it, the finest teachers, doctors and artists may be brought right into the school or home. The accumulated riches of man's educational, cultural and spiritual development can be spread right before the viewers' eyes in a convenient and attractive format. In fact, the sky of man's constructive imagination is literally the only limit on the good that can be derived from educational TV."[43] In the middle of her speech KNUZ executive Dave Morris's alarm wrist watch went off. "He just bought it, and he didn't know how to stop it. So he ran out the door."[44]

If that was her vision, Commissioner Hennock did not hesitate in identifying the leadership that made it come true. "One cannot expound on the vast potential of educational television nor thrill to the beginning of its realization at KUHT without paying tribute to Dr. W.W. Kemmerer, the President of the University of Houston, without whose foresight, vigor and determination KUHT would not have been possible. He is responsible—if any one person can ever be singled out of what must be a joint effort—for this major and vital step in the development of educational TV. This station is the practical fulfillment of his fondest hope. It represents the surmounting of a great challenge. Dr. Kemmerer has been 'Mr. Educational Television' in this city. To him, you in Houston as well as elsewhere throughout the country—including the FCC—have looked for and obtained leadership and guidance. KUHT is Dr. Kemmerer's magnificent contribution to this school, his community and his country."[45]

"As the first of its kind in a new species," NAEB President William G. Harley wrote 15 years afterward, "it carried special responsibilities. Now, all at once, for the first time in history, here it was: an actual, operating, honest-to-God educational television station. What hundreds of advocates had been talking about, what thousands of pages of testimony were written for, what educational broadcasters and interested citizens had been working toward for years was suddenly there. Eureka! It is not difficult to prophecy, to engage in wishful thinking or propound 'what could be if only.' But Dr. Schwarzwalder, his staff, and President Kemmerer didn't wait around for big foundation support or federal subsidy; they went ahead and acted and brought an ETV station into being by daring to make the dream so many had held for so long come true."[46]

INNOVATIONS ON THE AIR

Since early April, crews had been primed to go on the air with a full schedule, and with technical complications finally resolved, the first test pattern was telecast on 12 May 1953. Thirteen days later on Monday, 25 May 1953, KUHT-TV actually began programming. "We just wanted to slip quietly on the air," Schwarzwalder said. "No ceremonies until June 8, when we have our formal opening. By then we should have the rough edges worn off."[47] *The Houston Press*, spot checking reception, found that of 20 set owners contacted, eight were tuned to Channel 8. They reported a fine, steady picture free of white particles electronically cast across the screen called "snow." The signal compared favorably with KPRC-TV's, and according to one caller, KUHT could be seen clearly 30 miles away in Seabrook.[48]

The Monday schedule ran for two and a half hours, from 5:00 to 7:30 p.m. The first program was *It's Five*. It featured George Arms and a half dozen coeds in a variety format, including some "down-to-earth" advice for women giving

It's Five with George Arms and hostesses (l to r) Sally Stubling, Patsy Turrentine, and Caroline Richer was the first program, 25 May 1953.

parties, beauty secrets, flower arranging, instruction on making a convertible blouse in ten minutes, and how to prepare a child psychologically for a tonsillectomy. The program presented a regular five-minute newscast. At 5:30, Mrs. Evelyn Thompson began her *Bookland* series that encouraged children to read. It became very popular. At 5:45, anchors Jim Gardner and Donald Blavier rotated in reading AP news from script outlines accompanied by wire service pictures. At six, Patsy Magruder and Nancy Watchous appeared as hostesses, and at 6:03, Assistant Professor Curtis Rogers gave a geometry review for high school students taking final exams. He repeated his review the next night. At 6:30, *Man on the Land*, a film for *Know How*, and the Toronto Symphony Orchestra, also on film, provided a break from live programming. At 7:00, Assistant Dean of the College of Education Charles White presented an education course for administrators, as part of a twice weekly series, *Experiment in Teaching*. At 7:30, hostesses signed the station off the air.[49] *Houston Press* reporter Winston Bode wrote: "Academic humor, stagefright and amateurishness marred the debut only slightly."[50] The "sneak opening" with its staff of ten professionals and 25 students had begun to smooth out its rough edges.

Other live programs throughout the first week featured UH Athletic

First night congratulations were in order for (l to r) Bill Davis, John Schwarzwalder, Paul Owen, George Arms, 25 May 1953.

Director Harry Fouke, Clyde Lee, and Buddy Gillis reviewing last year's football games on film for *Spring Quarterback*. Tuesday was *Viz Quiz* with Bernie Burris and Marg Lea. At six o'clock Wednesday, *U.H. Open House* acquainted the public with how the university operates and departments function. Arms promised that future programs would feature faculty from all over the campus discussing contemporary issues. By Thursday night, the staff and students realized their goal of programming from five to nine nightly was in sight. *Let's Talk Sports* closed out Thursday, and on Friday, *University Forum*, already successful on KUHF radio, and frequently hosted by Schwarzwalder, completed the first week's programming.[51] Though these live originations were not unique, they utilized university resources and presented topics relevant to the Houston area.

After two weeks of trial programming—none of which was extraordinary—KUHT initiated various experiments in local programming. The programs fell into two categories: instruction that was live and/or filmed and was ostensibly the principal reason for the station's existence, and enrichment programs that were largely on film and featured subjects of interest within the urban area. These shows drew upon the university as its main resource. Alternating with its local originations, in part to enable the crews to change settings, were odd-lot programs on film and initially available at little or no cost. These "canned" or prepackaged enrichment programs from outside producers became within about a decade Channel 8's mainstream programs, replacing its attempts at substantial local production. As outside programming improved in quality and became available for leasing, KUHT's local programs further decreased.

Instructional programs attracted curious faculty participants and observers. Could hundreds, perhaps thousands, of students be taught by means of television as effectively as in the traditional classroom? The inference was controversial. Dr. R. Balfour Daniels, dean of the College of Arts and Sciences, and Dr. Horace J. Sawin, dean of the Graduate School and head of the Division of Sciences, expressed reservations. "These two gentlemen hated the thing from the beginning and were determined to destroy it from the very beginning" was Schwarzwalder's opinion.[52] By contrast, Dr. Richard I. Evans, a psychology professor, accepted the instructional television challenge. "We found in our data the humanities individual—the more traditional professor—resisted innovations including television instruction, the hard sciences were a little more receptive, the social sciences more receptive. But it seemed that traditional education consisted of a teacher in a class and some discussion, maybe ideally about 30, and they felt this technology broke down the relationship with individuals. They felt that by definition the medium is superficial, which is a kind of stereotypical, view of this, even though Shakespeare was being taught on television by a professor from Northwestern University.[53] I used to sit around with Daniels; and he used to say, 'How could a scholar like you do this?' He thought I was a traitor for doing it."[54]

Born in Chicago, Evans had received his degrees from the University of Pittsburgh and Michigan State College. He was familiar with forums and panels discussing psychology over MSC's WKAR and UH's KUHF. As a social psychologist, he saw that the potential of instructional television extended far beyond classroom teaching to continuous research and publication in new fields. He anticipated instructional television's considerable public impact and potential for personal involvement. Virtually everything Evans did on television, he tested, documented, and reported. Evans agreed to do KUHT's first instructional course. Prior to going on the air he planned a special half-hour lecture, "The Psychology of Propaganda," which he asked three colleagues to watch. The next day, as a panel, they discussed the merits and faults of the presentation with viewers. "In this way," Evans said, "a general audience reaction will be obtainable before the series actually begins on June 8."[55] During the first week of telecasting, Dr. Evans gave his propaganda lecture on *Open House* (27 May 1953). His telecourse—*Psychology 231*—began as announced and ran for 12 weeks. The series aired from 8:00 to 8:30 nightly, Monday through Friday. It was the only college course offered for credit on Channel 8 that first summer. Evans alternated three half-hour lectures with half-hour question and answer sessions that depended on viewers sending in questions by mail or phone. Once a week discussion sessions were held on campus, and those who wanted credit had to take examinations. Students who took the course by correspondence were required to fill out a specially prepared television manual and take a final examination given on campus. Evans immediately wrote a booklet entitled *Telecourse Guide for Introductory Psychology*. Papers followed. "An Evaluation of the Effectiveness of Instruction and Audience Reaction to Programming on an Educational Television Station," co-authored by H. Burr Roney and Walter J. MacAdams, and "Summary of Research Findings Concerning Educational Television at the University of Houston" were among the earliest research efforts.[56] In the fall of 1953, he appeared on a symposium at the American Psychological Association's meeting in Cleveland, where a course in psychology had already been offered on television at Western Reserve University. TV Critic John Crosby wrote that an audience measurement firm estimated the Cleveland course had an audience of about 55,000 people. About 550 persons had enrolled by sending in a small fee; a local survey estimated that "no fewer than 56,000 persons viewed the program regularly at 9:30 a.m."[57] Two years later, Schwarzwalder estimated the audience for Evans' course at 20,000. A coincidental telephone survey conducted by about 30 students under the supervision of Patrick Welch showed that Evans had "an audience of 8 people who took the course for credit, 21 audited it, and 40,000 people listened."[58] Evans taught the introductory course both summer and fall semesters, 1953, and an advanced psychology course was presented by John W. Love in spring 1954.

Research published by the psychologists was modest, but it was extrapolated to the advantage of Channel 8. Some conclusions were that (1) television is at least as effective in teaching subject matter as conventional classroom instruction, and in certain areas, may be a great deal more effective, (2) television has immense potential for saving teacher time and room space, which was an objective that sold instructional television to the university in the first place, and (3) no evidence supports the fear that television suffers as a teaching device because of the lack of direct teacher-pupil contact. However, these claims, more or less supported by this early research, are debated to this day in many detailed studies.

Other studies on a range of subjects are Pennsylvania State University's 1961 report *Newer Educational Media*; the U.S. Department of Health, Education, and Welfare's 1962 survey of *the needs of education for television channel allocations*; Stanford's 1962 Institute for Communication Research collection of viewpoints, *Educational Television, The Next Ten Years*; NAEB's 1964 *Educational Broadcasting Research, A Report of A Survey of Personnel, Projects and Publications*; Lawrence E. McKune's 1966 *Compendium of Televised Education*; NAEB's 1966 *Utilizing Instructional Television*, the Carnegie Commission's 1967 *Public Television a Program for*

Action, and the perspectives of leading educators in Allen E. Koenig and Ruane B. Hill's 1967 book, *The Farther Vision: Educational Television Today*.[59]

During summer 1953, workshops were held for potential television faculty. They became familiar with the basics of production behind and in front of the camera. Simultaneously, KUHT gave workshops for commercial and educational station personnel.[60] From fall 1953 through the spring of 1955, each long semester had eight or nine courses for college credit. The live instructional telecasts required 13 to 15 hours a week or approximately 38 per cent of the program schedule. Most courses were telecast at night, when presumably working students would take advantage of them. *Biology 131* and *English 231* were offered both morning and evening. Three home study courses in *Preparatory Spanish*, *Today's English*, and *Writing for Money* carried no credit. In this two-year period 36 three-hour credit telecourses were scheduled: agriculture, 3; biology, 4; economics, 1; elementary education, 9; English, 5; French, 2; German, 2; music, 1; photography, 1; psychology, 6; and Spanish, 2. "Enrollment in the non-credit English course is 850; in tuition courses it averages 50 to 70 students."[61]

At this point, the instructional television courses were taught by instructors already on campus. The exception, Dr. Harlan Burr Roney, who went by Burr Roney, had impressed his former student Dr. Sara Huggins. (Huggins had become associate professor and chair of biology.) So, she convinced Dean Horace Sawin to hire Roney from Western Reserve University where he was an experienced television teacher who liked to construct fine models as visual aids for his class. Dr. Matthew W. Rosa invited several lecturers to participate in teaching *English 231*, a basic cultural course designed to integrate literature, drama, art, music, architecture, and philosophy. Dr. John Owen, chairman of economics and finance, considered his telecourse an experiment. He wanted to determine through traditional recitation periods, use of the blackboard, charts, graphs, and appropriate visual aids whether television was as effective as the conventional classroom. Martha Pyke presented practical instruction in portrait photography. Paul Keopke and Harry Lantz taught *Listening to Music*, an introductory course utilizing live television performances, lectures, and recordings. Attendance at performances on campus was required. George Stout, with pianos furnished by manufacturers, taught the elementary education course in applied music required by the State Board of Education. Attendance at campus seminars was required. Two classes were offered in agriculture. *Dairying and Dairy Herd Management* addressed the profitable production of milk for large or small operators, and *Soil and Pasture Management* had Dr. John S. Williams discussing clovers and grasses, summer and winter pastures, profits from proper fertilizers, and managing sandy and clay soil.[62]

A sampling of courses offered in 1954 indicated enrollment results: *Beginning Piano*—3 credits, junior level, elementary education; $40 for credit, $10 for non-credit enrollment. Fifty enrolled for credit; 45 completed the course. *Home Nursing,* an American Red Cross course, had 365 out of 655 persons completing this non-credit course.[63]

Today's English, a pre-college, non-credit course enrolled 30 students at $10 each; 28 completed the course. A sophomore version of *Today's English* given for credit cost $40, enrolled 600; *Mental Health* had 50 out of 60 students completing the $40 credit course; and *Life Sciences,* a.k.a. the freshman biology course, also $40 for credit, enrolled over 600, with 445 completing the course.[64]

Interestingly, many television instructors soon gained local, if not national, prominence that resulted in administrative posts, promotion, and salary increases. By 1960, a typical salary for a television instructor was over $1,000 a month, placing that person among the three highest paid faculty members in the respective departments. The fortunes of a few are worth noting. Dr. H. Burr Roney's biology class, originating live and filmed in the quonset hut for distribution, was perhaps the most distinguished example of KUHT's instructional television classes.

On 16 June 1958, Dr. Huggins explained her department's pioneering role in instructional television to the regents: "Since the fall of 1953 our freshman biology course has been on the air continuously and has had the greatest total

Dr. H. Burr Roney gained national renown for his telecourse on biology filmed in the quonset hut, 1953.

enrollment of any standard college course given by television at any school in the nation. We are very fortunate in our choice of a teacher for this course, because Dr. H. Burr Roney has not only taught one of Educational Television's most successful courses but has become a nationally recognized authority in this field."[65]

Anthropology professor Allan Eister complimented Roney: "...I have seen several installments of a very interesting teaching film by one of your colleagues at Houston. His name is H. Burr Roney and the series is being used here in an experiment in the biological sciences. Dr. Roney does a marvelous job, with no notes apparently, and with considerable ease and control over the situation."[66] "As a result of his work with television," Dr. Huggins continued, "Dr. Roney has also become interested in the making of teaching films for both adult education and regular instruction. His series on the nature of life had been shown by educational stations all over the United States. He is currently engaged in two film projects; one a thirteen-film series for adult education, and the other a two-film pilot series for class instruction. In his plans for the next year there is the initial stage of a project of colossal proportions, even by Hollywood standards. This project will study the subject matter content of college biology courses and eventually produce a complete film library for direct teaching. The Ford Foundation will underwrite this work and expects to put several million dollars into it."[67] During 1958-59, Roney went on leave as professor and television instruction coordinator. Returning in 1960, he resumed his teaching role but left the university three years later.

In addition to being KUHT's first credit course instructor, Dr. Richard Evans attained international recognition for his filmed interviews with distinguished psychologists, discussed elsewhere. He received millions of dollars in grants, and years afterward was designated Distinguished Professor of Psychology for devoting his life's work to his discipline and remaining at the university. Dr. Matthew Rosa had a doctorate from Columbia University. While he was chairman of the English department from 1950 to 1954, he presented his basic English literature courses, English 231-232, on television. They were the result of a 1950 study conducted by Rosa and his wife, Jean. They were trying to formulate a new approach for freshmen. Dr. Rosa died in 1973, having attained the title of professor emeritus. Frequently, foreign languages were taught. Dr. Will McLendon taught French and became chair of that department. Dr. Alfred Neumann, who joined the faculty in 1953 as an assistant professor, taught German. Within eight years he became dean of the College of Arts and Sciences, and in 1972 was appointed Founding Chancellor of the University of Houston at Clear Lake, a position he held for ten years. Dr. Evelyn Thompson, already a widely read *Houston Chronicle* columnist, gained even larger audiences by means of her television courses on education.

KUHT-TV also attempted a potpourri of live, locally originated experiments in enrichment programming. Most of them drew little more than fleeting attention. The principal programs were film projects that were distributed nationally. The live news, sports, art, drama, and music programs imitated those already in the marketplace. *It's Five* and *It's Happening* in Houston were talk shows that spotlighted visitors to the city. Dancer Alexandra Danilova, of the Ballet Russe de Monte Carlo, the Metropolitan Opera's Lauritz Melchior, politicians such as Abraham Tulin, of the Hadassah, telling about the new nation of Israel, were typical guests. An interview with Bill Roberts, a gossip columnist for *The Houston Press*, introduced Maxine Mesinger to similar work for the *Houston Chronicle*. Mesinger's column keeps Houstonians up-to-date about the lives of celebrities and social events to this day. The most impressive of the discussion/interview formats was *University Forum*. Originating on KUHF in December 1951, the program was simulcast over televison and radio on Friday evenings and rebroadcast over FM on Saturdays to an estimated weekly audience of 120,000, about two-thirds of whom listened on radio. In 1955, Ann Hodges reported: "Further, it is the longest-running local panel discussion show, and the only one in the area dealing with international affairs."[68] Topics included "Unification of Germany," "Future of Asia," and "Recent Russian Diplomatic Maneuvers." A particularly memorable program had Eleanor Roosevelt as guest.

Local game shows, *Who Am I?* and *Viz Quiz* with Jack Bailey on Thursdays, could have been the forerunners of his hosting the highly popular *Queen for a Day* and *Truth or Consequences*. A series of spelling bees, sponsored by *The Houston Press*, drew champion spellers from 23 countries and regions. In studio, one hundred youngsters and guests saw Catherine Carl, a Pershing Junior High School student, become the grand champion, but thousands more viewed the event at home.[69] Ventures into live drama were presented by student actors who appeared in local writer Ann Nathan's original historical drama, "The Monument," on 29 May 1953, and Anton Chekhov's "The Boor," on 11 September 1953.

The most memorable of the local programs was its most controversial series—live meetings of the HISD School Board. Beset with many much-discussed problems and trends during the 1950s, the running of the HISD by its independently-minded elected members had become hotly politicized, with four liberals and three conservatives. Soon after his termination as University of Houston president, Dr. Kemmerer won a seat on the School Board. Knowing that the board had never funded KUHT as it had agreed to do and realizing that the public had little knowledge of the behavior of its members, in spring 1955 Kemmerer proposed that the HISD's first board session each month be televised over Channel 8. Of course, the HISD would have to pay the station to make this on-location pick-up. Mrs. Olon Rogers, board president, predicted that "television would cut down on intermember strife and that everybody would 'act like ladies and gentlemen,'" and the motion passed unanimously.[70] Indeed the meet-

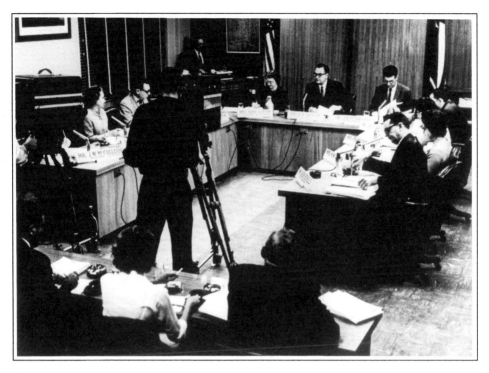

The Houston Independent School District first telecast its controversial board meetings in spring 1955.

ings, produced and directed by George Arms, began innocently enough at 7:30 p.m. on Monday, 14 March 1955. In attendance were Superintendent W.E. Moreland, Board President Rogers, Dr. Henry Petersen, James Delmar, Jack Tucker, Mrs. Frank Dyer, Mrs. A.S. Vandervoort, and Dr. Kemmerer. Also present for this televised event was a large spectator gallery.

At issue were personnel changes, free school lunches, forced retirement at age 60, how to abate pressures exerted by lobbiests, and even the fee Channel 8 was charging to televise the HISD meetings. As each matter was presented over several months, it became evident that the board and the pro-conservative audiences were vehemently partisan. The crowded chamber frequently erupted into cheers, hisses, and boos, creating a storm of dissension between conservatives and liberals. The melee immediately drew over 100,000 viewers.[71] "The last program ran for four hours and seven minutes; none less than three hours," *ETV News* reported.[72] One fascinated viewer objected to station interruptions for manditory identification. Public opinion expressed in the newspapers said the HISD programs "furnished more comedy than Milton Berle," "are the finest things we have ever had in Houston," "are the best programs on the air," and "are more interesting than any commercial program."[73] One writer told *The Houston Post*: "I thought such actions as were attempted on that meeting were only practiced in Russia, or some of its puppet states."[74] For a short time the HISD increased the frequency of its telecasts to meet popular demand, only to find the level of controversy increased. After sanctioning the series for more than two years, the board decided it had enough exposure on television, and anyway, Channel 8's charge of $130 per hour, reduced from $165, was still too expensive, for some programs exceeded $500.[75] Someone also floated the notion that it might not be legal to invest public funds in broadcasting the meetings. Still, KUHT's most talked about program continued well into the sixties.

Besides live instruction and enrichment programs, KUHT-TV produced several, perhaps its best, programs on film. On 1 January 1953, Dr. John W. Meaney was hired as head of Film Operations. He had proper credentials: a B.A. from the University of Notre Dame, M.A., the University of Chicago, and a doctorate from the University of Texas. With all of his degrees in English, he began teaching English at St. Edward's University, San Antonio. His curiosity for making films however linked him to George B. Storer, Jr., heir to Storer Broadcasting and manager of KEYL. "I walked in to Mr. Storer's office and told him I wanted to learn something about television. I told him my background and that I had an interest in film for a number of years. He happened to need a film director.... I had never turned on a TV set, and I was asking for a job in a TV station. He offered me the job as film director. I stayed there about three months."[76]

With this meager background, he was hired by Channel 8. KUHT now depended heavily on film as relief for its live schedule. If they could do a live program and then do a half hour film, they could change the sets and prepare for the next live program. "My first job was to get as many films as possible without too much commercial content. They were not too expensive. They were [ordered] from a book. The first one I remember was done by Texaco called *Man on the Land*. It was a cartoon, but a very interesting little cartoon. We ordered the films two or three weeks in advance."[77] In the first phase of his work, therefore, he built a film library and employed a small staff. The next year he went on leave for three months—15 May to 15 August—and began writing numerous requests for grants. In 1955, the Fund for Adult Education (FAE) granted KUHT-TV $34,500 for kinescope recording equipment.[78] Meaney persuaded the FAE to buy film equipment instead, insisting that the kinescope process—a method of filming the face of a television receiver—resulted in picture quality too poor for educational purposes. At this point black and white videotape had been introduced, but editing it was extremely difficult. Thus, the film unit came up with two Auricon sound-on-film cameras that were immediately assigned to a dozen small projects.

By 1956, Meaney started to look for ways to make money through color film production. "The university had no public relations film. So I wrote a script

The KUHT-TV staff (first row, l to r): Sarah Ewert Beach, Betsy Monday, Beth Potter; (second row) Ray Yelkin, Paul Schlessinger, Dr. Tom C. Battin, Lillian Thorson, Patrick Welch, Arvil Cochran, Paul Owen; (third row) Roy Barthold, O.C. Crossland, James Bauer, Pat Coakley, Dr. John Meaney, Dean Johnson, fall 1956.

and got the administration [alumni] to put up a little money to do a film called *Center of Learning* [1956]."[79] Like a film shot earlier at St. Edward's University, it reveals facets of campus life, including Frontier Fiesta; and it was narrated by the famous voice of *The March of Time*, Westbrook van Voorhies. Directed by Paul G. Schlessinger, "It contained within it a shot that I thought was absolutely tremendous," Jim Bauer remembered. "It was in the library with a young lady on the other side of the stacks, and a young man pulls out a book and takes a peek at her—very innocent. It was basically Paul's film. I shot a good share of it, but Paul was a very creative director."[80] It was screened by the UH Board of Regents on 12 June 1956."[81]

Aside from his modest films promoting universities, Meaney's film successes involve the sciences: anthropology, biology, medicine, and psychology. Often grant funded, these efforts received national attention and gained the most recognition the station has had for programming. By mid-1950s, the National Educational Television and Radio Center (NETRC) had a Ford Foundation grant

People Are Taught To Be Different, 1957, a pioneering series on black culture, was filmed at Texas Southern University.

of $6 million from which Channel 8 could get as much as $500,000 for film contracts. The first important film was a 17-part series, *People Are Taught To Be Different*, 1957.[82] It is an anthropological apologia on black life written by Dr. Henry Allen Bullock, a sociologist at Texas Southern University for 18 years (1950-68). "The idea was that racial discrimination has to be literally taught, that people are not naturally prejudiced."[83] Staged in the TSU auditorium, once a week equipment was hauled over in Audio Operator Pat Coakley's Volkswagen van to film Bullock's narrative, while black dancers interpreted the sequences amidst the clever arrangements of canvas, electrical wire, long rolls of wide paper, pools of light and shadows that George Collins extemporaneously fashioned into huts, trees, and space. The series was directed by Paul Schlessinger. "John [Meaney], George Collins and our white crew—because the University of Houston had no black students in those days—did the production on it."[84] *People Are Taught To Be Different* was distributed by the NETRC and won second place in a world competition.

Meaney aspired to producing significant programming and was less interested in station management and political maneuvering. "Economic realities force upon educational television a role of leadership," Meaney once wrote. "It is just too expensive to be used for anything but the best offering possible, and the moment that it is committed to the best it is inevitably in a leadership position, helping to transform education itself."[85]

Film projects overlapped, a new one began while the previous one was being completed. One series, *Doctors in Space*, began in 1956 with the shooting of the pilot, "The Unseen Burden," on the fifth floor, but most programs were filmed at remote locations.[86] The content concerned the School of Aviation Medicine at Randolph Air Force Base, San Antonio, the only such school in the country. Meaney wanted to tell about the exciting development of aviation medicine several months before Sputnik was news and long before Houston became a space center. He was particularly good at organizing projects and enlisting the services of key talent, in this case a humorous old German named Hubertus Strughold, M.D., Ph.D., and chief, Department of Space Medicine. Strughold had been in aviation medicine since Hitler came to power and was a virtual encyclopedia. With Strughold's contacts throughout the country, a series of black and white film programs evolved. *Doctors in Space*, 1958, was written by a civilian, Green Peyton, working at Randolph AFB as chief, Information Services, and hosted by Dr. John Rider, an associate professor of physics at the University of Houston. *Doctors in Space* described a "Flight toward the Stars," "Torrid Journey," "Atomic Barrage," "Collision Stations," "Eternal Day, Eternal Night," "Satellites and Missiles," and the irresistable, "Life on Other Worlds."[87]

At a preliminary meeting Meaney had met James Bauer, a motion picture expert who was about to be mustered out of the service. Subsequently, Meaney hired him, and Bauer operated one of the cameras, Paul Schlessinger the other. Pat Coakley solved the engineering problems; George Collins took a $39 Sears Roebuck photograph of a skyscape and worked his scenic magic in the fifth floor studio. Meaney rehearsed Rider, Strughold, and Colonel Henry M. Sweeney over the rough spots using "cheaters" to read from. Often filming took place from 1:30 to 3:30 afternoons so that the colonel could get back to the base.

With *Doctors in Space* in progress and with two semesters of biology— some 56 programs—completed or underway, Meaney unexpectedly received an $18,000 grant from the Ford Foundation to test the effectiveness of instructional television on students. Dr. Evans was particularly intrigued by the prospects. "He said, 'Why don't we call C.G. Jung right now. He's an old man, but it might be interesting getting him into the film. We could go over to Europe.' I said sure. So he called Jung and he was interested. So we went to Europe, Dick Evans and I."[88] When they arrived, they found that the biographer of Freud, Ernest Jones, from England, was going to be in Paris at the same time; therefore, they arranged to extend the series and do a few recordings with Jones. This marked the beginning of many filmed interviews conducted by Evans. The series was distributed all over the world, and Evans in particular drew such favorable attention that it shaped his future career. For Meaney, the Ford grant was followed by a Fulbright research grant that enabled him to study film and broadcasting in France for a year (1957-58).

Doctors in Space and People Are Taught To Be Different suggested the direction KUHT might have followed in providing imaginative and significant programming with adequate funds. In any case, programs like these formed the basis for the National Educational Television and Radio Center (NETRC) which aimed to assure that "the very best programs developed by any of the educational stations are available to all, that program ideas of merit are brought to fruition, and that the most significant and interesting programs produced anywhere in the world are added to the resources of these stations."[89] Later identified as NET, it would be instrumental in limiting local, original, and potentially national, programs produced by Channel 8. In the 1960s KUHT became largely an exhibitor of NET productions.

3

FUNDING

Programming, whether it was instruction or enrichment, live or recorded, was never educational television's biggest problem. It was funding. Legally prohibited in most instances from raising money through taxes or advertising, educational television stations were dependent on private donations, foundation and corporation grants, and government subsidies; to wit, complex patronage. Throughout the 1960s KUHT sought this patronage, desperately.

During the previous decade Dr. Kemmerer's dream of a Texas Television Center (1952) continued to make progress. He saw his proposal as a way of giving a home to Channel 8 and a means of providing a perpetual income from leasing space and facilities to as many as six commercial stations. By spring 1953, the regents had set aside 30 acres of land south of Wheeler Road and on the east side of Cullen Boulevard. Dr. Kemmerer had been given authority to negotiate a lease with KNUZ-TV, operating on UHF Channel 39.[1] "We built the building and put up the tower which we shared with Channel 8," David Morris said, as KNUZ-TV became the first occupant.[2] An unofficial estimate of the building, equipment and tower cost was $2 million.[3] By fall 1953, KNUZ-TV President Max R. Jacobs and General Manager Morris expected to be operating its 3 p.m. to midnight schedule, and to be a Columbia Broadcasting System (CBS) affiliate. When the FCC allowed KGUL-TV, Channel 11, Galveston, to move its transmitter to Houston, KNUZ-TV became a DuMont affiliate instead. Within a year KNUZ-TV ended broadcasting, deeding the building and 749-foot transmitter tower to the university, and selling its equipment to KTRK-TV, Channel 13, an American Broadcasting Company (ABC) affiliate, owned by Houston Consolidated Television Company. With promotional flair before going on the air, KTRK-TV's remote truck simulcast six hours of election night coverage from the city room of the *Houston Chronicle* over KTRH radio, both owned by John T. Jones, and KUHT-TV on 2 November 1954.[4] In newly renovated space KTRK-TV became the second tenant in the Texas Television Center on 20 November 1954. Within two years, KTRK-TV built a 36 by 40-foot addition at the back of the main structure, and later the regents authorized $30,000 for a 4,000 square foot film operations building behind the transmitter site, the cost of which was to be returned within three years.[5] In 1961, KTRK-TV moved to new quarters, and the prospect for a shared commercial and educational television center never materialized.[6] For a time the

National Aeronautics and Space Administration (NASA) occupied the building as a computer center. The main building with its expansion, the transmitter building, and the film operations facility—all built between 1953 and 1956—constituted thereafter the physical plant for KUHT-TV, when in 1964 it moved from the fifth floor of the Ezekiel Cullen Building.

After Kemmerer resigned, the vision faded; after Schwarzwalder left, the dreams for a television center and college vanished altogether. Temporarily replacing President Kemmerer, while the regents sought a permanent university head, was Charles Flemming McElhinney (1908-1978). Hired as an assistant to HISD Business Manager H.L. Mills, McElhinney moved through the ranks to become, by 1953, vice president and business manager, the second highest ranking administrator at the University of Houston. "Mr. Mac" accepted a one-year appointment as acting president. He had no ambition to be president, but he had a zealous desire to watch over every dollar of university funds, as if it were his own.

McElhinney's responsibility was primarily to maintain the status quo until a permanent president could be found. He avoided policy decisions regarding Channel 8, but he meticulously guarded the budget. "I used to go round and round with Mr. Mac," Schwarzwalder recalled. "'We're devoting all the time to Mr. Burr Roney and biology, and there is a hell of a lot of tuition on that—' but I never was able to convince him. Never got a nickel on that. He would grin and say, 'Yeah, yeah, John.' But I knew this was in the back of his mind. He was a very sharp man."[7] More likely McElhinney was smiling at Schwarzwalder's optimism in the face of financial reality. Aside from a $10,000 gift from the Emerson Radio and Phonograph Corporation, New York, for being the first station on the air, KUHT-TV depended on local university sources, especially benefactors like Cullen, commercial broadcasters, student tuition, and services it could sell.[8] Although KUHT was never "loaded with money," as John Crosby wrote in *The New York Herald Tribune*, it seemed that way, for the stations were financed largely by the Cullen fortune.

A 1954 report listed KUHT's initial capital costs: $135,000, including space at $9,000, transmitter tower at $20,000, equipment at $56,000, antenna and transmitter at $50,000. Its annual operating expense programming 13 live and seven filmed hours per week was $73,000, including payroll at $50,300, and rentals, replacements and supplies at $22,700.[9] Several benefits to the station allayed higher expenses. First, the availability of unlimited student and voluntary help. Second, availability of two rooms (20 x 20 x 10 feet and 15 x 15 x 8 feet). Third, availability of a site for the transmitter. Fourth, distribution of films from ETRC (NETRC) in Ann Arbor. Fifth, a modest 20-hour program schedule. Sixth, a minimum signal capable of only ten-mile Class A and 13-mile Class B coverage, inadequate for growing Houston's urban sprawl.[10] Four often cited KUHT benefits to the university were reduced need for teachers and classrooms, student training in communications, university public relations, and programming service to the Houston community. KUHT's drawbacks some detractors were willing to identify. *Houston Press* columnist Carl Victor Little wrote: "Because the University of Houston, gulled into accepting the dubious honor of setting up the first of Frieda's passions, the people of the Metropolitan Area, which will be 1,000,000 strong in population at high noon July 3 by fiat of the Chamber of Commerce, are being deprived of a commercial channel that would offer programs, many of which would be of real merit." He referred to KUHT as "KNUT" and in a later paragraph complained: "At the time, if you will allow a modest man to quote himself, we stated in a column, 'After KUHT performs for, say two years—if it lasts that long—then the world will have been shown whether it is a boon to education hungry (ha ha) people or just another plaything of our friends, the power-obsessed educators.'"[11]

For the most part Channel 8 and its leader John Schwarzwalder were a big success, enjoying a national reputation. Mentioned in *Newsweek*, he received a letter from Senate Democratic Leader Lyndon B. Johnson: "As you know, Houston is a fabulous name all over the Nation. I wanted to make sure all the members of Congress had an opportunity to read the Newsweek article, so I had it inserted in the Congressional Record."[12] Despite its recognition KUHT-TV's longevity was by no means assured. The year-long appointment of C.F. McElhinney was to end on 31 August 1954. A search had been more or less underway, but in fact, Colonel Bates had heartily recommended to H.R. Cullen an acquaintance who was retiring from a distinguished career. After 37 years of active Army duty, Lieutenant General Andrew Davis Bruce (1894-1969), a Texas A&M graduate, had an impeccible military reputation with assignments at Fort Hood, as commander of the 77th Infantry Division in the South Pacific, as post-war military governor of Hokkaido, and as commandant of the Armed Forces Staff College, Norfolk. "A.D.," as his friends called him, and his wife of 35 years made a striking couple. Bruce, Bates, and Cullen all admired Dwight D. Eisenhower and Douglas A. MacArthur, distinguished generals and Republicans. In such conservative company, the General was compatible with the dominant power structure, a welcome contrast to Kemmerer and Schwarzwalder.

Although General Bruce was able to administer the overall necessities of the university, he wanted a strong vice president and dean of faculties who was far more familiar than he with academic life. He was fortunate in hiring Clanton Ware Williams (1903-1975). A professor at Vanderbilt and the University of Alabama for many years, Dr. Williams had been called to active duty during World War II and the Korean War. He rose to the rank of colonel, serving on the staff of General H.H. Arnold, as chief historian for the Air Force, and as head of international studies at the Air War College of the Air University, Montgomery, Alabama.

Prior to Williams arrival in January 1955, President Bruce noted his main concerns: television was prominent among them, along with faculty salaries, nursing, agriculture's demonstration farm, photography, modeling and charm courses, Frontier Fiesta, and McElhinney's speeches. "Everything on there I've heard about in negative or controversial terms, either on campus or around town except for Mr. Mac's speeches to the faculty," he confided to his ambitious assistant, Patrick J. Nicholson.[13] "General Bruce was perhaps one of the nicest, most polite men, I have ever known, and surely one of the stupidest" was Schwarzwalder's blunt complaint.[14] What he meant was that they disagreed about the future of television and a college of communications. Schwarzwalder attempted to convince Bruce of the importance of the college by enlisting the aid of Roy Hofheinz. After getting the concurrence of the chairmen of speech, journalism, drama, and speech correction, "I went to Roy Hofheinz, who was my good friend, and proposed that he might be willing to raise two million dollars for such a facility. He was ready to do it, if he could secure the 'full' cooperation of the university. He believed R.E. (Bob) Smith and others would help."[15]

Schwarzwalder told General Bruce that the college would not only balance the budget, but it would become a money-maker, assuming the continued growth of all departments and the use of common courses. The General looked at the proposal and said: "'Four out of these six departments are losing money for the university.' I agreed. 'And they are going to keep right on doing it. But two of them are making a good deal of money for the university. If we have common survey courses and other economies of scale, the whole college will make money.' He said, 'John, four of six departments are losing money. We can't have a whole college losing money.' I said, 'General, the college would not lose money. It would be a financial asset.' 'John, we can't have a whole college losing money.' It was at that moment I despaired that anything could be done about a college of communications in the foreseeable future.... That's when I finally decided that it was time for me to move on."[16]

President Bruce was also troubled about the deficit Channel 8 had accrued during its first four years; it amounted to over $625,000. Vice President McElhinney's memo reported the realities of KUHT-TV's operation: From 1952 to 1956, KUHT-TV's "excess expense over income" totaled $513,148; and the Radio-TV Department, which included the radio station that did not make any money, totaled $112,817. The net loss of the Radio and Television Department and stations amounted to $625,965.[17] The expenses, including operations and overhead at 43 per cent of direct expenses, revealed a steady rise of $6,000 to $9,000 a year in the academic department and increases in KUHT's cost each year, as depreciation set it. The only area with modest income was KUHT's Film Operations. McElhinney noted: "We have not taken into consideration any indirect income due to Radio-TV, such as students taking other courses; income from students studying English and Biology by TV; saving in classroom space; and other matters mentioned by Dr. Schwarzwalder."[18] The original investment as of 31 August 1954 in the station was $301,022, with capital additions in 1954-1955 of $7,227 and 1955-56 of $8,737; the building cost was $90,247 in 1954. The station and the building combined cost $407,233.[19]

For public benefit, President Bruce and Dr. Schwarzwalder exhanged pleasantries in prepared statements: "Constant support by the Board of Regents for educational television has been an inspiration to all of us who have worked for the establishment and operation of the station. The administrators of the university under whom I have served have been most helpful in every way. I believe that the staff of KUHT is the best in the country. It is undoubtedly the most industrious. Finally, the community and its leaders have helped greatly in maintaining this educational medium."[20] But his comment to *The Houston Labor Journal*—he strongly supported labor's causes—was closer to his real feelings. He said that he would have stayed for considerably less money, "if the University had shown a desire to get off 'dead center'."[21] In fact, President Bruce was not on dead center; he did not intend to support construction of a college of communications and he would carefully monitor the expenses incurred by KUHT.

With various newspaper editorials lamenting the loss of Schwarzwalder, President Bruce used his departure to his own advantage: "We are very sorry to lose Dr. Schwarzwalder, although we can understand his desire to accept a position which involves other challenging problems in the field of educational television and a substantial raise in salary. [It was about a one-third rise.][22] This is another example of the number one problem at the University of Houston, the need for increasing faculty salaries. The University, and the community it serves, will be continually faced with the possible loss of key faculty members unless we can bring our salaries more into line with competing institutions."[23] Schwarzwalder's resignation became official 30 September 1956. He had decided to extend his leadership to the Twin Cities of Minnesota.[24]

"John was responsible for putting these various elements together, getting the thing to work, and then staying on the air! That should very definitely be given to him," Roy Barthold once said, "putting this student and faculty operation together was a major chore. This was something that [required] executive ability, push, initiative, and exerted continual pushing; it wouldn't have worked otherwise. John was interested in the overall thing. When it settled down to detail stuff—which is what it did for some twelve years—John was ripe for a new opportunity, which St. Paul was, of course."[25]

From Schwarzwalder's September departure until early in 1957, KUHT-TV was in a holding pattern awaiting a new mandate from Vice President Clanton Williams. Staff filled the void, but no manager was named. On 1 November 1956, Assistant Professor Paul Owen (d. 1994) was promoted to program director and assumed many of the manager's duties. Associate Professor Patrick Welch chaired the Radio-Television Department and managed KUHF. In some ways their backgrounds were similar. Owen had a more impressive professional background; Welch had a better academic record. Both were highly regarded for their experience in radio production, particularly in performing. Owen, a former Navy pilot appeared as a soloist with Fred Waring's Pennsylvanians, *Duffy's Taven*, and *Burns and Allen* radio shows. He was hired in 1953 at the same time as George Arms, who had departed for KETC, St. Louis a year earlier (15 November 1955).[26] Owen said he joined KUHT-TV for three reasons: He was suffering from rheumatoid arthritis, he was persuaded by Schwarzwalder, and "I knew I was never going to replace Bing Crosby."[27] With three years as a radio operator in the Air Corps and some professional stage acting and radio announcing, Pat Welch had completed his master's degree at Tulsa University. He joined the University of Houston as a teacher, a role he always preferred, yet assumed various posts with KUHT-TV and KUHF-FM. Both Welch and Owen were married, well liked, gregarious, good looking individuals. Eventually they both obtained doctorates: Owen from the University of Houston, Welch from The Ohio State University.

As Bruce neared the end of his second full year as president, it was rumored that Williams was being sought for the presidency of the University of Alabama. So, on 10 December 1956, General Bruce avoided losing Dr. Williams by convincing the regents to name Williams as president and the General as chancellor and chief executive officer. Over the holidays President Williams made plans to completely reorganize the radio-TV areas.[28] Effective 15 February 1957 a newly organized Radio-Television-Film Center was established. Heading the center was the only staff member holding a doctorate, Dr. John W. Meaney. Named to head divisions under him were Roy E. Barthold, program director, and James L. Bauer, director of Film Operations. James J. Byrd was retained as chief engineer and Patrick Welch continued to chair the instructional department. Paul Owen, however, accepted an appointment as program director for Schwarzwalder. "Mr. Owen is a true pioneer in the educational television movement in this country," President Williams said, "and all of his colleagues at the University wish him well in the task of helping put on the air another educational station in the Twin Cities.[29]

Meaney, who as head of KUHT Film Operations was noted for his grant-supported film projects, was director only six months when he received the aforementioned Fulbright research grant to study in France for the year beginning 14 July 1957-58. When he returned to campus, he was promoted to full professor and continued as director of the Radio-Television-Film Center. KUHT was coming up for license renewal. "So here I made what I regard as my key contribution to KUHT and the University of Houston."[30] He alerted Chancellor Bruce and President Williams that this was the crucial period in which the University of

Houston should make a bid as sole licensee. "They recognized how unfair the sleeping dog position of the HISD was to the university. So they arranged for a joint meeting of the two boards at which the matter was decided."[31] In preparation, the University of Houston Board of Governors unanimously agreed on the either-or position it presented to the HISD School Board: the university notified the School Board earlier, as the deadline for relicensing approached, of a unanimous Board of Governors vote in favor of the university becoming sole licensee of KUHT-TV, in the best interests of educational television in the community. As an alternative, the university proposed that the School District become the sole licensee.[32] About a week later—28 April 1959—the HISD agreed that the University of Houston should be the sole licensee.[33] The School Board was still offered "a minimum of 15 hours a week telecast time, in addition to School Board telecasts, at a computed facility charge."[34] In the original application the HISD claimed it had a $9 million fund it could draw upon; however, when, after six years, it was finally pressured to financially support the station, HISD School Board President James Delmar said: "This station would not have been possible if it were not for the university, because the Independent School District was not financially able to bring it here at this time. We need every dollar for building classroom space."[35] "The separation from HISD allowed the university to guide future developments at KUHT with much greater freedom than it would otherwise have had," Meaney believed.[36] Chancellor Bruce predicted this decision would open doors for participation by many more school districts in the Gulf area, and it did.

More grants continued to improve Channel 8. To assist the station with new video recording equipment the NETRC provided an Ampex VR-1000B and technical training to operate it at a cost of $52,950.[37] In 1957, after the Russians launched Sputnik I, the first artificial satellite, Congress assumed the United States was technologically behind and needed to accelerate and strengthen education. In 1958, it passed the National Defense Education Act, authorizing low-interest, long-term tuition loans to colleges and graduate students. This Act to improve education had several different titles including new media. The new media section was under the Office of Education in Washington, D.C., as part of the Department of Health, Education and Welfare (HEW). The Office of Education sought someone to advise it on educational television applications, to supervise a series of grants for experiments, and to document the capability of television for student instruction. Its search identified, Dr. John Meaney who accepted the position of Educational Research and Program Specialist, a Civil Service post. "I was the only [ETV] representative on the staff of the U.S. Office of Education. It was such an exclusive kind of position that I felt it was a very strategic appointment and something I should take."[38] Again—this time on 1 March he went on leave.

In Meaney's absence, the managerial duties of KUHT-TV fell to Roy E.

Barthold (d. 1982). Barthold once described himself to the author as "one of the hardy group of eccentrics assembled by J.C. Schwarzwalder to invent ETV." In 1953, at his initial interview with Dr. Kemmerer, the president asked, "I see there is a gap here of about ten years in your employment record. I see you're alive. You must have done something." Barthold mumbled, 'I did the first thing I could. I stayed alive.'"[39] Kemmerer laughed and Barthold got the job as an instructor and writer. During the 1960s, Barthold's main task, as station manager, was keeping KUHT alive. Prior to World War II he attended Hamline University in St. Paul, Minnesota and the University of Houston. He served as a non-commissioned officer during the war, returning to the University of Houston for a bachelor of science degree in 1952. A short, dark haired, single man with a warm smile and a quiet manner, he rode the roller coaster fortunes of the fledgling station with a touch of humor. In 1954, he advanced to Senior Technical Instructor, a title he would retain. By 1956, he was promoted to program coordinator and in 1957 program director, the title he held during the Meaney administration. In 1960, when Meaney departed for Washington, D.C., Roy Barthold was made station manager of KUHT-TV and KUHF-FM, and still carried the second title, Senior Technical Instructor. The job paid $760 a month.[40]

That same year, 1960, President John F. Kennedy told a convention of educational broadcasters: "American progress and even our national survival is directly dependent on what we as a nation do now about the shameful weaknesses and deficiencies of our educational system. Television, a device which has the potential to teach more things to more people in less time than anything yet devised, seems a providential instrument to come to education's aid."[41] The message was inspiring, but at Channel 8 reality was wrenching. Lack of money threatened KUHT in every direction.

Roy Barthold had hardly assumed his new manager's title when the university's consultant firm—Cresap, McCormick and Paget—wrote an extensive opinion about Channel 8's financial status. In Chapter VIII of the CM&P report: "It suggested that the university devote one year to evaluating the [primary mission] of the television station, to planning programs aimed at self-support, and to developing policies in regard to the televising of instructional courses. If it is clear at the end of one year that self-support cannot be achieved the consultants recommend discontinuance of the television station at a claimed saving of about $159,000 a year."[42] The CM&P report caused a flurry of university studies that refuted the consultants' recommendation. Barthold said the cost of teaching classes was less than they reported and that, in fact, mathematics, accounting, and biology were profitable. It was true, however, that McElhinney's figures showed a deficit in 1958-59 of $159,000; but the deficit was reduced in 1959-60 to $58,325.[43] The 1960 projection anticipated a rise in expenses unless a fresh flow of research funds came to the university; new courses being planned such as General Chemistry, General Biology, and American Government were potential revenue sources.[44]

The report suggested funding plans. One alternative was a non-profit community organization under full state support, but obtaining state support was impossible. On 10 May 1957—when the University of Houston was still a private school and educational TV was in its infancy—the 55th Texas Legislature passed a special provision to the appropriations bill (H.B. No. 133, Article V, Section 13): "TV stations prohibited. None of the moneys appropriated in this Article may be expended for the acquisition, construction, or operation of television transmitter stations; provided, however, this prohibition shall not be construed so as to prevent the medical schools, dental school, general academic teaching institutions or other agencies of Higher Education named in this Article from using closed-circuit television for purely instructional purposes."

This law would become the guiding prohibition against using tax dollars to fund Channel 8 after the university came under state support, and remains in effect to the present day.[45] Another fund-raising suggestion sought a special committee to pursue the possibility of using credit lines on public service programs, for a fee. This was the origin of institutional spot announcements that eventually appeared on Channel 8. A solicitation of donations was made through KUHT's printed schedule, *KUHT Program Previews*, in November 1962.[46]

KUHT's funding quandry was turned over to President Williams' vice president and dean of faculties, Dr. Philip G. Hoffman, who had been appointed in June 1957. The CM&P report was studied intensely for a year. Dr. Hoffman had expressed his thoughts about KUHT previously. In 1958, he gave the main address televised on the occasion of the station's fifth anniversary. He reiterated the dominant conclusions of the time: television supplemented a shortage of fine teachers and classrooms, higher education was experiencing higher enrollments, television utilized well trained professors who were confronted with a wholesome reevaluation of course content in preparation for television, programs could be distributed anywhere in the world, and that there was no significant difference between learning achievement by television or in the traditional classroom.[47] Hoffman described what he termed "The Houston Plan," which offered Instructional Television (ITV) courses for large enrollment sections at the freshman and sophomore levels. These courses were repeated at different times, and the lectures were mixed with on-campus live discussions. He viewed this approach as beneficial to students who wanted to see the lecture more than once. He mentioned advantages for the faculty, too. A trigonometry course, for example, which was on film, could release faculty to spend time on research and writing.[48] "University of Houston courses using television had had 13,000 class enrollments, principally in courses of from two hundred to eight hundred students, for a total of about 3% of University teaching."[49] In light of university experience, he thought perhaps 15 to 20 per cent of the total class enrollments, including some of the general education first-and-second year required courses could be presented on television. Ultimately, this large percentage would save money for the university, and in turn, the savings could raise teacher salaries. "It is the expectation of the University," he concluded, "to so expand its program of TV application that appropriate utilization will be fully in effect by the time a projected new plateau of freshman enrollments is established in the academic years beginning in 1961 and 1962."[50] Few of these goals were realized.

FUNDING KUHT-TV WITHOUT STATE SUPPORT

After a lengthy and complex campaign in the Texas Legislature culminating in the passage of Senate Bill 2, the University of Houston became part of the state supported system of higher education on 1 September 1963. As part of the transition that spring Governor John B. Connally formally thanked the board of governors that was in existence since 1957 for its service and instated a newly appointed nine-member University of Houston Board of Regents, six of whom were already serving as governors, including Colonel W.B. Bates who carried on as chairman. This heralded a positive new era in the fortunes of the university, but devastated the fund-raising outlook for Channel 8. The private school deci-

Governor John B. Connally (l) paid tribute to UH President Philip G. Hoffman and the outgoing board of governors as UH became a state institution, 4 April 1963.

sions, sometimes quickly made behind closed doors and accountable to a few wealthy powerbrokers, were a thing of the past. Public money would enrich the rest of the campus, but Channel 8, which never had tax dollars anyway, would have to struggle harder for attention, priority, and funding. The principal figure in leading the university for the next two decades was Dr. Philip G. Hoffman. Stately, distinguished looking, married with four children, Hoffman was born in Kobe, Japan on 6 August 1915. He was graduated from Pacific Union College and the University of Southern California before obtaining his doctorate in history from The Ohio State University in 1948. During the early 1950s he was an officer in the U.S. Navy. Since beginning his career in education, he combined teaching history with various administrative roles. A cordial relationship between Hoffman and Clanton Williams developed over four years when they taught history at the University of Alabama. Then Hoffman became dean of faculties at Portland State College, Oregon. Shortly after Williams became the University of Houston president, he asked Hoffman to become vice president and dean of faculties, allowing Williams to free himself of routine duties. On 11 April 1960, a power struggle between Chancellor Bruce and President Williams ended when Williams was placed on leave. Meanwhile, Hoffman's role strengthened. When the governors accepted Bruce's request to retire on 31 August 1961, Dr. Hoffman was the unanimous choice for swift elevation to the presidency and the title of chancellor was eliminated.[51] Hoffman's formal inauguration took place on 27 April 1962. He was poised for the task of leading the university from a private to a state institution.

President Hoffman had the vision, desire, opportunity, and ability to build an outstanding physical plant. With the infusion of tax dollars, the Hoffman administration began a remarkable construction program. Although one of the last buildings he would authorize—a Humanities Building—consisted of a School of Communication, a modest version of Schwarzwalder's communication college, and a drama department, neither KUHT-TV nor its radio counterpart benefited greatly from his vigorous building program.[52] Hoffman assigned the welfare of the broadcasting properties largely to Vice President Patrick J. Nicholson. In 1956, with an MBA from Harvard University, "P.J." Nicholson was named Executive Director of Development. He quickly became a trusted assistant to President Bruce; and in two years was Vice President for University Development, while he studied for a doctorate in psychology. Although Nicholson's role was mainly that of a facilitator who carried out programs credited to others, his relentless efforts enabled the university to become a state school; and he was, in President Hoffman's opinion, "one of the best friends Channel 8 had. I think he saw that Channel 8 had tremendous potential in terms of the development of the university and its public relations."[53] As the Hoffman administration began, however, neither Hoffman, Nicholson nor Barthold knew where the money would come from to support Channel 8.

When asked about the future of KUHT-TV, a frustrated Barthold responded: "The University as a private institution conducted the most far-reaching program of continuing and cultural education that has ever been mounted in Texas. I'll try to develop a tenable idea or two of what might happen. [But] nobody in his right mind would tackle that [question]. The only people who ever made predictions about ETV were those who didn't know anything about it."[54] Barthold was right. The turbulent sixties would thrust the administration into a series of unforeseeable changes. These changes forced the trio to react rather than act on behalf of the television station. Circumstances would compel the station to relocate, to terminate its college credit courses, to relinquish its daytime schedule to school district programming, to finally emerge from the decade as a regional rather than a local station seeking federal grants for greater power and color capability.

In 1961-62 memos—the final year before becoming a state school—Barthold contemplated the uncertainties. To Nicholson, his immediate supervisor, he wrote: "Possible consideration should be given to revising the Spring, 1962, budget requests to show greater commitment to Radio and less to TV, and possibly even to strengthen FM programming."[55] He feared that federal aid to educational television in the form of equipment appropriations would be administered under the Texas Education Agency, and that "it is possible the TEA would move in on the whole state appropriation and preclude any participation by colleges and universities."[56] He recommended: "We will, under the present law, need to substantiate the position that broadcasting is a privately supported extension of closed-circuit instruction."[57] In another memo Barthold could identify funds for on-campus, closed circuit instructional courses and for studio costs for HISD programs, but there was no money for NETRC affiliation fees for enrichment programs and transmitter operating costs. They required non-state funds in the amount of $32,000. On the other hand, with federal legislation pending for educational television facilities and with the University of Texas planning to operate Channel 9, which it did on 10 September 1962, he speculated that the legislature would lift its ban against the use of tax dollars for educational television by 1963 in order to get federal money.[58] However, it didn't.

Seeking influential persons who would listen, Barthold expressed his many concerns to Scott Red, of the Education Committee of the Houston Chamber of Commerce. He reviewed the "fluid" state of nearly everything affecting ETV: local public school use, federal aid, industrial education, and state support for KUHT-TV and the University of Houston. In regard to the latter he suggested to Red: "This is perhaps a proper concern of the Education Committee in its contacts with the Harris County legislative delegation."[59] Barthold recognized that he was in a delicate position. To improve the station's financial future from his low position in the chain of command, he would have to do what he could to

r student training ended. RTFC engineer and former student Arvil
laced him with a different approach for radio.
nwhile, the failure to meet student laboratory requirements in radio
sly generated a debate over television laboratories. Vice President
n his role as Director of Development, had to juggle academic de-
those of Channel 8. KUHT consistently won, as in this memo from
Vice President and Dean of Faculties, Dr. John C. Allred: "We look
priated dollars as a relatively small percentage of the far larger total
operating the overall RTFC. You apparently see the $55,000 [money
contracts] as a large and generous sum which should permit the
ible use of RTFC facilities, equipment, supplies and personnel to
instruction of Communications students."[73] "This is a complex but a
standable problem which centers around the unavoidable conflict
RTFC administrators under a mandate to produce from projects the
essary to keep the Center afloat; and (2) members of the Department
ications with the laudable ambition to provide the best instruction
their students. The underlying difficulty is the refusal of the State
to fund directly either operations of the RTFC or laboratory instruc-
o and television. An appropriate solution should obviously accommo-
fering objectives and attendant difficulties obtaining for all concerned;
me more and more apparent that any viable resolution must include
ion of production/broadcasting from laboratory instruction; and (2)
on of separate budgets."[74]
though Dr. Battin continued to teach students in KUHT's Studio B to
he sixties, the situation was doomed. Accounting studies were under-
HT-TV wanted several thousand dollars a year for use of Studio B;
had budgeted $3,000 for laboratories. He said he had no other money.
2, the situation reached a stalemate. Without funds, KUHT terminated
laboratories.[75] Consequently from 1972 to 1978, with the administra-
tal impasse, the communication students were denied access to Chan-
UHF as laboratories. The perception that KUHT-TV, particularly, was
ative, overpriced, and failed to meet its obligations to the academic
y penetrated the Houston community. For the next 15 years no one on
pus could articulate the reasons for Channel 8's failure to fulfill the
he campus that held its license. Commercial station contributions de-
part, with the gift of the Alvin site, discussed later, and because KUHT
trained potential employees. In 1972, an internship program that still
established between the Communication Arts Department and media
s. The first intern, Johnny Almendarez, went to KTRK-TV, Channel 13.
mercial stations, however, gave no monetary support to the academic
nt. During the 1970s, weak support from the university administration,

maneuver politically the university administration, the Houston community, and
eventually the Texas Legislature. Even though Barthold remained optimistic and
resilient, the immediate present was bleak.

On 27 March 1962, Vice President Nicholson told the governors that his
office was about to have responsibility for the Radio-Television-Film Center under Hoffman reorganization, and he had taken steps to rectify the causes of the
CM&P recommendation for Channel 8's termination by constituting and consulting with a Television Advisory Board consisting of managers of the three
commercial television companies. Nicholson's claims for improvement were,
first, that a substantial breakthrough was imminent in faculty utilization with the
beginning of instructional television in political science, and second, that various
external funding sources would help the station become self-sustaining. For example, two of the three commercial television stations had paid their $10,000
annual commitments and a $300,000 contract with HEW was pending. Third, a
new community support program asking for individual donations was being
launched by brochure.[60] Fourth, a former staff man [Paul Owen] skilled in securing industrial contracts was rehired.[61] Based on this progress, Nicholson asked
the board to extend the period for the continuance of KUHT-TV until 31 August
1963, the last day the university would be a private school. The likelihood of
terminating Channel 8 was moot. By now, the regents, led by Colonel Bates,
considered KUHT-TV a mainstay of the university and never seriously considered discontinuing its service to the public or turning over its control to another
governing entity, for that might have been a public relations disaster. Yet, to the
contrary, such a decision might have been in the best interests of the public and
the university.

It seemed that everyone wanted Channel 8; but no one knew how to pay
for it. As KUHT neared its tenth birthday, the station's decline was evident in
personnel, programming, and contracts.

Most of the staff who maintained the original vision and dedication had
departed. Most of those remaining were caretakers, as Barthold alluded to when
commenting on Schwarzwalder's departure. In 1953-54, the roster listed a staff
of 17; in 1958, it peaked at 28; in 1963—the tenth anniversary, KUHT had 16 full
time employees and 10 part-time students.[62] They produced 44 per cent locally
originated programming and depended on 56 per cent programming from other
sources.[63] Roy E. Barthold was station manager. The two remaining producer-
directors were Fred Smith (a.k.a. Carter Smith) and Ainslie Bricker. Bricker, a
music specialist formerly at the National Music Camp, Interlochen, the District
of Columbia Public Schools, and the Oregon School of the Air soon departed.
Smith, whose background included teaching and commercial announcing, sought
a career in acting. James Page continued as production manager, George Collins
as artistic head of production, and Charles (Phil) Zimmerman, Jr., who got a

bachelor's degree, began working his way toward program director. In May 1962, Paul Owen was rehired as a television consultant for special projects, while still pursuing a doctorate in psychology. Six employees were engineers. Counted separately were those in Film Operations. Director Paul Schlessinger, who had a bachelor's degree from Amherst, Army film experience, and was the artistic force behind most of KUHT's nationally distributed series, left in 1959. Editor Arnold Bergene, after 12 years in Hollywood, proved to be a valuable asset; and Pat Coakley remained steadfast as chief audio engineer while getting a bachelor's degree. James Hunt and Bill Henry were once student interns. KUHT internships, military experience, and bachelorhood characterized many young filmmakers at Channel 8.

Even the relationship between KUHT and the academic department deteriorated.[64] So long as they shared the fifth floor, KUHT had plenty of faculty and student volunteers; but by the mid-sixties physical separation of the station and the department resulted in increased isolation. Fewer faculty participated in activities at KUHT, and few Channel 8 employees taught classes. Volunteering ended as students were scheduled into formal laboratory classes. The Radio-Television-Film Center has no interest in KUHF-FM, and so it became a student operation under the supervision of a faculty member. During the late 1950s radio-TV and journalism were merged as a single department, and in 1963 renamed Communication Arts, chaired by now "Dr." Patrick E. Welch. Communication Arts was part of the College of Arts and Sciences, headed by Dean Alfred Neumann. Welch said combining the areas would enable students and faculty to share similar interests, would be more economical to operate, and would lead to a broader knowledge of print and broadcasting within a liberal studies background that a student of the sixties should have. He predicted: "Over the next two or three decades, various schools teaching mass communications can make a profound difference in the level of media personnel. They can do so, if they utilize their facilities at full potential, allowing maximum access by students. They can do so if they are geared for not only vocational training, but also for a liberal education of breadth and depth which very few other occupations require."[65] This view—media taught within a liberal arts context—is supported to this day.

The merger resulted in radio-television and KUHF-FM moving into the acutely inadequate "temporary" building shared by journalism and Student Publications. While radio-television and KUHF were on the fifth floor, on 15 July 1955 journalism moved from the Recreation Building to a 1,500 square foot, air-conditioned "residential" structure built for about $15,000.[66] It had one classroom, offices, minimal space for *The Cougar* and *Houstonian*, and was located near the printing plant, also in "temporary" quarters. To accommodate the 1962 merger, a two-classroom wing was added. Faculty shared offices. One office was so small

that students could not sit down for counsel[ing] Strader was in charge of Student Publicatio[ns] about 425 majors in 1968, Welch and Strader n[radio-television teaching load, besides Welch C. Battin, who acquired an early doctorate i[n] Michigan. He came from the University of Flo[rida] a visiting professor (1954) and remained at the of his career.[67] Like others, he initially produc[ed] drama workshops for Channel 8, in addition t[o]

To supplement this modest faculty, the doctorate, was added in 1965. Previously he duties, especially in FM, at Texas Christian U[niversity] North Carolina at Chapel Hill. KUHF had been format, but with the move, students resisted cla[ssical] ming more compatible with the industry they e[nter] sity financial support, the students became invo[lved] to life in Houston, such as live freshmen baseba[ll] news and documentaries, occasional dramas, a[nd] times featuring student artists.[68] With 10,000 wa[tts] ful educational radio station in Texas, and was than Channel 8 had viewers.[69] A coincidental [study by] Wilbur Schramm showed that KUHT was viewe[d at some] p.m. in 23 per cent of Houston, 47 percent of Alv[in] homes each week.[70] In May 1968, the Student A[ssembly] that sought "A more effective voice in the contr[ol] and more unified and sensible financing for p[ublic] station."

KUHF-FM was relegated to a pitiful, cl[oset] behind a sheetrock wall with a large window loo[king] private entrance, an unbelievable descent from i[ts] fact, the relationship of student training to the stat[ion] correspondence at the university's highest levels.[71] position was clear. KUHF was looked upon as a[n asset] primarily for possible RTFC expansion, and at th[e time] avoid interference with a commercial station by sh[ifting] megacycles. FM was so tenuous that in applying fo[r a grant] neys asking the station's location were given the u[niversity's] 3801 Cullen Boulevard, no one being certain wher[e it would be] next. Student concerns prompted a professional br[oadcast] Alpha, to file a protest with the FCC that sought [years as station manager, the author resigned, and[

KUHF-FM f[Cochran rep[

Mea[simultaneou[Nicholson, [mands with[Nicholson t[upon appro[required for[earned fro[m widest pos[assist in the[quite unde[r between (1)[income nec[of Commu[possible fo[Legislature[tion in radi[date the di[it has beco[(1) separat[the provisi[

Al[the end of[taken. KU[Neumann[By fall 197[all studen[tion at a t[nel 8 and [uncooper[communi[or off ca[needs of [clined in [no longer[exists wa[businesse[The com[departme[

on-going troubles with Channel 8 and FM contributed to the department's not seeking continued accreditation from the American Council for Education in Journalism.[76]

Besides staff and voluntary losses that helped to offset operational expenses, instructional television was terminated. In 1966, *Effort Toward Excellence: The University of Houston Self Study*, prepared for the Commission on Colleges of the Southern Association of Colleges and Schools, the university's accrediting organization, declared that by the mid-1960s more than 100,000 semester hours had been taught on television.[77] "In view of the existing classroom space, use of television teaching will permit the accommodation of more qualified students in a rapidly growing university."[78] Instead, before the ink was dry on the *Self Study*, KUHT suspended telecourses at the university on 1 September 1965. Students were advised they would have to enroll in "super lectures" of 200 or more students with "live" instructors.[79] President Hoffman said that the sudden increase in enrollment from 11,000 to 17,000 in the two years after becoming a state institution required a massive building program. "The reason for phasing out instructional TV programs, which I had supported strongly as vice president was the very simple fact that whereas the state formula for support per credit hours applied to courses given in the classroom, we could not get it applied to courses given through television."[80] He saw only continuing expense for professors with no off-setting revenue, and he faced another reality: lack of enthusiasm among the faculty. In a 1967 study, Dr. Richard Evans summarized the reasons for instructional television's failure on 11 college campuses: (1) professor insecurity, (2) traditional sanctity of the classroom, (3) psychological aspects of teacher-to-television, and (4) lack of feedback. Evans claimed that the argument "that TV teaching is not as effective as teacher-to-student instruction is erroneous."[81] Television instruction demands updating material. "There have been more than 200 different studies made around the country since UH initiated this technique. They show there is no significant difference in the the knowledge gain."[82]

From 1960 to 1965, KUHT had fewer contracts. It had no new NETRC contracts; it produced less than six programs a year for national distribution.[83] Few local contracts utilized the talents of staff filmmakers. HISD, UH, Fleming Company, Greater Houston Action for Youth, and Playways funded three to six programs. The biggest single contract came from the Texas Education Agency for *Education for Survival*, 1960, a 12-program civil defense series. The entire film output for 1963-64 was five films, but activity with HISD, GRETA, UH alumni and public relations offices increased thereafter. Dr. Richard Evans continued his interviews with world famous behavioral scientists such as Eric Fromm, B.F. Skinner, and J.B. Rhine, and playwright Arthur Miller. By 1965, the outlook improved. Film Operations began producing short features for NET's *Regional Reports*, among them "H.L. Hunt: the Richest and the Rightest," "L.B.J.," "The

Republicans," "The Democrats," "The New Morality," "Prayer in the Public Schools," and "Drugs on Campus." For NET's *What's New* it filmed "Wonder in the Eighth," describing the Astrodome, and "Spaceport, U.S.A." In 1966, NET gave an award to KUHT for "The Wrong End of Main," a local documentary. In June 1968, the station received a $153,000 Ford Foundation grant for a 12-program series that attempted to motivate low income consumers from detrimental economic practices. *The Way It Is* included three live town meetings that were "stimulating experiments in the use of television." In each, a searching dialogue-in-depth was established between consumers and experts in various areas: small loans, food purchases, home buying, apartment rental, furniture buying, new and used cars, home remodeling, and the family budget. A 4 November 1969 special, "The Heartmakers," produced for NET, showed current developments

The Arts in Houston, originating in 1956, spotlighted (l-r) James Johnson Sweeney, Nina Vance, Sir John Barbirolli, Tatiana Semenova with host Dr. William Lee Pryor on its fifth anniversary.

in artificial and mechanical hearts and featured Dr. Denton Cooley and Dr. Michael DeBakey, who had gained worldwide attention in a controversial and growing field.[84]

As the station's schedule broadened from five days a week in 1966 to include Sundays in 1967, KUHT-TV could point with pride to its local live discussion programs and townhall meetings. "If anyone ever bothered to compile a list of Houston's most valuable local TV shows, 'Critical Issue' would have to be at the top of the heap," reported the *Houston Chronicle*.[85] Funded by the Texas Education Coordinating Board and hosted by former Channel 11 News Anchor Nick Gearhart, *Critical Issue* premiered on 17 October 1967 with a two-hour open-end live discussion on mass transportation. Each month Gearhart conducted candid exchanges between local and national experts and viewers whose phone calls were taken by volunteers from the League of Women Voters during the telecast. Racial understanding, the Mexican-American, drug abuse, the nursing shortage, and Houston slums were some of the topics. Another bright spot was *The Arts in Houston*, premiering in January 1956. The arts prototype had English Professor William Lee Pryor interviewing major local and national figures in music, theater, and the arts. By mid-1960s, the series consisted of occasional specials.[86]

Recognizing the need for more and better local programming. Roy Barthold consistently expressed his complaints about the station's funding: "But, the bitterest lesson of ten years with Channel 8 has been realization that adequate performance of these functions simply cannot be budgeted by a university or school system. A broader base of organizational and financial support is necessary to activate the 50 per cent unused potential of KUHT—in program areas perhaps more vital to the community than any that have been dealt with in depth so far." "This is our frank evaluation of the status and prospects of Channel 8 now—a statement of the basic problem of financing non-instructional programming on an ETV station. We must deal with this problem decisively the next few months, and we will need cooperation from interested individuals and organizations, and from business and industry."[87] Modest efforts throughout the decade were made to attract public support; however, no major fund-raising project materialized during Roy Barthold's administration.

A SEARCH FOR NEW VIEWERS

In order for Channel 8 to survive the 1960s, it had to reinvent itself. This time it would not originate many local programs or offer college credit courses. Instead, it would hire out its services to organizations seeking to broadcast their own programs and messages: HISD, NET and PBS, and institutional commercial sponsors. In return for virtually abdicating its local service contribution, for being an independent voice, for serving local needs by identifying community problems and solutions, and for encouraging local talent through original broadcasts,

KUHT-TV would distribute programs produced by non-station personnel. To accommodate outside producers and to find new audiences, Channel 8 expanded its studio space and acquired a new transmitter. In September 1964, Channel 8 moved from its single studio facilities on the fifth floor of the Ezekiel Cullen Building to the university's Texas Television Center at 4513 Cullen Boulevard. (The historic original studios would become administrative offices.) The new location had ample space to simultaneously telecast live on-air programming from one of them, to videotape another program in the second studio, and to telecast two telecourses over closed circuit to other buildings on the campus.

KUHT-TV was off the air June through July 1964 to relocate. It returned with a rejuvenated spirit and facilities. If the public wanted local programming, it would have to financially support it. Although increased revenue from instructional programs was anticipated, Barthold said, "This security of the basic operation does not include a large segment of programming that *ought* to be done—programs dealing with local issues and cultural interests which cannot be produced with State, University, or public school funds. We have contended with this impasse since 1953, trying to provide creative local programs with marginal personnel and funds from formally budgeted activities. As we enter this period of physical expansion, we realize that concurrent planning must go on for establishing local live programming as something more than a petty cash drawer operation. This will require cooperation and support from organizations and individuals representing a cross-section of the community's interests and needs."[88]

In order for Channel 8 to be utilized by a larger population, its 11-year-old transmitter, which was no longer manufactured, had to be upgraded. In 1964, the principal coverage area was about 40 (some claimed 60) miles from the on-campus transmitter site, alongside the studios on Cullen Boulevard.[89] At distances of one to 20 miles many factors affected reception. In southwest Houston some homes and schools had trees and tall buildings interferring with the signal. A properly tuned outside antenna was essential for a decent picture.

Dr. Nicholson, two years earlier, said KUHT was applying for an HEW grant to improve its facilities, but the money was slow in coming. This period went by before he was able to present a confidential report to the board of regents indicating that local support was being sought; so that a grant in the range of $500,000 could be obtained from HEW under the ETV Facilities Act of 1962, the first federal bill recognizing educational television's financial difficulties and providing funds on a matching basis.

A promising prospect was suggested by Channel 13 General Manager Willard Walbridge. Walbridge, a Channel 8 advocate, once said: "KUHT has given the public some milestones in television history and literally thousands of hours of interesting, mind-stretching fare."[90] He had heard that Channel 11 was moving from its transmitter site in Alvin, about ten miles south of the central maneuver politically the university administration, the Houston community, and eventually the Texas Legislature. Even though Barthold remained optimistic and resilient, the immediate present was bleak.

On 27 March 1962, Vice President Nicholson told the governors that his office was about to have responsibility for the Radio-Television-Film Center under Hoffman reorganization, and he had taken steps to rectify the causes of the CM&P recommendation for Channel 8's termination by constituting and consulting with a Television Advisory Board consisting of managers of the three commercial television companies. Nicholson's claims for improvement were, first, that a substantial breakthrough was imminent in faculty utilization with the beginning of instructional television in political science, and second, that various external funding sources would help the station become self-sustaining. For example, two of the three commercial television stations had paid their $10,000 annual commitments and a $300,000 contract with HEW was pending. Third, a new community support program asking for individual donations was being launched by brochure.[60] Fourth, a former staff man [Paul Owen] skilled in securing industrial contracts was rehired.[61] Based on this progress, Nicholson asked the board to extend the period for the continuance of KUHT-TV until 31 August 1963, the last day the university would be a private school. The likelihood of terminating Channel 8 was moot. By now, the regents, led by Colonel Bates, considered KUHT-TV a mainstay of the university and never seriously considered discontinuing its service to the public or turning over its control to another governing entity, for that might have been a public relations disaster. Yet, to the contrary, such a decision might have been in the best interests of the public and the university.

It seemed that everyone wanted Channel 8; but no one knew how to pay for it. As KUHT neared its tenth birthday, the station's decline was evident in personnel, programming, and contracts.

Most of the staff who maintained the original vision and dedication had departed. Most of those remaining were caretakers, as Barthold alluded to when commenting on Schwarzwalder's departure. In 1953-54, the roster listed a staff of 17; in 1958, it peaked at 28; in 1963—the tenth anniversary, KUHT had 16 full time employees and 10 part-time students.[62] They produced 44 per cent locally originated programming and depended on 56 per cent programming from other sources.[63] Roy E. Barthold was station manager. The two remaining producer-directors were Fred Smith (a.k.a. Carter Smith) and Ainslie Bricker. Bricker, a music specialist formerly at the National Music Camp, Interlochen, the District of Columbia Public Schools, and the Oregon School of the Air soon departed. Smith, whose background included teaching and commercial announcing, sought a career in acting. James Page continued as production manager, George Collins as artistic head of production, and Charles (Phil) Zimmerman, Jr., who got a bachelor's degree, began working his way toward program director. In May 1962, Paul Owen was rehired as a television consultant for special projects, while still pursuing a doctorate in psychology. Six employees were engineers. Counted separately were those in Film Operations. Director Paul Schlessinger, who had a bachelor's degree from Amherst, Army film experience, and was the artistic force behind most of KUHT's nationally distributed series, left in 1959. Editor Arnold Bergene, after 12 years in Hollywood, proved to be a valuable asset; and Pat Coakley remained steadfast as chief audio engineer while getting a bachelor's degree. James Hunt and Bill Henry were once student interns. KUHT internships, military experience, and bachelorhood characterized many young filmmakers at Channel 8.

Even the relationship between KUHT and the academic department deteriorated.[64] So long as they shared the fifth floor, KUHT had plenty of faculty and student volunteers; but by the mid-sixties physical separation of the station and the department resulted in increased isolation. Fewer faculty participated in activities at KUHT, and few Channel 8 employees taught classes. Volunteering ended as students were scheduled into formal laboratory classes. The Radio-Television-Film Center has no interest in KUHF-FM, and so it became a student operation under the supervision of a faculty member. During the late 1950s radio-TV and journalism were merged as a single department, and in 1963 renamed Communication Arts, chaired by now "Dr." Patrick E. Welch. Communication Arts was part of the College of Arts and Sciences, headed by Dean Alfred Neumann. Welch said combining the areas would enable students and faculty to share similar interests, would be more economical to operate, and would lead to a broader knowledge of print and broadcasting within a liberal studies background that a student of the sixties should have. He predicted: "Over the next two or three decades, various schools teaching mass communications can make a profound difference in the level of media personnel. They can do so, if they utilize their facilities at full potential, allowing maximum access by students. They can do so if they are geared for not only vocational training, but also for a liberal education of breadth and depth which very few other occupations require."[65] This view—media taught within a liberal arts context—is supported to this day.

The merger resulted in radio-television and KUHF-FM moving into the acutely inadequate "temporary" building shared by journalism and Student Publications. While radio-television and KUHF were on the fifth floor, on 15 July 1955 journalism moved from the Recreation Building to a 1,500 square foot, air-conditioned "residential" structure built for about $15,000.[66] It had one classroom, offices, minimal space for *The Cougar* and *Houstonian*, and was located near the printing plant, also in "temporary" quarters. To accommodate the 1962 merger, a two-classroom wing was added. Faculty shared offices. One office was so small that students could not sit down for counseling. Assistant Professor Noel Ross Strader was in charge of Student Publications. While enrollments climbed to about 425 majors in 1968, Welch and Strader managed the complex. Carrying the radio-television teaching load, besides Welch and part-time faculty, was Dr. Tom C. Battin, who acquired an early doctorate in the field from the University of Michigan. He came from the University of Florida on a one-year appointment as a visiting professor (1954) and remained at the University of Houston for the rest of his career.[67] Like others, he initially produced and directed programs such as drama workshops for Channel 8, in addition to teaching.

To supplement this modest faculty, the author, who also had a Michigan doctorate, was added in 1965. Previously he taught and held administrative duties, especially in FM, at Texas Christian University and the University of North Carolina at Chapel Hill. KUHF had been a classical music and information format, but with the move, students resisted classical music in favor of programming more compatible with the industry they expected to enter. Without university financial support, the students became involved in programs directly related to life in Houston, such as live freshmen baseball, international student activities, news and documentaries, occasional dramas, and contemporary music sometimes featuring student artists.[68] With 10,000 watts, KUHF was the most powerful educational radio station in Texas, and was believed to have more listeners than Channel 8 had viewers.[69] A coincidental audience survey conducted for Wilbur Schramm showed that KUHT was viewed occasionally from 7:30 to 9:30 p.m. in 23 per cent of Houston, 47 percent of Alvin, and 21 percent of Texas City homes each week.[70] In May 1968, the Student Association Senate drafted a bill that sought "A more effective voice in the control of KUHF and more effective and more unified and sensible financing for planning and expansion of the station."

KUHF-FM was relegated to a pitiful, closet-like 19½ x 9½ foot studio behind a sheetrock wall with a large window looking into a classroom, and no private entrance, an unbelievable descent from its original $400,000 facility. In fact, the relationship of student training to the stations was already the subject of correspondence at the university's highest levels.[71] By 1969, the administration's position was clear. KUHF was looked upon as a minimal operation retained primarily for possible RTFC expansion, and at the moment its interest was to avoid interference with a commercial station by shifting KUHF from 91.3 to 87.8 megacycles. FM was so tenuous that in applying for the frequency change, attorneys asking the station's location were given the university's general address at 3801 Cullen Boulevard, no one being certain where the studio might be located next. Student concerns prompted a professional broadcasting fraternity, Phi Chi Alpha, to file a protest with the FCC that sought a public hearing.[72] After four years as station manager, the author resigned, and the era of attempting to use

KUHF-FM for student training ended. RTFC engineer and former student Arvil Cochran replaced him with a different approach for radio.

Meanwhile, the failure to meet student laboratory requirements in radio simultaneously generated a debate over television laboratories. Vice President Nicholson, in his role as Director of Development, had to juggle academic demands with those of Channel 8. KUHT consistently won, as in this memo from Nicholson to Vice President and Dean of Faculties, Dr. John C. Allred: "We look upon appropriated dollars as a relatively small percentage of the far larger total required for operating the overall RTFC. You apparently see the $55,000 [money earned from contracts] as a large and generous sum which should permit the widest possible use of RTFC facilities, equipment, supplies and personnel to assist in the instruction of Communications students."[73] "This is a complex but a quite understandable problem which centers around the unavoidable conflict between (1) RTFC administrators under a mandate to produce from projects the income necessary to keep the Center afloat; and (2) members of the Department of Communications with the laudable ambition to provide the best instruction possible for their students. The underlying difficulty is the refusal of the State Legislature to fund directly either operations of the RTFC or laboratory instruction in radio and television. An appropriate solution should obviously accommodate the differing objectives and attendant difficulties obtaining for all concerned; it has become more and more apparent that any viable resolution must include (1) separation of production/broadcasting from laboratory instruction; and (2) the provision of separate budgets."[74]

Although Dr. Battin continued to teach students in KUHT's Studio B to the end of the sixties, the situation was doomed. Accounting studies were undertaken. KUHT-TV wanted several thousand dollars a year for use of Studio B; Neumann had budgeted $3,000 for laboratories. He said he had no other money. By fall 1972, the situation reached a stalemate. Without funds, KUHT terminated all student laboratories.[75] Consequently from 1972 to 1978, with the administration at a total impasse, the communication students were denied access to Channel 8 and KUHF as laboratories. The perception that KUHT-TV, particularly, was uncooperative, overpriced, and failed to meet its obligations to the academic community penetrated the Houston community. For the next 15 years no one on or off campus could articulate the reasons for Channel 8's failure to fulfill the needs of the campus that held its license. Commercial station contributions declined in part, with the gift of the Alvin site, discussed later, and because KUHT no longer trained potential employees. In 1972, an internship program that still exists was established between the Communication Arts Department and media businesses. The first intern, Johnny Almendarez, went to KTRK-TV, Channel 13. The commercial stations, however, gave no monetary support to the academic department. During the 1970s, weak support from the university administration, on-going troubles with Channel 8 and FM contributed to the department's not seeking continued accreditation from the American Council for Education in Journalism.[76]

Besides staff and voluntary losses that helped to offset operational expenses, instructional television was terminated. In 1966, *Effort Toward Excellence: The University of Houston Self Study*, prepared for the Commission on Colleges of the Southern Association of Colleges and Schools, the university's accrediting organization, declared that by the mid-1960s more than 100,000 semester hours had been taught on television.[77] "In view of the existing classroom space, use of television teaching will permit the accommodation of more qualified students in a rapidly growing university."[78] Instead, before the ink was dry on the *Self Study*, KUHT suspended telecourses at the university on 1 September 1965. Students were advised they would have to enroll in "super lectures" of 200 or more students with "live" instructors.[79] President Hoffman said that the sudden increase in enrollment from 11,000 to 17,000 in the two years after becoming a state institution required a massive building program. "The reason for phasing out instructional TV programs, which I had supported strongly as vice president was the very simple fact that whereas the state formula for support per credit hours applied to courses given in the classroom, we could not get it applied to courses given through television."[80] He saw only continuing expense for professors with no off-setting revenue, and he faced another reality: lack of enthusiasm among the faculty. In a 1967 study, Dr. Richard Evans summarized the reasons for instructional television's failure on 11 college campuses: (1) professor insecurity, (2) traditional sanctity of the classroom, (3) psychological aspects of teacher-to-television, and (4) lack of feedback. Evans claimed that the argument "that TV teaching is not as effective as teacher-to-student instruction is erroneous."[81] Television instruction demands updating material. "There have been more than 200 different studies made around the country since UH initiated this technique. They show there is no significant difference in the the knowledge gain."[82]

From 1960 to 1965, KUHT had fewer contracts. It had no new NETRC contracts; it produced less than six programs a year for national distribution.[83] Few local contracts utilized the talents of staff filmmakers. HISD, UH, Fleming Company, Greater Houston Action for Youth, and Playways funded three to six programs. The biggest single contract came from the Texas Education Agency for *Education for Survival*, 1960, a 12-program civil defense series. The entire film output for 1963-64 was five films, but activity with HISD, GRETA, UH alumni and public relations offices increased thereafter. Dr. Richard Evans continued his interviews with world famous behavioral scientists such as Eric Fromm, B.F. Skinner, and J.B. Rhine, and playwright Arthur Miller. By 1965, the outlook improved. Film Operations began producing short features for NET's *Regional Reports*, among them "H.L. Hunt: the Richest and the Rightest," "L.B.J.," "The

Republicans," "The Democrats," "The New Morality," "Prayer in the Public Schools," and "Drugs on Campus." For NET's *What's New* it filmed "Wonder in the Eighth," describing the Astrodome, and "Spaceport, U.S.A." In 1966, NET gave an award to KUHT for "The Wrong End of Main," a local documentary. In June 1968, the station received a $153,000 Ford Foundation grant for a 12-program series that attempted to motivate low income consumers from detrimental economic practices. *The Way It Is* included three live town meetings that were "stimulating experiments in the use of television." In each, a searching dialogue-in-depth was established between consumers and experts in various areas: small loans, food purchases, home buying, apartment rental, furniture buying, new and used cars, home remodeling, and the family budget. A 4 November 1969 special, "The Heartmakers," produced for NET, showed current developments

The Arts in Houston, originating in 1956, spotlighted (l-r) James Johnson Sweeney, Nina Vance, Sir John Barbirolli, Tatiana Semenova with host Dr. William Lee Pryor on its fifth anniversary.

in artificial and mechanical hearts and featured Dr. Denton Cooley and Dr. Michael DeBakey, who had gained worldwide attention in a controversial and growing field.[84]

As the station's schedule broadened from five days a week in 1966 to include Sundays in 1967, KUHT-TV could point with pride to its local live discussion programs and townhall meetings. "If anyone ever bothered to compile a list of Houston's most valuable local TV shows, 'Critical Issue' would have to be at the top of the heap," reported the *Houston Chronicle*.[85] Funded by the Texas Education Coordinating Board and hosted by former Channel 11 News Anchor Nick Gearhart, *Critical Issue* premiered on 17 October 1967 with a two-hour open-end live discussion on mass transportation. Each month Gearhart conducted candid exchanges between local and national experts and viewers whose phone calls were taken by volunteers from the League of Women Voters during the telecast. Racial understanding, the Mexican-American, drug abuse, the nursing shortage, and Houston slums were some of the topics. Another bright spot was *The Arts in Houston*, premiering in January 1956. The arts prototype had English Professor William Lee Pryor interviewing major local and national figures in music, theater, and the arts. By mid-1960s, the series consisted of occasional specials.[86]

Recognizing the need for more and better local programming. Roy Barthold consistently expressed his complaints about the station's funding: "But, the bitterest lesson of ten years with Channel 8 has been realization that adequate performance of these functions simply cannot be budgeted by a university or school system. A broader base of organizational and financial support is necessary to activate the 50 per cent unused potential of KUHT—in program areas perhaps more vital to the community than any that have been dealt with in depth so far." "This is our frank evaluation of the status and prospects of Channel 8 now—a statement of the basic problem of financing non-instructional programming on an ETV station. We must deal with this problem decisively the next few months, and we will need cooperation from interested individuals and organizations, and from business and industry."[87] Modest efforts throughout the decade were made to attract public support; however, no major fund-raising project materialized during Roy Barthold's administration.

A SEARCH FOR NEW VIEWERS

In order for Channel 8 to survive the 1960s, it had to reinvent itself. This time it would not originate many local programs or offer college credit courses. Instead, it would hire out its services to organizations seeking to broadcast their own programs and messages: HISD, NET and PBS, and institutional commercial sponsors. In return for virtually abdicating its local service contribution, for being an independent voice, for serving local needs by identifying community problems and solutions, and for encouraging local talent through original broadcasts,

KUHT-TV would distribute programs produced by non-station personnel. To accommodate outside producers and to find new audiences, Channel 8 expanded its studio space and acquired a new transmitter. In September 1964, Channel 8 moved from its single studio facilities on the fifth floor of the Ezekiel Cullen Building to the university's Texas Television Center at 4513 Cullen Boulevard. (The historic original studios would become administrative offices.) The new location had ample space to simultaneously telecast live on-air programming from one of them, to videotape another program in the second studio, and to telecast two telecourses over closed circuit to other buildings on the campus.

KUHT-TV was off the air June through July 1964 to relocate. It returned with a rejuvenated spirit and facilities. If the public wanted local programming, it would have to financially support it. Although increased revenue from instructional programs was anticipated, Barthold said, "This security of the basic operation does not include a large segment of programming that *ought* to be done— programs dealing with local issues and cultural interests which cannot be produced with State, University, or public school funds. We have contended with this impasse since 1953, trying to provide creative local programs with marginal personnel and funds from formally budgeted activities. As we enter this period of physical expansion, we realize that concurrent planning must go on for establishing local live programming as something more than a petty cash drawer operation. This will require cooperation and support from organizations and individuals representing a cross-section of the community's interests and needs."[88]

In order for Channel 8 to be utilized by a larger population, its 11-year-old transmitter, which was no longer manufactured, had to be upgraded. In 1964, the principal coverage area was about 40 (some claimed 60) miles from the on-campus transmitter site, alongside the studios on Cullen Boulevard.[89] At distances of one to 20 miles many factors affected reception. In southwest Houston some homes and schools had trees and tall buildings interferring with the signal. A properly tuned outside antenna was essential for a decent picture.

Dr. Nicholson, two years earlier, said KUHT was applying for an HEW grant to improve its facilities, but the money was slow in coming. This period went by before he was able to present a confidential report to the board of regents indicating that local support was being sought; so that a grant in the range of $500,000 could be obtained from HEW under the ETV Facilities Act of 1962, the first federal bill recognizing educational television's financial difficulties and providing funds on a matching basis.

A promising prospect was suggested by Channel 13 General Manager Willard Walbridge. Walbridge, a Channel 8 advocate, once said: "KUHT has given the public some milestones in television history and literally thousands of hours of interesting, mind-stretching fare."[90] He had heard that Channel 11 was moving from its transmitter site in Alvin, about ten miles south of the central campus, to a new tower. Nicholson was greeted sympathetically by Channel 11's Vice President and General Manager James C. Richdale, Jr., who like other Houston boardcasters, had kept an interest in Channel 8 and the academic department, sources for many employees. Nicholson sought a tax write-off and gift, which required the approval of Channel 11's owners at Corinthian Broadcasting in New York. "KUHT with its wide range of cultural and educational offerings is a powerful and important voice in the Houston community. It is a gigantic classroom, a drama theatre with unlimited seating capacity, and an outlet for meaningful community dialogue. KUHT makes a daily contribution to our highest needs—our emotional, intellectual and aesthetic satisfactions," Richdale wrote in support of the station.[91] "With all this in mind, our purpose in donating the KHOU-TV Alvin tower and transmitter was to expand the reach of KUHT so that its fine offerings could touch more people, and thus expand the intellect of our coummunity.[92]

KHOU-TV's extraordinary donation included a 1,171-foot tower, a newly secured antenna, 18 acres of land and a transmitter building valued at around $280,000. "With help from the ill but still hard-wroking Congressman Albert Thomas, and his colleague Bob Casey, the HEW grant in the amount of $294,966 was approved August 26, 1964."[93] The grant enabled Barthold to award contracts to the General Electric Company on its low bid of $206,726 for a new antenna

NET's *Cancion de la Raza* appeared in 1969.

system and transmitter, and a contract to Sarkes Tarzian in the amount of $17,377 for related microwave equipment.[94] Its tower at nearly 1,200 feet and move from 46 to full power at 316 kilowatts (302 kw visual, 30.2 kw aural) increased KUHT's coverage to over 80 miles from the Alvin site.[95] KUHT could be seen throughout Houston, Galveston and most of the upper eastern Gulf coast. By October 1965, KUHT—with a current investment of $1.3 million—had become a regional, instead of a local, station. Its potential audience rose from 1.5 to 2.3 million viewers. This was a major turning point in its history.

Despite considerable effort by RCA/NBC and KPRC-TV, color was not widespread in Houston as late as the mid-1960s. The first interconnected colorcasts on other public stations was unavailable in Houston. Then in 1967, KHTV, Channel 39, owned by Gaylord Broadcasting of Oklahoma City, came on the air as the city's first all-color UHF station. Channel 39 broadcast "The Game of the Century," when Elvin Hayes and the University of Houston Cougars ended Lew Alcindor and the UCLA Bruins' 47-game winning streak in the Astrodome. Rapid conversion to color took place thereafter. The following year KUHT-TV sought another federal grant. "If local funds in the modest ratio of about one-to-five can be found," KUHT-TV could broadcast in color.[96]

Some colorcasts were not noted in Channel 8's *Program Previews* in 1967. But within two years about a dozen programs appeared in the schedule: NET's *Sounds of Summer, NET Journal, Speaking Freely, Washington Week in Review, Book Beat, NET Playhouse, NET Festival, Cancion de la Raza, Black Journal, Spectrum,* and *All the President's Men.* By 1969, the only locally originated program produced in color on Channel 8 was *News on Campus,* a showcase for student talent and a laboratory for production students in the Communication Arts Department.[97] The series, supervised by Dr. Battin and the author, began in January 1967, when Channel 39 went on the air, and was delivered to KUHT for a repeat broadcast. On 10 November 1969, *News on Campus* was scheduled a half-hour earlier to make room for the premier of *Sesame Street,* also in color. "The first color program to originate from KUHT studios was *Talk Point: Houston Reaction* on 16 February 1970."[98] It was made possible by a partial donation of two RCA cameras. Within the year, a second HEW grant was obtained.[99] Afterward, all KUHT local programs were in color. Color transmission and production had become a reality.

NEW FUNDING SOURCES

Instructional television for the public schools was hampered by KUHT's low power and limited coverage area. Some schools developed Instructional Television Fixed Service (ITFS).[100] As a co-licensee in the 1950s, the HISD had aired instructional and enrichment programs. In 1960, the HISD began some in-service programming for teachers and gradually added some in-school programs, such as chemistry and physics, to supplement teachers' classroom activities.[101] Soon the Harris County Department of Education initiated instructional television in Spanish; and representatives from 14 school districts decided to appropriate 25 cents per child for supplementary instruction by television.[102] By 1964, many school districts in Harris and surrounding counties agreed to fund four courses on a cooperative basis: Spanish, modern mathematics, science, and a combination art and music course for grades four through six. The formation of this cooperative group, these funds, and the installation of the more powerful transmitter at Alvin enabled Gulf coast schools to use Channel 8. KUHT-TV proposed to the HISD that it would broadcast school programs, if HISD would pay for actual operational costs. To implement the deal, the University of Houston offered $20,000 for administrative and development functions.[103] "Well, when we were cut off from our only source of funds, this very small public school thing that had been dawdling along for about two or three years, we had to use that as an immediate transfusion," Barthold claimed.[104] On 23 February 1965, some 40 school administrators met at the Channel 8 studios to consider the financial problems and program potential of the proposed Gulf Region Educational Television Affiliates, referred to simply as "GRETA."[105]

Sufficient commitments were made within a few weeks to provide minimal programming in the first year. GRETA produced eight series for a total of 105 programs. Simultaneously, the 59th Texas Legislature passed Senate Bill 149 that designated $250,000 per year to match local participation of schools in Houston, Austin, and Dallas served by educational television stations.[106] Administered by the Texas Education Agency, $78,000 was made available to schools in the Gulf region and the schools put up $88,000 based on 40 cents per student's average daily attendance (ADA). Private and parochial schools paid 40 cents per child, but the state did not match the money. GRETA's total projected budget for 1965-66 was $166,000.[107] These developments made it possible for a comprehensive schedule of five hours a day of in-school and school-related programs. By 1966, GRETA listed 31 private and parochial schools and 33 school districts with 300,000 students in 16 counties.[108] The 1967-68 operating budget was $149,000. In 1968, 35 hours of supplementary programming reached 460,000 children in over 60 districts in 23 counties.[109]

GRETA was a self-governing organization operated by the authority of a board of school administrators chosen from representatives of the participating districts. The board was composed of a president, vice president, secretary, four standing committee chairmen, and the coordinating director of GRETA, Mrs. Dorothy Sinclair, the only non-expiring term member. Since 1953, Sinclair had produced and directed HISD programs on Channel 8. She also contributed innovative specials, such as the 1963 series, *Los Pastores* that included "The Shepherds," the annual Mexican Christmas pageant in San Antonio, narrated in English by Joe Coffer. By the late sixties one projection suggested that enrollments would eventually reach 600,000 or 700,000 pupils; and Sinclair was advocating a second television channel: "We have literally reached the saturation point of available time for in-school programs, yet increasingly favorable attitude on the part of teachers and administrators makes it imperative that the University of Houston make application for a second channel so that GRETA can anticipate and meet the needs of the schools in the area."[110] Satisfying the ever-changing schools, administrators, teachers, and students required an incredible amount of insight, care, understanding, and expertise, which Mrs. Sinclair handled astutely from her Channel 8 office until her retirement in 1984.

Although instructional television was no longer utilized by the University of Houston, the public schools monopolized about one-third of KUHT's day to: "1. Help strengthen and control district-wide curriculum. 2. Strengthen and enrich the subject matter taught. 3. Provide through the redevelopment of teaching staff and student body more opportunities to take full advantage of the individual strength of the staff. 4. Provide opportunities to effectively utilize team teaching concepts. 5. Provide for more education per dollar through such areas as foreign language, music, driver education, etc. 6. Offer unlimited opportunities for in-service training of teachers. 7. Allow for unique opportunities to strengthen and improve the communication process throughout the district. 8. Reduce costs and strengthen all areas of the audio-visual services of the district. 9. Provide opportunities to reduce class size at no additional costs in selected subject areas. 10. Give every student a front row seat in science and demonstration type subjects. 11. Provide opportunities for every student in the district to gain the benefit of a highly trained and skilled teacher. 12. Reduce graphic arts cost; demonstration materials will be more effectively utilized. 13. Strengthen and enrich community relations programs. 14. Provide the opportunity to bring outstanding personalities and programs directly to the classroom."[111]

"Both teachers and pupils discovered that television can be a dynamic tool in the learning process when the program on the air makes use of its unique attributes for visualization and motivation and when the classroom teacher adapts the material to the needs and abilities of her class."[112] With careful, deliberate planning, administrators and teachers from the schools, the GRETA staff, and Channel 8 personnel developed ways the programs were integrated into the curriculum without imposing tone or substance that would be offensive to the participants. GRETA materials were primarily considered supplementary to classroom instruction, although in some cases they were dominant.

The process began with the formation of a program committee for each instructional series. The committee consisted of one or two supervisors and about ten members. The committee identified the nature of the subject matter, determined the relationship the television teacher would have with the classroom teacher, and auditioned the teachers. Teachers with past experience in the subject matter were most likely selected. Finding good television teachers was difficult, because a pleasing personality and communication skills were essential, along with a cooperative attitude in structuring the printed materials. The challenge to the teacher was formidable. Basically, she had to write a complete *Teacher's Television Manual* or program guide outlining every lesson in the series.[113] The series ran from 15 to 30 lessons. Usually each lesson lasted 20 minutes for elementary school programs and 30 minutes for secondary classes, which were believed to be optimum attention spans. The television teacher had the responsibility for developing the outline, including all necessary research, "and most important, the outline should contain enough information for the teacher to answer student questions." Once the *Teacher's Television Manual* was perfected and received final approval from the program committee, it was printed and distributed to the school districts. The teacher, program, and guide were continuously monitored by means of evaluation forms given to those teachers who incorporated the telecast in their classrooms. The evaluation forms were reviewed by the program committee and the teacher. Program guides and telecast content were revised if necessary for upcoming editions. The process—from committee to teacher to study guide to printer to distribution to in-class use to feedback to committee and back to the teacher—was never-ending so long as the series was distributed.

The television teachers were dedicated, stimulated, and highly competent individuals. Many spent from ten to 20 hours on each 20- or 30-minute lesson on a subject in which she was already an expert. Compensation was stipulated in separate contracts. Generally, teachers of the shorter elementary school lessons received $100 per program; those teaching the longer secondary school sessions were paid $150, in addition to their normal annual salaries. If the *Teacher's Television Manual* they wrote or the programs they appeared in were distributed beyond their district jurisdictions and income was generated, they were entitled to small fees. According to Pat Reumert, GRETA's program coordinator: "The publication of the teacher's guides is the most expensive part of the preparation process. Every year the cost of printing amounts to about ten percent of the entire budget for the Gulf Region Educational Television Affiliates."[114] The first printing was for 25,000 copies.

The *Teacher's Television Manuals* included outlines for three or four classes and detailed for the in-class teacher in advance the purpose and preparation, concepts and content, and review and activities recommended for each lesson. The television teachers were carefully screened, but they were not highly publicized. By 1966, Mrs. Betty Lester's class, *English Composition*, had been accepted for national distribution by Great Plains Instructional Television Library, Lincoln, Nebraska, a major center.[115] This class was designed for Grades 7, 8 and 9. The lessons were tested with the assistance of seventh grade students. The series generated techniques in effective writing of description, narration, and exposition. Later lessons were an extension of the skills developed originally for the seventh grade. Mrs. Audrey Graves presented the series, *Once Upon a Printing Press*. It intended to help teachers instruct students in the skills and techniques of reading critically factual and fictional material. Sixteen programs were based on the fourth grade supplemental reader *Peacock Lane* and 15 programs made use of the fifth grade supplemental reader *Silver Web*. *A Is for Art* demonstrated techniques for teaching art in the primary grades. The programs used crayon, tempera, simple crafts, clay, puppets, and cut, torn or folding paper to motivate youngsters.[116]

Not all of the programs were produced by GRETA. *Music Appreciation* for grades four through six was a combination of live and filmed performances that acquainted children with the instruments in an orchestra. This series depended on NET and the Houston Symphony. A current events series, *Places in the News*, was telecast weekly by WNDT-TV, New York. It featured a host with several guest experts. *Exploring* offered documentaries on the history of America that held the attention of juniors and seniors. Produced by NBC in cooperation with the National Council for the Social Sciences and the American Library Association, it won many awards.

Prompted by a rare request from Colonel Bates, Dorothy Sinclair, who was designated assistant director of the Radio-Television-Film Center, introduced Mrs. Francis Hipple, a classroom teacher from Garden Villas, to testify before the regents on 29 October 1968. "Mrs. Hipple, alluding to her own experience in the classroom stated briefly that GRETA was a very effective means of providing valuable supplementary material."[117] GRETA quickly received a special grant of $55,000 to create three 28-minute color pilot videotapes and to devise study guides for a Project Promoting International Understanding of Latin America. Funded under Title V of the Elementary and Secondary Education Act, six KUHT staff members chose to record Christmas and customs in Guatemala as their first foreign assignment in December 1966, a project reminiscent of the Mexican Christmas filmed three years previously. "By showing the daily life of a Guatemalan child—his methods of recreation, holiday activities, religious ceremonies, mode of dress, daily duties, games, etc.—GRETA plans to supplement local social studies programs, emphasizing international understanding."[118] The goal was to devise a series so innovative and stimulating it would serve as a model for other groups interested in producing programs for international education. GRETA maintained a rigorous schedule of programs designed for teachers in elementary and secondary classrooms. The schedule completely filled broadcast daytime hours whenever schools were in session. Ten years later (1977), GRETA was broadcasting 35 hours of in-school programming to 60 area school districts at a cost of $212,000, comprising about 20 per cent of Channel 8's one million dollar budget.[119]

About the same time GRETA was in its successful third year, a similar vehicle was sought so that KUHT-TV could offer production and broadcasting services to universities and colleges, junior colleges, selected cultural organizations, government and community projects, businesses and industry. A pilot project, already operating at Texas Technological College, Lubbock, called the Western Information Network, was allowed under HB 692, passed by the 60th Texas Legislature and approved by the Texas Coordinating Board. President Hoffman asked the regents to seek approval for a similar project at the University of Houston. He believed "such an association would not involve any expenditures on the part of the University."[120] It would benefit Channel 8, however, through indirect financial support and the opportunity to make its services available to appropriate users. This new organization was named the Southwest Texas Information Network Association (SETINA).[121] In September 1969, KUHT-TV claimed SETINA as another first for the station, because SETINA was providing programs for the university and 14 other state-supported institutions of higher education in a 31-county area in East Texas and along the Gulf coast. SETINA estimated its potential audience at more than 100,000 college and university students. By 1977, although SETINA was an official state agency, it still had not been funded. Headquartered at Channel 8, its members included 16 junior and senior colleges and universities in the region that wanted a distribution link for joint programming and broadcasting operations.

No matter how hazy Channel 8's future looked as the 1960s began, on balance, good fortune had prevailed. As the decade ended, KUHT-TV was ensconced in new quarters, had a new transmitter site, and color was imminent. Its daytime programming shifted from unfundable college credit courses to funded public school instruction, and its night time programming had broader choices as the federal government decided to support public broadcasting. With a regional approach to programming as Houston exploded into a dynamic oil-driven economy, Roy Barthold's persistent argument for more investment in quality night time programming supported by viewers and institutional short announcements began to materialize, even though the programs would be produced largely outside the city. To accomplish this goal, a formal method of fund-raising had to be established.

4

NETWORK INUNDATION

As the obvious role for educational television, namely instruction, faded in prominence, its other major role as alternative enrichment programming gained more attention. During the 1960s most cities across the country had only one or two commercial television stations. A community was very fortunate to have all three network affiliates, one or two independent stations, and an educational station. The multiple channel choices offered on cable television were, of course, in the future.

After nearly 15 years, educational television had now proven its value by providing programming that commercial broadcasters were unwilling or unable to support. These programs included those that drew small audiences with special interests, that were controversial and sponsors wanted to avoid, that were experimental and required time to nurture and develop. Children's programming seemed to be particularly handicapped on commercial stations. Educational television had shown that it could deliver programs of local and national interest that were decidedly different, yet professionally competitive with those aired by the national commercial networks. As mentioned earlier, KUHT-TV had always depended on external program sources.

By the 1950s, responsibility for the Ford Foundation that emerged from handling the private philanthropies of Henry Ford, had been inherited by Henry Ford II, who turned its presidency over to the former president of Studebaker Corporation, Paul Hoffman. Hoffman, a believer in decentralization, established organizations for dispensing foundation money.[1] One organization was the Fund for the Advancement of Education (FAE). FAE provided money for the [National] Educational Television and Radio Center (ETRC), founded in 1953, later NETRC, to administer and distribute educational programs. "KUHT-TV was one of the four founder stations which received NET's first program on January 1, 1954," NET President John F. White wrote.[2] It was "Frontiers of the Sea," produced by the University of Miami, but NET's inaugural program was "Vision," televised 16 May 1954.[3] Its first major distribution was *Science in Action*, 1954, that debuted with "How Man Measures," on 27 September, followed by such diverse topics as rainmaking, volcanoes, bridge building, ant life, detergents, plutonium, and the animal of the week. Numerous programs joined a growing list: *Great Plain Trilogy, Of Men and Ideas, American Economy, Ballets de France*, and

Shakespeare on TV. Some programs were especially for young people: *Youth Forum*, *Magic Window*, and *The Friendly Giant*. "By 1958, 30 stations were getting a minimum of six hours a week from this cooperative, chiefly as kinescope recordings or film. By 1959, having lost interest in radio, it supplied members with eight hours of programming a week—a quarter of all educational television programs. Major producing stations were WGBH (Boston), WQED (Pittsburgh), WTTW (Chicago), and KQED (San Francisco)."[4]

By 1961, NETRC became the headquarters and programming agency for a "fourth" network of noncommercial stations across the country that had risen to 62 educational television stations, 57 of them holding noncommercial licenses. In 1963, NETRC shortened its title to National Educational Television or N.E.T.[5] Its programs were recorded on tape and film and distributed to affiliates by mail. "NET counted 53 of these stations as affiliate outlets, claimed 10,000,000 regular viewers and a potential national audience in excess of 26,000,000 people. Alabama, Florida, and Oklahoma were operating state-wide television networks. WGBH in Boston was the key outlet in a projected regional network which would link East Coast cities from Philadelphia to Montreal. KTCA-TV in Minneapolis had completed similar plans for a six-state network in the central Middle West. Kansas, Nebraska, Maine, and Ohio had engineered state-wide network plans, and the Southern Regional Educational Board in Atlanta proposed a microwave system which would link each of the educational stations and all of the four-year colleges in a 16-state area."[6] Many programs were produced by the stations under contract with the Center; some were produced by commissioned independent producers; some were obtained from abroad through exchange agreements.

In January 1967, the Ford Foundation invested money in interconnecting educational stations so that they could offer several hours of evening programming, and later that year NET, again with Ford Foundation support, initiated a two-hour experimental series of cultural, informational, and public affairs programs. On 5 November 1967, "to stir things up" Executive Director Av Westin and Host Edward P. Morgan, veterans of commercial television news, produced a pivotal series for NET. It was a live experiment in color called *Public Broadcasting Laboratory* or *PBL*. The first broadcast was "Day of Absence," a drama written by Douglas Ward Turner, a black author. Played in whiteface by an all black cast of the American Negro Ensemble Company, the fantasy comedy commented on black life in the rural south premised on the assumption that all blacks had disappeared for one day. Following the play, *PBL* presented a view of black life in the north. A national black leader took the audience on a filmed tour of Chicago's Westside and then confronted a racially mixed audience to present viewpoints on what was happening in northern American cities. The entire broadcast was put into perspective by Dr. Robert Coles, a Harvard expert on race relations. Channel 8's film unit contributed segments for the two-year *PBL* series: "Murder," "O.E.O. Gunsight," "Chamizal Revisited," "Gas Buggy," and "West House." One program on the theological, medical, legal and sociological aspects of euthanasia and organ transplants included a live KUHT studio segment with Dr. Michael DeBakey, a noted heart surgeon (21 January 1968). By the

NET's *Mister Rogers' Neighborhood*, starring Fred Rogers, debuted on KUHT-TV in 1966.

mid-1960s, Channel 8 spent ten per cent of its annual budget—$30,000—on film and taped programs. NET supplied about two-thirds of the schedule.[7] Included were the Emmy award-winning children's series *Mister Rogers' Neighborhood*, *NET Playhouse*, cited as the nation's best dramatic series (1969), *NET Festival*, a kaleidoscope of music, dance, film and documentaries, and *NET Journal*, a current events digest.[8]

As NET programming improved during the 1960s, the Carnegie Corporation, in addition to Ford, became a major contributor to educational television by setting up the Carnegie Commission on Educational Television (1965) that soon published a benchmark report: *Public Television: A Program for Action*. President Johnson wrote the commission: "From our beginnings as a nation we have recognized that our security depends upon the enlightenment of our people; that our freedom depends on the communication of many ideas through many channels. I believe that educational television has an important future in the United States and throughout the world."[9] The statement reiterated his enthusiasm expressed to Schwarzwalder a decade earlier. Two of the 15 members of the commission were influential Texans: Oveta Culp Hobby, owner and publisher of *The Houston Post* and KPRC radio and television, and J.C. Kellam, president of

President Lyndon B. Johnson, who signed the Public Broadcasting Act into law, was portrayed in both drama and documentary on PBS.

the Texas Broadcasting Corporation that ran President Johnson's broadcasting properties.

The Carnegie Commission began its report by separating educational television programming into two parts: "(1) instructional television directed at students in the classroom or otherwise in the general context of formal education, and (2) what we shall call Public Television, which is directed at the general community."[10] Among its 12 recommendations were that a Corporation for Public Television be formed to receive and disburse funds mainly from governmental and private sources, that it support at least two national production centers and independent producers at local stations, that it encourage interconnection of stations, that it stimulate experimentation in television and the recruitment and training of personnel, that federal funds from a manufacturer's excise tax on television sets be used to set up a trust fund for the Corporation.[11] The report was widely read. On 28 February 1967, President Johnson recommended to Congress that it pass the Public Broadcasting Act of 1967, and by November, the bill was enacted along the lines recommended in the Carnegie report; and thereby, the Corporation for Public Broadcasting (CPB) was established.[12]

Industry reaction was favorable. CBS President Frank Stanton pledged one million dollars to the proposed Corporation: "The report of the Carnegie Commission on educational television provides the American people a balanced, realistic and practical approach to a more adequate non-commercial television service. The report's reasoned safeguards give assurance that educational television will be pluralistic in the sources of its support and its programming and in its administrative controls."[13] Using television as a tool for public education was agreeable, but whether the government should fund educational television was debatable. Once again Rosel Hyde was chairman of the FCC. Before Congress he endorsed legislation proposed by HEW Secretary John W. Gardner: "This is an opportunity you must accept when it is available or it will be gone and probably politically and financially irreversible. This not only serves the educational purpose, there is a broader advantage to it. What we need is a service that is competitive to the one we have in the interests of diversity, operated by people whose approach to television is different from that of the commercial operator, those who have educational purpose and [are] financed from those other than advertisers."[14]

CPB was prohibited from producing programs itself; therefore, in 1969, the Public Broadcasting Service (PBS) was set up to allocate monies for productions from individual educational television stations, now referred to as "public broadcasting" stations. Heading PBS was former WGBH-TV Manager Hartford N. Gunn, Jr., who devised a plan for financing public television.[15] CPB and PBS then proceeded to give production contracts for program concepts they judged acceptable. These program concepts were funded at much higher levels than single stations could afford. Prompting the selection of programs was a dramatic increase in foundation support to public broadcasting during the early 1970s. This support came largely from foundations located along the East Coast mainly in the middle Atlantic states. The Carnegie Corporation initiated the Children's Television Workshop with $4 million, and four key production centers were identified: WGBH, Boston; WNET, New York, which had consolidated the NET operation; WETA, Washington, D.C.; and KCET, Los Angeles. WTTW, Chicago, and KQED, San Francisco, were centers also, but they received far less financial support.[16] The result was a small number of stations, for the most part already furnishing programs to NET, attracted PBS money for major program series. All stations depended on venture capital to start projects that sometimes put them in debt before they could realize financial returns. By and large the designated production centers had grander facilities. For example, WTTW, part of the Chicago Educational Television Center, had three studios (1965). Studio A, the largest was 60 X 80 feet with a 34-foot ceiling—large enough to hold an entire symphony orchestra and high enough to permit dramatic productions requiring quick scene changes.[17]

Comparatively, KUHT was no competitor, having only two small studios 40 X 50 and 40 X 25 feet with a total of two color cameras and one black and white camera; a switcher with special effects but no chroma key; two color capable hi-band video tape machines without editing facilities; and two black and white film chains. "We have parts on order to repair and install one used color film chain. The other three black & white cameras, the GE switcher, and the IVC 1" tape recorder are used for student laboratory purposes only. At the transmitter we have one black and white chain with an old slide projector used for trouble slides and test pattern only. We have no remote facilities," Jim Bauer reported in 1970.[18]

A great deal of criticism concerning the relationships of CPB, PBS and the participating stations persisted throughout the decade. Key figures in the Carnegie Commission study like Stephen White and Arthur L. Singer, Jr., agreed: "The likely outcome is that...the Corporation for Public Broadcasting will be formed, that Ford's Public Broadcasting Laboratory will dominate its program production, and that it will fall into a simple fourth-network operation. Let it be clear that if this happens, or if anything much like it happens, the intentions of the Carnegie Commission will have been largely ignored."[19]

Reminders of what Public Television's programming goals ought to be appeared frequently. TV Guide's Richard K. Doan wrote that he thought the better, the more important, and realistic objectives of Public Television were: "To be determinedly inventive in your thinking, and hence in your programming; to have a strong propensity for doing the unexpected; to be exceedingly topical—as topical as today's weather; to be acutely sensitive to your fellow human beings' wants, woes and worries; to be steadfastly dedicated to helping civilization survive and making life understandable; to have the courage of your convictions when the chips are down; to make us feel you are striving more to enlighten and encourage us than to confuse and discourage us, and along the way, to entertain us without sullying our sensibilities."[20]

With the PBS designated production centers getting most of the work, "the rest of the more than 200 stations got very few production grants or none at all," John Schwarzwalder, in his role as KCTA executive vice president, complained.[21] By 1972, he recommended immediate changes at CPB and PBS, including replacement of those in charge, a fairer policy of distributing funds, strengthening the concept of education on television, prohibiting CPB/PBS from forcing programs on stations, and new policies formulating that at least two-thirds of appropriated federal dollars go directly to educational television stations.[22] Schwarzwalder's complaints were echoed by many stations, including KUHT.

KUHT's dwindling contracts contributed to its growing financial plight. Not only was the lack of income damaging to Channel 8's operation, but the public perception of KUHT's staff was downgraded. If it could not successfully compete for national contracts, perhaps its staff was incapable, unimaginative or incompetent.

In 1973, "after almost a year of bitter struggling, an Agreement was reached between CPB and PBS."[23] The Agreement stated that CPB would contract PBS to operate the interconnection, make direct grants to the stations, and fund programs it wanted on the interconnection. PBS would operate the interconnection, pay for its own activities, and for the programs it wanted on the interconnection.[24]

After President Johnson decided not to run for reelection, his program in regard to public broadcasting mentioned earlier, fell into the hands of a less supportive Nixon administration. Domestic unrest and the Vietnam war had President Richard M. Nixon's attention. Then too, disagreement among educators as to whether public television should be centrally or locally controlled posed important hindrances to the viability of public television. Maintaining a priority for federal tax dollars was difficult. CPB, nevertheless, was funded on a year-to-year basis. After President Nixon resigned, President Gerald Ford signed a five-year $634 million authorization for public broadcasting, but stations had to raise matching money to obtain federal grants. "Between 1951 and 1974 the Ford Foundation awarded over $268 million in grants to noncommercial broadcasting. No other foundation even remotely approached support on this scale."[25] Because of government and foundation support, a plethora of NET and PBS programs were funded, produced, and broadcast. By contrast, KUHT found little local funding or venture capital of any kind throughout the 1960s. Instead, KUHT had to strive very hard to obtain enough money just to lease PBS programs for broadcast.

A sampling shows a wide range of NET/PBS programs serving diverse interests. NET had already set the pace for offering an alternative service. Julia Child's *The French Chef*, William F. Buckley's *Firing Line, The Advocates, Black Journal*, and *The Great American Dream Machine* were among them.[26] PBS programs really took hold in the late 1960s. After more than a year of testing and production, *Sesame Street* premiered on 10 November 1969. The first experimental season consisted of 130 programs designed "to help bridge the intellectual gap between the disadvantaged and middle-class child." This outstanding $8 million project was produced by the Children's Television Workshop (CTW), under the direction of Joan Ganz Cooney. Unlike successful traditional formats, *The Friendly Giant*, 1955, or *Mister Rogers' Neighborhood*, 1966, the hour-long *Sesame Street* borrowed commercial television techniques for educational objectives.[27] Letters of the alphabet, displayed in highly repetitious forms, sponsored programs. Staged in an urban street setting, it relied heavily on puppets and animated characters, some of which had to deal with imperfect personal qualities. Sequences were brief, and thus they held the attention of young children. The series was continuously undergoing research on its effectiveness and impact. It was soon supplemented by *The Electric Company*, debuting on 25 October 1971. The series' multi-segments focused on second to fourth graders, were shot in a Manhattan theatre, and directed for a season by former University of Houston communication student John Tracy, who is now one of the nation's top sitcom directors. *The Electric Company* using similar production techniques concentrated on spelling, vocabulary building, and numbers.

Adult viewers, although relatively small in numbers compared with commercial television viewers, were considered a well educated leadership group within a market and worth influencing. In the early 1970s, many programs were issue-oriented discussion formats and feature news, such as *World Press, Realities, Book Beat, The Nader Report, The Black Frontier, Our Vanishing Wilderness*, and *Washington Week in Review*. British suppliers, never far from American television screens, returned with new collections of literature-inspired dramas. Produced by the British Broadcasting Corporation (BBC) or British production companies, these programs were subsequently leased to PBS. Premiering on 5 October 1969 was the BBC's "all time smash hit," *The Forsythe Saga*. Based on the work of John Galsworthy, the 26-hour serial traced the intrigues, romances, and financial dealings of a Victorian family. It was the last major series in black and white.[28]

Already familiar to viewers for his 1960s series on man and the arts, Oxford University art historian Kenneth Clark narrated what he called his autobiography in 13 one-hour episodes. Beginning on 8 October 1970, *Civilisation*, two years in production and requiring 80,000 miles of travel, was a stunning account of Western Man from the fall of the Roman Empire to the twentieth century.[29] *The Ascent of Man*, a spectacular and throught-provoking 1971 series took Dr. Jacob Bronowski and a BBC crew to 27 countries to pursue its central issue: dogma versus scientific process. On 10 January 1971, *Masterpiece Theatre*, a broad title encompassing various serials and mini-series requiring viewers to watch succeeding programs, continued the fare popularized by *The Forsythe Saga*. *Clouds of Witness, Cousin Bette, Elizabeth R, The First Churchills, Poldark, Upstairs, Downstairs*, and *Vanity Fair* were some of the early dramas. *Masterpiece Theatre*, produced with a delicate aura of snobbery and English tradition, attracted faithful and substantial American audiences. For the 1972-73 season the English-American host of *Masterpiece Theatre*, Alistair Cooke, chronicled in addition a personal history entitled *America*.[30]

With the CPB/PBS Agreement in place, PBS had become the national distribution agency for public stations, after combining with the existing distributors, NET and NAEB. For an annual membership fee stations received coordination and scheduling of the national program service, fund-raising for national programs and support of local stations, technical and statistical research, system planning and financial management, legal counsel, and institutional and national program promotion.[31] PBS priorities and objectives were set by a 52-member board of directors elected by station licensees. Thirty-five were lay representatives who served as local station trustees. Fifteen were professional public television station managers. Everyone was elected for a three-year term. The PBS president and vice chairman were salaried.[32] In 1978, the administrative budget for PBS was paid for by the membership at a cost of $4.5 million. A contract from CPB gave PBS approximately $12.5 million to maintain and operate distribution facilities.[33]

Funding for programs came mainly from the stations themselves through a cooperative called Station Program Cooperative (SPC), grants from CPB, the National Endowments, private foundations, corporations, and individual station donations.[34] Initially, 27 public stations contributed programs; however, by 1977, 40 stations supplied programs for distribution. Twenty-eight per cent of the national programs were independently produced; 94 per cent were produced in the United States. PBS membership in 1977 was comprised of 157 independent local licensees operating 270 public television stations.[35] Programs were largely distributed over cable and microwave from the PBS main terminal located in Washington, D.C.; but expansion was underway in suburban Virginia. Within two years, PBS facilities would involve regional transmission and reception terminals utilizing the communication satellite WESTAR, which would link domestic stations in every state except Wyoming and Montana where there were none. PBS stations were in Puerto Rico, the Virgin Islands, Guam, and American Samoa.[36] Although nonprofit community organizations held the lead with 38 per cent of the stations, colleges and universities came in with 34 per cent, state authorities had 16 per cent and local school districts, 12 percent.[37] By providing viewers in the 1970s with such attractive programs, public television became a showcase for prestigious institutional linking with international corporations that wanted to favorably influence educated, politically astute American viewers. In the power politics of the time *Masterpiece Theatre* through its sponsor, Mobil Oil Corporation, would be a major factor in enabling WGBH, Boston, during the Nixon administration to replace WNET, New York, as the most prominent production/distribution center for PBS.[38] The wealth of New York cultural venues commanded attention however in such series as *Great Performances*, which

In the mid-1970s Willie Nelson gained national prominence on *Austin City Limits*.

began on PBS in 1972. Underwritten by Exxon, it absorbed *Theatre in America*, *Dance in America*, *The Shakespeare Plays*, and *Live from Lincoln Center*.[39] Or it became "a solid, thoughtful broadcast that unravels the news one issue at a time" in *The Robert MacNeil Report*, beginning in 1975, with Executive Editor MacNeil at WNET, New York, and Associate Editor Jim Lehrer at WETA, Washington, D.C. In 1976, the three-day-a-week series expanded to five half-hour programs. Within two years the title changed to *The MacNeil Lehrer Report*, and soon Charlayne Hunter-Gault and Judy Woodruff joined them.[40] *Nova*, 1974, a decendent of BBC's *Horizon*, had Michael Ambrosino as executive producer for WGBH. The episodes cost on average $250,000, and made some extraordinary cinematic observations through fiber optics, such as the human sperm entering the egg for "Miracle of Life."[41] *The National Geographic Specials* that debuted in the 1960s, are filmed all over the world, produced at WQED, Pittsburgh, and sponsored by Gulf Oil. One of the most expensive science series was *Cosmos*. It featured Carl Sagan, and cost $300,000 to $900,000 because of special effects. Some programs were directed by former KUHF Program Director Rob McCain at KCET, Los Angeles. According to Executive Producer Adrian Malone, *Cosmos* "tells in a brave way man's relation to the universe. It stands upon the beautiful concept that we are made of starstuff—that every atom in our bodies was once an atom in a star and may have been part of many children of stars—trees, people, comets, and planets."[42] During the decade some fine series did not originate at PBS designated centers. *Austin City Limits*, produced at KLRN by the Southwest Texas Public Broadcasting Council, San Antonio/Austin began 2 January 1976 with "Asleep at the Wheel" and classic renditions of Bob Wills and His Texas Playboys. It was funded by Budweiser Beer.[43] *American Indian Artists*, premiering on 8 August 1976 and produced by KAET, Phoenix, featured six successful jewelers, painters, sculptors, and potters illustrating their complex blend of tribal, Anglo and electic backgrounds.[44] *Wall $treet Week*, originating in 1969, with its "cheerful pundit" Louis Rukeyser and produced by the Maryland Center for Public Broadcasting, was destined for longevity.[45] KUHT promoted the the reputations of these programs, threatening that the public would be unable to view them if it did not support the station. During the 1970s this was probably true.

FUND-RAISING FOR PBS

Not being a PBS production center, Channel 8 became an exhibitor of PBS programs, and raising money on its ability to exhibit them was, to an extent, a major reason for Channel 8's existence. Meanwhile, its local programming obligations were eclipsed and production activity was minimal. GRETA programmed KUHT-TV until the public schools let out at 3 p.m.; but late afternoons and evenings had to be filled with alternative programs. KUHT's few talk shows emphasized local activities and issues. They depended on inexpensive or volunteer host/producers, guests who did not charge fees, modest sets, and the in-house Channel 8 crew, for even these low budget shows cost something to produce.

The move toward community support for Channel 8 and its schedule had been contemplated throughout most of the 1960s. Direct public support was nothing new. Door to door drives for station operating funds were launched in Chicago, St. Louis, and Pittsburgh a decade earlier (1953). As early as 1962, Channel 8 mailed program guides with enclosure envelopes asking viewers for $10 to $100 or more. But a permanent KUHT "viewer sponsor" plan was not started until 1966, when Channel 8 incorporated "I Luv Channel 8 Week" with its fall schedule.[46] The objective was to obtain local donations to support public affairs and cultural programming at night. KUHT claimed "the basic equipment and operating costs of Channel 8 are budgeted, with difficulty, by the University of Houston; the daytime in-school programming is paid for by a cooperative organization of school districts; but the evening programming is supported entirely by local [non-state] funds which contribute less than 10% of KUHT's total budget."[47] Channel 8's entire annual film and tape cost for Monday through Friday evening programs was about $30,000, a sum it hoped individuals would contribute. The station did not ask viewers to support local programs, however. Instead it raised money on network programs by asking viewers whether specific programs like NET's *The French Chef* or the *Festival of the Arts* were worth a $10 annual donation.

In 1967, when CPB came into existence, one of the first things it did was allocate $10,000 in seed money to every station for whatever project it chose. "Well, we stashed that away with about the same amount from somewhere else," Barthold once remembered, "and a month or so later I went to see McElhinney again. I told him, 'I'm about to retire in a couple of years and I think the station is going to peter out if you don't get some new financial blood in it while there's still some management left.' He said, 'Well, what have you got in mind?' I said, 'I've got $10,000 I'd like to spend to get out into the community and stir up something.' Mac said, 'What have we to lose?' Well, that green light enabled me to get Pat Nicholson, vice president for Development, into the act and help put together a Community TV Board, which became the Association for Community Television (ACT), a relatively exciting climax to our first fifteen years, and one I could retire with comfortably."[48] Meanwhile, Barthold was fighting cancer of the larynx. After a laryngectomy, he depended upon an electrical laryngeal prosthesis for several months prior to his retirement, as head of the Radio-Television-Film Center and general manager of KUHT-TV and KUHF-FM, in August 1969.[49]

Once again the University of Houston administration looked to an incumbent employee for leadership. A glance at the employee roster indicated that aside from Dorothy Sinclair, who headed up the GRETA project, no one had much administrative experience, except possibly James L. Bauer, director of Film Operations. "If I recall correctly Dr. Nicholson came over one day to the quonset building [Film Operations]. He said he thought I was doing a good job, and he was going to make the recommendation [for station manager] and wanted to know if I would accept it. And I did," Bauer said. "I was very happy where I was. I didn't want to be the oldest film producer in Houston. It sure wasn't the money [$16,100 a year]. There was the realization I was being given a heck of an opportunity. I was either going to do that or move on to something else."[50] At the School of Aviation Medicine, where he met John Meaney, Bauer had become an expert in high speed camera recording, explosive decompression, in making many experimental and some regular training films.[51] Married, with two children and one on the way, when he came to Channel 8 looking for a job, he found neither the time nor the money to obtain a college degree. After graduation from high school in Kingman, Kansas, he joined the service, completing basic training at Lackland Air Force Base. A shy man, the one aspect of film production he disliked the most was raising money for each project. Ironically, raising money was what the role of station manager required. As Bauer pondered the responsibilities, he said: "I think I had a feeling of inadequacy [as far as] my background was concerned. I felt I did have a business sense, and I believed that the station was going to be a major challenge and a lot of opportunity. I was aware of the financial situation. At that time I certainly was aware of what was happening nationally in the system. As a producer I had a good run of programs off the system, but the financial challenge was the pressure CPB, which was just in its infancy, and of course, PBS [put on the station]. The emphasis was toward community stations and the next step was the strong state networks [like those funded by the states of Georgia and South Carolina] that were very successful. That, as I saw it, was probably one of the things that, as an institutional station given the restrictions we had, we [would not have major production contracts]. I saw a good share of the production opportunities going to those stations that CPB had designated as producer stations."[52]

The university could have sought an outside candidate, but the key decision-maker was Vice President Nicholson, who wanted someone he felt he could work with as a subordinate, for Nicholson fancied himself as the real head of the broadcasting properties. In fact, his first move after Barthold's retirement, was to appoint himself as acting director of the Radio-Television-Film Center, a title he kept for the next decade.[53]

Nicholson, though not wealthy himself, persistently associated with wealthy potential contributors, hoping to take advantage of possible gifts.[54] How effective the quiet spoken Nicholson was in raising money for Channel 8 is difficult to assess. Many could share some credit, but many more attribute Channel 8's success to his contacts and tireless energy. In any case the main fund-raising group was the University of Houston Foundation, established in 1960. It had raised more than $1.2 million in its 1969 Excellence Campaign. Vice chairman of the campaign was S.I. Morris, a principal supporter of Channel 8. On 13 November, a black tie dinner was held in the Texas Room of the Houston Club to honor the 500 university benefactors and to announce KUHT-TV's status as a "public station." Channel 8 "now moves into a new and expanding era, with partial color capability added to full power, a new and most interesting range of programs and—of special significance for the future—the formation of the Association for Community Television," President Hoffman told the elite gathering.[55]

Association for Community Television that was to become KUHT's principal fund-raising organization was introduced at the UH Foundation dinner on 13 November 1969.

Weeks before, Nicholson had asked John T. Jones, an important media figure and an advisor to Channel 8 since 1955, to help organize a support group that would raise the money needed to keep Channel 8 on the air and to provide quality programming that was becoming available through PBS. At the dinner Nicholson introduced John O. Emmerich, Jr., editor of the editorial page of the *Houston Chronicle* as ACT chairman, and it was anticipated that 15 to 20 directors—Jones included—would be appointed to the ACT Board within weeks.[56] Emmerich had come to the *Houston Chronicle* in 1965. He was a graduate in history and journalism from the University of Mississippi. He had been in the Army and served on other newspapers. A Neiman Fellow, he had studied at Harvard University and the Sorbonne, Paris. "I concur with the whole theory behind ACT—that public TV has a tremendous role to play in community activities and a vast potential that is unfulfilled," Emmerich said. "And public envolvement can do a whole lot more."[57] By spring Emmerich was named president and CEO, and Frank M. Wozencraft, an attorney with Baker, Botts, Shepherd and Coates and former assistant attorney general of the United States, was designated ACT's board chairman. The group known as the Association for Community Television (ACT) immediately enlisted the aid of a cross section of influential citizens. The founding officers included Mrs. Joseph R. Mares of Dickinson, vice president; Patrick J. Nicholson, secretary, Robert L. Grainger, treasurer, and Dorothy Sinclair, assistant secretary. They planned a March membership drive "to publicize the purposes of the new organization, elicit community interest in present and potential programming and generally expand support."[58]

Channel 8's budget for 1970 was quickly drafted by Jim Bauer. He could count on the University of Houston to provide housing, maintenance, accounting, and administrative service estimated between $150,000 and $200,000; but the rest of the money had to be raised elsewhere. His anticipated operational costs were summarized as follows: Total anticipated operating budget, including salaries, was $408,500: administration, $81,600; programming, $121,100; engineering, $205,800. The funding sources he identified totaled $483,700. They included University of Houston cash allocation, $100,000; GRETA, $177,000; Hobby Foundation, $10,000; Houston Endowment, Inc., $10,000; Community Services Television Project, $10,000; ACT, $150,000; production services and contracts for CPB, $22,000; sale of GRETA study guides, $1,200, and non-broadcast activities, $2,500.[59]

On 24 March 1970 ACT's first membership drive signed up 455 members who became the basis of on-going public support, and netted $8,412.[60] During breaks between programs running from 5 to 10 p.m. viewers were asked to pledge a minimum of $15. Aside from a membership drive which usually took place in late winter, the principal means of getting money from the public was a teleauction, a device introduced years before at KQED, San Francisco. The teleauction collected donated gifts ranging from art works to travel services to dinners at various restaurants. These items were displayed at remote locations or at the station and put up for bid. No one realized how incredibly complicated and time-consuming this undertaking would become. Mrs. Max (Marty) Levine, an ACT director, agreed to be vice president and chairman of the teleauction, a critical appointment. Dr. Nicholson then went to President Hoffman for seed money and authority to go ahead with it.[61] "He looked at me just a little askance and asked, 'This teleauction, PJ, will it fly?' I assured him it would, and it did."[62]

It took nearly two years to put an effective group together to assume the work of the auction. Bauer credited Marty Levine as "the first chairman to put her name to the line, and said she'd get the volunteers to go out and canvass merchants to get items and volunteers to help with the broadcast."[63]

By 1971, ACT was ready to launch Auction I under the guidance of Levine who enlisted the aid of one thousand volunteers to gather items, to present them for bidding on the air, to carry out the multitude of tasks necessary for distributing the items, and to collect the money. That first auction raised $122,000, resulting in the university reducing its KUHT contribution to $75,000, which was only three-fourths of the amount Bauer expected.[64] Within a few months the university allocated its final cash sum of $25,000, in addition to utilities, maintenance of the buildings, grounds, and transmitter.[65] "The ACT Board felt strongly about this decision as they felt their commitment was to provide money for programming and the university should provide operating expenses and equipment."[66] "In my looking back over the books, it was 1972," Bauer has stated, "the university pulled out completely as far as any cash contribution to the station.[67] [KUHT's building and property remained rent free.] So from that point forward we were totally on our own."[68] The responsibility of the university to provide KUHT operational funds, and thus, enable ACT to apply its fund-raising to programs is a point of contention to this day. In 1972, the auction, under the chairmanship of Mrs. Robert U. (Ann) Haslanger and Alex Chesser, of Houston Natural Gas Corporation, and of course, with hundreds of volunteers, came to KUHT's rescue with an amount well over $200,000.[69] The next year with increased experience, more valuable objects, and more "art nights," the sum rose to about $252,000 (1973).[70]

The third teleauction raised over $250,000 in 1973.

By 1975, for every $1 of federal funds, the public broadcasting system would have to raise $2.50, or 60 per cent of the total. For Fiscal 1976, KUHT had to contribute $78,000 to the PBS Station Program Cooperative.[71] ACT took ten evenings in March 1975 to increase pledges to 10,000, raising an income of $90,000. Channel 8 viewership was at record levels. Paid memberships and bids from auctions continued to grow. Sums derived from the KUHT teleauction show a steady increase: 1971, $122,000; 1972, $207,000; 1973, $252,000; 1974, $303,000; 1975, $340,000; 1976, $341,000; 1977, $407,000.[72]

ACT's success drew considerable attention. A University of Houston planning committee was established that same year to study the accomplishments, organizational effectiveness, and long range potential of ACT to generate community support for Channel 8, and to consider its future relationship with the university and the station. In other words, the time had come for the university administration to take over responsibility for such a high income generating organization. To this point the staff required to run the increasingly complex ACT operation was not under the jurisdiction of the university. It was a team of enthusiastic, interested volunteers. On 3 August 1977, the university demanded control over it, and President Hoffman and ACT Chairman Levine signed an Agreement enabling all ACT staff workers to become employees of the University of Houston.[73] Thereby, the university assumed control over the Association for Community Television, and ACT assumed direct support for the station. With the exception of a small retainer to cover ACT board expenses, all donated funds were turned over to the station and then forwarded to the university on a monthly basis.[74]

By 1977, Nicholson announced that ACT was able to grant $600,000 to KUHT-TV for its 1976-77 budget, estimated at $1,122,942. GRETA provided $212,000 and CPB/PBS $214,700. This was the first time Channel 8's budget exceeded one million dollars.[75]

In 1978, the eighth teleauction, headed by Auction Chairman Rollie McGinnis, with Bauer, the station's staff, and 1,100 volunteers, brought in a record $507,865. The April membership drive increased the list from 17,000 to 26,000 members, adding more than $400,000. A separate drive in May, chaired by Mrs. Harris Masterson, raised $87,000. Before the year ended, ACT had raised $1,336,000, a sum 30 per cent higher than Channel 8's projected 1978 budget of $1,030,000.[76] In addition, one ACT vice president donated the accounting services of his firm to study receipts and internal cash flow. A major accounting firm continued to do the external audit, however. ACT had become indispensible to Channel 8's existence. ACT Board Chairwoman Marty Levine, recognized as a charter director and chair of the first teleauction, was appointed lay representative to PBS in Dr. Hoffman's place (1977), and she became first vice chairman of the National Association of Public Television Stations (NAPTS).[77] As important federal legislation loomed in 1978, namely U.S. House Bill 12605 that would provide one billion dollars for PBS over the next five years, Chairman Levine, along with President Hoffman and General Manager Bauer, conferred in Dallas with PBS Board Chairman Newton N. Minow, an outspoken critic of commercial television, concerning the impact of the legislation. The increasing importance of the ACT chairman's role illustrates how significant ACT had become to KUHT-TV in just eight years. "Public television is very nearly the only serious broadcasting game in town," John J. O'Connor wrote in *The New York Times* in 1978. Public Television was highlighting 25 years on the air, because, he said, "It seems some enterprising executive discovered that the first station in the present system was established in Houston in 1953, and the anniversary hoopla was put into orbit." He warned however: "But the system, if it is to continue providing a 'marked contrast' to the commercial alternative, must be allowed to keep its primary focus on programming. As matters stand at present, public TV is wasting too much of its energies on financing. The system's primary incentives are being redirected to the raising of money. And in that direction lies the formula for disaster."[78]

FORECASTS AND REALITIES

The unhappiness that resulted when Channel 8 management abruptly terminated all student laboratories in the fall of 1972, leaving the Communications Department completely without on-campus television laboratories, took six years to alleviate. From 1972 to 1978 all laboratories for students studying television were held, however inadequately, at KHTV, Channel 39, through the production of the university's weekly workshop series, *News on Campus*, currently called *Video Workshop*.[79] Frequently, this meant that three students were competing for each position on the crew. By the mid-1970s, enrollments in communication courses had increased so substantially that Dr. John Guilds, who eventually succeeded Dr. Alfred Neumann as dean of the reorganized College of Arts and Sciences, retitled the College of Humanities and Fine Arts, considered separating certain areas to form a College of Communication, as John Schwarzwalder had advocated many years earlier.[80]

Alternatively, Guilds suggested the college might incorporate these areas within its title, as the College of Humanities, Fine Arts, and Communication. In 1975 the university was in the midst of its ten-year report to its accrediting agency, The Southern Association of Colleges and Schools, and so it launched Mission Self-Study.[81] In its Preliminary Report, the Steering Committee said it was "deeply troubled by our failure to develop fruitful cooperation between the station and the academic departments of the Central Campus." It recommended the development of "a plan to more effectively relate the educational television and radio operations with the academic programs on the Central Campus."[82] Special attention should be given to defining a "learning laboratory" role for the stations, the report said. To the contrary the stations became less involved with the central campus.

While indecision prevailed, Dr. Barry Munitz became vice president and dean of faculties in April 1976; and about a year later, on 6 June 1977, he proposed to the regents the creation of a School of Communications, combining the existing departments of communications and speech. "The School of Communications, including appropriate research and learning resource programs, would be able to serve as a catalyst for interdisciplinary development, and professional service. This School would reflect the University's effort to achieve excellence through the discovery and application of knowledge, to sponsor and support distinguished interdisciplinary research, and to establish strong cooperative and service bonds with the academic community."[83] Dr. Munitz, who was about to become head of the central campus, explained that the proposal would seek approval of the Texas Coordinating Board and then recruit a director. The director would be responsible for the implementation of the curriculum, assignment of faculty, creation of specific goals and programs, and needs assessments.[84] The proposal passed unanimously. Within a year Dr. Kenneth A. Harwood was hired as Founding Director of the School of Communication at a salary of $45,000.[85] At the time, Harwood was dean of the School of Communication and Theater at Temple University, Philadelphia. His leadership set the standards for areas that were redefined as radio-television, journalism, speech communication, and communication disorders. Simultaneously, a Humanities Building at a cost of about $4,145,000 was being constructed to house drama, a theater, student publications, KUHF-FM, laboratory studios, offices, and classrooms for the School of Communication.[86] Soon the west wing of the Humanities Building was referred to as the Wortham Theater, named after regent and benefactor Lyndall F. Wortham, and the east wing was known as the Communication Building.[87] The School of Communication was formally dedicated in June 1978, with the main address presented by University of Houston graduate, former LBJ adviser, and president of the Motion Picture Association of America, Jack Valenti.[88]

A few days earlier, KUHT-TV celebrated its Silver Anniversary. It was a glittering affair held at the Museum of Fine Arts on 25 May 1978. An elegant crowd of 370 invited guests enjoyed a $100-a-plate dinner—cocktails at 6:30 p.m.—and were entertained by witty PBS talk show host Dick Cavett, who donated his services as master of ceremonies, and renowned jazz vocalist Ella Fitzgerald, who brought her guitar, bass, and drum trio.[89] The public was invited via television to watch the elite have a grand time. At 8:30, *The 25th and All That...from Cowtown to Countdown and Beyond,* a retrospective of still and moving pictures from the early days on the fifth floor of Ezekiel Cullen, showed faculty teaching courses, students interning, and staff presenting programs that some-times included celebrities.[90] Several segments from NET and PBS, along with greetings from local and national figures, reminded everyone that educational television had become very sophisticated since KUHT-TV went on the air. At 9:00, the guests assembled in Cullinan Hall where a live show, produced by Robert Cozens and directed by Mark Schiebl, was colorcast. The evening cost about $40,000: one-half for entertainment, one-fourth for the dinner, and one-fourth for the telecast. The event, sponsored by the university and ACT, at-tempted to showcase Channel 8's importance to the Houston community and its support from prominent citizens.[91] Sandra S. Mosbacher was the 25th Anniver-sary coordinator and Mrs. Robert L. Gerry, III, chaired the dinner committee. By now, the ACT Board consisted of 40 members, 15 of them were women. Six corporations helped underwrite the activity: Armco Steel Corporation, Pogo Producing Company, Shell Oil Company, Southwestern Bell Telephone Com-pany, Texas Commerce Bank, and United Gas Pipe Line.[92] Institutional support had become synonymous with quality television that Channel 8 initiated and symbolized. Wealthy patrons who contributed to the station could do so with considerable pride.

By 1978, KUHT-TV had reached a cumulative audience of 300,000 house-holds, a potential audience that ranked 14th among the nation's 270 public tele-vision stations.[93] The splendid reunion suggested that the communication re-naissance at the University of Houston had arrived at last. Dr. Philip G. Hoffman was not only head of the central campus but had become Founding President of the University of Houston System (1977). In his KUHT address Hoffman pro-jected an impressive future: "Our objective will be to move our broadcasting operations into the first rank for educational public stations, and to further es-tablish KUHT-TV, which is probably the single strongest link between the Uni-versity of Houston and the area the System campuses serve, as an anchor station for the Public Broadcasting Service in the Southwest."[94] KUHT-TV was already receiving PBS programming over a new satellite system. When increased to four transponders, he said the satellite would allow system-wide programming trans-mission from Channel 8 to the central campus, Clear Lake City, the Downtown College, Victoria, and perhaps a fifth campus at The Woodlands. He anticipated greater service to the Gulf coast region and the nation, a view that may have been directed toward the evening's special guest, PBS Board Chairman Ralph B. Rogers.[95]

Hoffman envisioned numerous major goals. First was doubling the memberships in ACT from 26,000 to 50,000. Second, he wanted to get a $1.2 million grant for a new transmitter and equipment by means of a matching grant from ACT. Third, he sought a stronger relationship between the stations and the new School of Communication. His fourth goal was a sharp increase in the number of locally produced programs. Fifth, he advocated an expansion of GRETA to reach as many as 75 school districts and 750,000 students. Lastly, he anticipated more simulcasts with KUHF-FM, which was going to be a full power, stereophonic station through HEW grants matched by an anonymous donor. He praised Vice President Nicholson, who was chairman of SETINA and served as liaison officer between the University of Houston System, ACT, and GRETA, and recognized contributions of Jim Bauer as general manager of Channel 8, Arvil Cochran as manager of KUHF-FM, and Dorothy Sinclair as director of GRETA—all of whom reported directly to Nicholson.[96] Excitement had reached a pinnacle, the outlook for the stations and the academic area was bright. There was however one flaw—President Hoffman planned to retire. Hoffman supported the view that, except for tenured faculty, retirement of university employees should be at age 65.[97] After 19 years of distinguished service as president of the University of Houston and four years as vice president and dean of faculties, he announced he would retire on 31 August 1980.[98] Somewhat similar to LBJ's endorsement of public television before he decided not to seek reelection, Hoffman would leave execution of much of his vision to his successors. Of the six goals previously mentioned, to date memberships in ACT are in excess of 63,000, the "tall tower" transmitter was installed in the early 1980s,[99] KUHT-TV is again providing production time for the School of Communication's *Workshop* series, the lack of locally produced programs remains a principal deficiency, GRETA was terminated in the mid-1980s, and the sixth goal—KUHT-KUHF simulcasts have gradually increased. The Hoffman-Nicholson leadership of Channel 8 effectively ended on 31 August 1980, with the former's retirement and the latter's title change.[100]

5

SURVIVAL ON THE SUPERHIGHWAY

By the mid-1970s, a complex University of Houston System (UHS) emerged consisting of largely autonomous, scattered campuses serving more than 40,000 students in traditional classrooms. Thousands of other students depended on KUHT-TV through the GRETA program and the Open University. Channel 8's future anticipated extended regional coverage through cable television, satellites, and increased transmitter power, telecommunication systems of fiber optics linking the campuses, an Instructional Television Fixed Service for students outside the central campus, a possible second channel, an expanded physical plant, and an increased budget.

KUHT was also confronted with serious problems. Foremost was the confusing shift in leadership from the central campus to University System administration. Second was increased public criticism of programming, especially from minorities, and third, in that same regard, criticism for the lack of local original programming. Fourth was complaints filed by employees concerning hiring, job practices, and low wages. Fifth was clarification in the Agreement between the station, the University System and the Association for Community Television. Sixth was the necessity for upgrading its transmitter and in-house equipment.

THE UNIVERSITY OF HOUSTON SYSTEM AND THE STATIONS

To understand the status of the University of Houston System by 1980, a summary of its development is helpful. At a meeting of the Texas Coordinating Board in San Antonio on 29 May 1968, the staff recommended that the University of Houston develop branch campuses to its north and south.[1] The central or main campus was irregularly referred to as University of Houston-University Park(UHUP). A campus to the southeast, near NASA, became the University of Houston at Clear Lake City (UHCLC). Another serving the business community in the heart of the city is known as the University of Houston-Downtown (UHD), and a fourth campus was developed at Victoria. Smaller campuses or "institutes" are located in growing suburbs, especially at Cinco Ranch, The Woodlands, and in Fort Bend County. Jurisdiction and coordination of these campuses and institutes gave rise to the University of Houston System (UHS), which was formally recognized by statute, House Bill 188, promoted largely through the efforts of State Representative Craig Washington, and passed by the Senate on 27 April 1977.[2]

Within a year, the University Board of Regents, now controlling a "system," had approved a new organization designating important shifts in power, as previously mentioned. At the top of the UHS was a "president," (the title would change to "chancellor") and various officers including the System Vice President for Academic Affairs, who would evolve as the principal administrator over the stations.[3] As the 1980s began, the UHS had a new president, Dr. Charles Edward Bishop, who held a similar administrative post in Arkansas. Although in the latter years of his academic career, Bishop, UHS Information Director Farris Block once told the author, was perceived as "a long awaited freight train coming down the track," a signal that awesome changes would take place when he assumed his duties on 1 February 1980. The shuffling of administrators and their titles in this formative period was confusing. Dr. Barry Munitz, promoted to interim, then permanent, chancellor (the title would change to "president") of the central campus by 1977, retained control over the School of Communication and shared jurisdiction with the UHS over the radio station.[4] The UHS kept full control over KUHT-TV; but it forced the main campus to house the radio station that remained in the Communication Building despite efforts to relocate it.

Legal and engineering aspects of both broadcast properties were administered by UHS through its Vice President for Academic Affairs. This office was held by Dr. Joseph E. Champagne for about one year after Bishop's arrival.[5] It was the failure of the board of regents to appoint Dr. Champagne as head of the Downtown campus, which Hoffman had recommended, that encouraged him to accept the presidency of the University of Michigan Oakland campus.[6] As an interim move, Bishop quickly appointed Dr. Martha Piper, an associate professor of curriculum and instruction in the College of Education on the central campus to serve as special assistant to the president for academic affairs. This office placed her over KUHT-TV and KUHF-FM. "We are pleased to have Dr. Piper on our system staff," President Bishop announced as he cited her work as a teacher, administrator, and faculty senate leader.[7] Meanwhile, Champagne was scouting for someone to take over the supervision of the broadcasting stations under a new UHS title: associate vice president for public service and telecommunications. This position at a lower level than the full vice presidency Nicholson had retained, turned out to be temporary. The position was offered to Dr. Florence Monroe. She noticed the listing on a job placement board, while attending an NAEB convention in Las Vegas. She contacted Champagne; and afterward received a call from President Bishop. Monroe had been in commercial telecasting since its embryonic days at WABD, the DuMont station in New York. Having earned her doctorate at New York University, she developed award-winning radio and television programs for the New York Board of Education, eventually becoming manager of Channel 25. In 1976, rather than preside over what she described as fatal budget cuts, she moved to Birmingham, Alabama as assistant vice president for telecommunications and general manager of WBHM, an educational FM station.[8] By June 1981, Monroe, like Bishop within six years of retirement, joined the UHS to oversee the stations, as associate vice president for public service and telecommunications.

While KUHT-TV received most of the attention, KUHF-FM, with Arvil Cochran as station manager, quietly increased its listenership by converting from a student-programmed station(1969) to a respected jazz and National Public Radio (NPR) format with a small professional staff and a few students. KUHF-FM had held a unique place in the community for about ten years. When the Humanities Building was constructed in 1978, a small suite, designed mainly by Cochran, was reserved for KUHF-FM. He had also applied his substantial engineering skills to the design of all radio-television space in the School of Communication.[9] By March 1980, KUHF-FM's full power transmitter was installed and operating, which extended its jazz/NPR programming to most of the upper Gulf coast. The staff numbered ten, including three minorities. Cochran's report to the University of Houston Board of Regents showed that KUHF-FM had made impressive favorable progress under his management. Then, unexpectedly, Cochran with nearly 30 years of university service was abruptly terminated by Associate Vice President Monroe.[10] Cochran was replaced by her long-time friend and former employee Judy Jankowski. Jankowski had spent the previous three years at WBHM, as program director for Monroe, and was now acting general manager. The decision to hire Jankowski was easy for Monroe because "she was very talented, very bright...and more than anything the staff reacted so well to her.... We interviewed a lot of people, at least 20. And she was one of the finalists. When we got down to the last five people or so—and the staff was in on the interview— they were the ones who said she's the one we'd love to see coming."[11] So, on 1 September 1981, Judy Jankowski became KUHF general manager at the same salary Cochran received: $28,000 for 12 months. And Cochran sued the university in a case that would not be settled for more than a decade.[12]

Jankowski, who was working on a master's degree in broadcast management at Ohio University, Athens, expanded contemporary talk programs along with the jazz format.

In fall 1982, NPR offered the news magazine, *All Things Considered, Washington Week in Review, Firing Line,* and America's Spanish-language news magazine, *Enfoque Nacional.* Locally, KUHF-FM introduced *KUHF Reports,* a discussion of issues facing Houstonians and Harris County residents, *Beyond the Box Score,* a look at changes in professional sports such as player injuries, contracts and changes in the power structure of athletics, *The State of the Arts,* a program covering Houston's visual and performing arts community, and *Curtain Call*, which reviewed local theater productions. Two programs—*Medicine for Every-body* and *Food for Thought*—reported on better health and nutrition.[13] On Christmas Day 1982, KUHF and a commercial classical music station, KLEF-FM, 94.5 MHz, simulcast in stereo a locally produced version of "The Messiah: A Complete Baroque Rendition," and *Live from the Met: Hansel and Gretel*.[14] These classical music programs foreshadowed what was to come.

During the waning months of Monroe's tenure, "The administration of KLEF came to me and said, 'We want to go off the air.' And I got very upset. 'But,' they said, 'we are hoping that you would pick up. If you want to consider it, we would give you our library.' ... I said, 'Let me ponder it. This is a major decision, because I am certainly very fond of jazz music myself.' And I talked to Judy about it. I said, 'We could sort of do the thing we did at WBHM where we retained jazz.' All our evening programs were jazz. She quickly looked up the surveys and found that most of our jazz listeners were at night anyway.... So I said, 'Let's make the switch because then we can serve both the classical music audience and the jazz audience."[15] In March 1986, the primary conversion serving jazz and classical music listeners took place. However, by September, classical music had completely replaced jazz.[16] With the changeover negotiated, Monroe retired on 31 August 1986, and Jankowski left for WDUQ, Rochester, another radio station with a similar format. John Proffitt succeeded her. Proffitt was with KLEF during the late 1970s and in public radio at WXXI, Rochester, in the early 1980s. KLEF's music director, Rohn Steelman, joined him at KUHF.[17] The conversion was lauded in the halls of the University of Houston System and praised by the board of regents. In addition to KLEF's library, KUHF-FM inherited a devoted audience that is willing to financially support listening to classical music, thus enabling KUHF to reach consistently its fund-raising goals.

On 1 September 1989, at the instigation of System Vice Chancellor Hugh Walker, KUHF-FM was formally transferred to the jurisdiction of the central campus.[18] Legal responsibilities for maintaining its license remained with the UHS, however. The rationale was ostensibly to "improve opportunities for interaction between the radio station and the academic departments, particularly in the arts, that would have the effect of strengthening relations with the Houston arts community and involving the KUHF staff in the cultural life of the university."[19] This goal, already well underway, has been expanded in that KUHF-FM identifies the finest arts activities in the area and promotes them on the air and by means of its monthly *KUHF Radio Guide* that is distributed to listeners who support the station. Distinguished musical events, theatrical productions, international arts festivals, and museum displays are among the activities the radio station identifies for listeners.

A second objective of the UHS policy was to "enable the need for more physical space for the station to be more systematically addressed in the context of the development of the overall campus physical plan."[20] In other words, maybe the station could improve its physical quarters more rapidly by being part of the central campus. As its staff grew to over 30, however, improvement in KUHF-FM's cramped space was obtained only through encroachments into academic space belonging to the School of Communication.[21]

LICENSE RENEWAL, PROGRAMMING, AND PERSONNEL PROBLEMS

While changes in administrators held some public attention, the UHS inherited bigger problems concerning KUHT programming and employment. During the last week of January 1977, the ABC Television Network ran an eight-part adaptation of Alex Haley's novel, *Roots*. The week-long serial was hailed for years as the most watched drama on network television. In February, traditionally designated as Black History Month in Texas, Haley came to the University of Houston's central campus as a featured lecturer sponsored by the Program Council and the Black Student Union.[22] About four months later, on 30 June, 12 individuals representing themselves and various organizations filed a petition with the FCC to deny license renewals for KUHT-TV and KUHF-FM. They were Pluria Marshall for the National Black Media Coalition, Thomas Wright for Operation Breadbasket of Texas, Incorporated, Jan West for Black Citizens for Media Access, Lucious New for Texas Southern University; Madgelean Bush for Martin Luther King, Jr. Community Center, Ernest McGowan, Sr., for the Conference on Minority Concerns, David Hilliard for Pilgrims United for Progress, Arenia Edwards for the Welfare Rights Organization, Barbara Marshall for Urban Theater, Deloyd Parker for Shape Community Center, Sandra Thomas for Alpha Kappa Alpha Sorority, and Elaine Taylor for Creative Artists Society of Houston. The petitioners claimed they would show that:

"1. KUHT-TV/FM has abandoned its obligation to the Black community of the Houston Area.

2. KUHT has intentionally and deliberately employed a 'revolving door' plan to weed out Black employees and has discriminated in its employment practices;

3. KUHT has refused to serve the interest and needs of its total community and has discriminated against the Black community in its programming practices;

4. KUHT has followed a pattern and practice of racial exclusion and has refused to air the activities of Texas Southern University in a meaningful way.

5. KUHT has engaged in commercial practices or activities in the nature of commercial practices which are prohibited by the commission's rules."[23]

The "Introduction" to the petition described frustrations particularly among the city's black citizens. The concerns of nearly 25 percent of Houston's total population were understandable. Apparently they looked to media to do something about "the dichotomy between the circumstances of the white and black residents."[24] According to 1970 census statistics, the income of black families was only two-thirds that of white families and about 78 per cent that of Mexican-American families. Forty per cent of unemployment was black.[25] In Houston, the largest city in the South with a metropolitan area reaching nearly two million and seemingly a strong economy, they believed significant problems existed that needed to be addressed in public forums. License challenges were also presented to three other television stations (Channels 13, 26, 39) and two radio stations (KMJQ, KIKK). Basically, the petitioners' complaints fell into two categories: programming content and control, and employment practices. They wanted more programs that would address poverty and other issues vital to the black community and would encourage discussions between blacks and whites. They sought more involvement in programming decisions. Another issue concerned the hiring and retention of blacks in significant roles at the stations.

Linking the plight of the black economy and its relevance to denying Channel 8 a license was impossible to support. Many of the facts presented in the petition were inaccurate, in part, because the complaining parties were not intimately acquainted with details. The only weekly local public affairs program dealing with minority issues, *Minority Report*, was accused of failing to invite "legitimate" black leaders. The station's response listed 128 black participants appearing within a year, including one of the petitioners.[26] Mexican-American leaders were also on the program. Ten other series often focused on topics important to the black community. Two complaints implied that ACT spent large sums on subjects that might have been better spent elsewhere, when in fact, outside philanthropic groups provided the money. ACT merely administered it.[27] Texas Southern University was named as a petitioner, when in fact, TSU President Granville M. Sawyer wrote that "filing the Petition on behalf of Texas Southern University is unauthorized and does not represent an official position on the issues comprehended by the Petition."[28] The petition claimed that "KUHT is controlled in part by lily white organizations and boards that oppress Black and poor people every day."[29] In fact, from 1 September 1976 through 31 August 1977, ACT's board had "12 women, three black and one Spanish-surnamed individual."[30] One of the black board members was the wife of TSU President Sawyer. After review, on 22 March 1978, the FCC renewed the KUHT and KUHF licenses for three years, finding no reason the stations would not broadcast in the public interest.[31]

About a year after the matter was resolved, Pluria Marshall, executive director, Operation Breadbasket of Texas, Incorporated, reiterated black views to

President Hoffman: "As a state supported institution centrally located in the black community (Third Ward) and having significant input in the development of the inner city, our concerns lie in the areas of the university's responsiveness to blacks, other minorities and women as an urban institution.... However, critical issues within the black community have been virtually ignored and what feedback you have received has been used to justify a continuation of 'window dressing' projects and activities that have failed to address the real problems. Thus, the university has fallen short of its public service commitment. The areas of concern are: ... [among eight] "the availability of the TV station (KUHT) for student training, its shortcoming in terms of accessibility and accountability to the black community, and discrimination in employment at the station; ...Our major concern today is that the university's basic commitment to the enhancement of the quality of life in Houston, the state or in the very community in which it exist [sic] has not been realized."[32]

The FCC, moreover, did show concern for the stations' hiring practices, especially those of Channel 8, and issued only a temporary Certificate of Renewal that was valid until August 1980. It will serve no purpose to review individual black employment decisions that are a matter of record during this period. No government agency ultimately supported any individual claims against the stations.[33] Let it be sufficient to say that under the Bauer administration employment of blacks increased. "In 1974, the station had 47 employees, only two of whom were minorities," the *Houston Chronicle* reported. "The percentage of minorities increased and by 1977, the staff totaled 67, 12 of whom were minorities."[34] Nevertheless, license renewal was contingent upon reporting hiring practices. KUHT was required to provide quarterly reports and to meet three conditions by submitting information to the commission (on 1 April 1979 and 1 April 1980) that included (1) a list of employees hired by the station from the date of the grant (1979) with a breakdown of date of hire, sex, race, and national origin, (2) demonstration of station efforts to recruit minorities in the positions filled during the period, and (3) a report on the final actions in a pending discrimination suit.

The First Quarter Reports filed by KUHT on 1 April 1979 and 1 April 1980 showed a total of 87 employees in 1979 rising to 102 in 1980. Of the total, 19.5 per cent were minority and 39 per cent were women in 1979.[35] These percentages rose to 22.5 per cent and 38 per cent respectively in 1980. An audit of KUHT's hiring practices from 1981 to 1986 showed that the station consistently hired 20 to 25 per cent minority employees; approximately 60 per cent were fulltime, 40 per cent were part time. Women held 42 to 48 per cent of the positions.

Minority complaints had apparently been resolved before the arrival of Dr. Florence Monroe in 1981. "I never had any trouble.... They settled that problem before I got here, and I never had any trouble with the minority community."[36] Instead, other personnel problems required immediate attention. A majority of Channel 8 employees presented General Manager Bauer with a petition asking for higher salaries and improved managerial procedures. "We had a fairly major revolt," Bauer recalled. "There was a lot of unhappiness. A lot of salary unhappiness and unhappiness with some of the individual department practices."[37] Part of it had to do with scheduling programs and auction times.

The salary question was dealt with immediately. "They were losing people," Monroe said. "When I got here I took a look at their budgets. The salaries they were paying the broadcast staff were abysmally low. They were not in keeping with other stations, and I thought that was a disgrace. I mentioned that to the President [Bishop] within the first couple weeks I was here. I said, 'I'm surprised you have anybody. They must be really very dedicated people, but those salaries are so out of line....' So, we got that situation straightened out in a hurry."[38] Typical salaries for principal 12-month staff were in the mid-twenties. The program director, who presumably held the second highest position in the station, made $36,600 (1983). In addition, managerial complaints were overcome by dividing up the responsibilities that had been acquired by Program Director Virginia Mampre. While Mampre retained her role as program director, an executive producer, Miriam Korshak, and a public information director, Jill Pickett, were hired. A development director was already in place—Yvonne Menuet.[39] They had direct access to Bauer. In summer 1983, Mampree was dismissed. She was replaced the following April by N. Steven Gray. Employee departures in 1980 were 39. About half as many employees left in 1985. Personnel concerns lingered as management reported significant strides in the hiring of women and multi-cultural employees during 1991. Yet, key personnel like Bauer, Menuet, Korshak, Pickett, and Senior Producer Robert Cozens remained at Channel 8 beyond the 1980s, providing valuable continuity for station operations. But in 1993, as a budget saving measure, KUHT CEO Jeff Clarke ordered major reductions in staff. "Twelve full-time positions out of a total of 83 and about 20 part-time and contract positions out of 30 were cut. We now have a staff of about 71 full-time employees and 10 part-time employees."[40] From a staff high of over 100 about a decade earlier to just over 70 people illustrated the lean hiring practices and the shift to part-time and temporary workers in the 1990s.

THE IMPORTANCE OF "DEATH OF A PRINCESS"

In 1980, while its license renewal was still pending, its discrimination suits remained unresolved, and its staff was in revolt over wages and internal management practices, KUHT-TV faced a public outcry over its decision not to show "Death of a Princess." PBS was scheduled to feed the program to about 100 stations for telecasting on 12 May 1980. "Death of a Princess" was based on a five-month investigation by journalist and filmmaker Antony Thomas into the execution of a 19-year-old Saudi Arabian princess and her young lover.[41] The two were accused of committing adultery, a capital offense under Islamic law. The story was well documented and filmed on location in London, Egypt, and Lebannon with a cast of leading Arab and European actors. Vice President Nicholson, in what would be his last significant act on behalf of the station, said the program would not be aired: "Certain scenes might easily insult not only the Saudi government but others in the Middle East at a time of great turmoil in that part of the world."[42] *Houston Chronicle* TV-radio editor Ann Hodges agreed: "The problem with *The Death of a Princess* is not production, but timing."[43] President Bishop said Nicholson had complete authority to decide whether the show would run; and University of Houston Board Chairman Leonard Rauch said he personally approved of Nicholson's decision, but no one on the board had any input to it.[44] The controversial docu-drama had already played in Great Britain, where as a result the incensed Saudi Arabian government expelled the British ambassador.

This view was certainly not shared by everyone. Station Manager Bauer and Program Director Mampre felt the two-hour film should be shown, but they went along with their boss.[45] Neither could recall Nicholson canceling a program and overruling their authority. Nicholson said it was the first time he had done it in 17 years.[46] Some critics claimed PBS stood for the "Petroleum" Broadcasting Service, because major oil companies exercised too much influence on public stations through large contributions. After the cancellation former HISD School Board trustee Gertrude Barnstone filed suit against the station. The long-time activist once told the author: "We couldn't let them get away with that." "She and her lawyer, David Berg, argued that state educational TV officials canceled the program for political reasons," *The Washington Post* reported on 10 May 1980.[47] District Judge Gabrielle McDonald issued a temporary order from the bench. She ruled that the Texas decision to cancel the program on state-owned KUHT-TV by an officer of state government was politically motivated and constituted government censorship. KUHT-TV lawyers appealed the judge's decision to the 5th Circuit Court of Appeals which supported Nicholson's position.[48] That afternoon the case was taken to U.S. Supreme Court Justice Lewis Powell who said: "I have consulted informally with each of my brethren who was present at the court when these papers arrived late this afternoon. Although no other justice has participated in the drafting of this order, I am authorized to state that each of the three whom I consulted would vote to deny this application."[49] The station's view was sustained just 80 minutes before air time. "Death of a Princess" was not shown. (At the same time the Turkish community requested and received airtime for two programs.) During the Second Quarter of 1980, Channel 8 received 311 complaints, the most complaints it had ever received. About 100 complaints, many asking to see "Death of a Princess," were filed throughout 1981.[50]

The initial decisions were reaffirmed as the case proceeded through the courts in full trial. In a landmark decision on 30 October 1982 the 5th Circuit Court of Appeals in New Orleans, Louisiana ruled that KUHT-TV would not be legally required to broadcast the film. The U.S. Supreme Court let stand that decision.[51] On 8 April 1983—one month after the final decision—Channel 8 decided to air the program.[52] "It was accompanied by a wrap-around presentation in which Bauer explained the controversy concerning the legal issues and the content of the program.

More than a decade would pass before another PBS program would create such a controversy. In July 1991, *P.O.V.* or *Points of View,* scheduled "Tongues Untied: An Unprecedented Exploration of Black Gay Life," a documentary by Marlon Riggs. Even though the series was scheduled for 11:30 p.m., KUHT management, along with about 20 PBS stations in the 50 top markets and eight state networks, decided not to broadcast it.[53] The film was promptly screened at Houston's Museum of Fine Arts, where interested persons packed the auditorium for two nights. Once again, Gertrude Barnstone and attorney David Berg filed suit, and once again they lost legally, but resurrected the point that KUHT-TV must serve diverse audiences.[54] Homosexual content had appeared on Channel 8; but management insisted this explicit material, shown in other cities, was not appropriate for telecasting on Channel 8. The failure of KUHT to broadcast the few PBS programs that have not lapsed into formula suggested how carefully Channel 8 had to measure the content of its broadcasts so that it did not offend anyone, especially wealthy viewers and corporations. Evidently, KUHT had not established a sufficiently admired and trusted place in the community to air really controversial, and often political, programs and standby them.

PBS TRADEMARK SERIES

Regardless of KUHT's administrative, technical or fund-raising problems, its raison d'etre has been to serve the public interest. Since Channel 8 locked into public fund-raising through ACT, it has managed to sustain itself, in part, by threatening to terminate favorite PBS programs, if viewers did not support them. PBS had provided an array of quality programs. In 1989, PBS celebrated 20 years as the main distributor of enrichment programs, and these fine programs occupied most of Channel 8's evening schedule. Some PBS programs had been so successful that they are still being reedited and re-distributed as special series, "best of" formats, and reruns. Three prominent PBS program categories are the arts, especially theater and music; sciences, mainly human or environmental insights; and information, principally contemporary issues and news. Each program requires funding for the production itself and additional money to distribute and put it on the air. "Underwriters," a term deemed more palatable than "sponsors," are corporations, foundations, individuals, the CPB, and "viewers like you" through memberships obtained in the station's fund-raising campaign.

Attractive as PBS programs may be, a Neilsen report over three randomly chosen months—February, May, July—in 1990 indicated that Channel 8 broadcast about 18 hours each weekday: 33 per cent (6 hours) received a below one rating, 55 per cent (10 hours) were at one, and 11 per cent (2 hours) had a two to five rating. Time periods below one were noon to 5 p.m. and midnight to 1 a.m.; periods with a one rating were 7:30 a.m. to noon and 5 p.m. to midnight, except for prime time hours of 8 to 10 p.m. that ranged from two to five points. A rating point represented about 14,000 households. May was an auction month. A program sampling showed that *American Experience, National Geographic Specials,* and some *Novas* had 4-5 ratings; *American Masters, Adventure, Great Journeys,* and *Mystery!* had 3-4 ratings; *Evening at the Pops, Masterpiece Theatre,* and *Austin City Limits* were mainly at 2; PBS talk shows, childrens' programs, and all local programs had a one or less rating.[55] According to a 1991 KUHT survey, viewers watched *Masterpiece Theatre, Mystery!, Nova, MacNeil/Lehrer NewsHour, Nature,* and how-to programs in that order.[56] PBS earmarked nearly $89.9 million to bring 20 "trademark" series back for the fall of 1992: *"Sesame Street, Mister Rogers's Neighborhood, Nova, American Experience, National Geographic Specials, Nature, Great Performances, American Playhouse, Austin City Limits, Mark Russell Comedy Specials, Evening at the Pops, MacNeil/Lehrer NewsHour, Frontline, Wall $treet Week, Washington Week in Review, The Frugal Gourmet, Victory Garden,* and *P.O.V.*[57] The last program, *P.O.V.,* already mentioned, is an anthology of perspectives—few are controversial—from various producers. By contrast, the works of Ken Burns are vintage PBS, high quality and sponsored by a major corporation, General Motors. Burns produces historical compilations using literary, visual, and sound materials meticulously arranged into an articulate narrative. *The Civil War, Empire of the Air,* and *Baseball* are accounts of American history reminiscent of such early PBS series as *America.*[58]

1992 was a bonanza year for PBS and Channel 8, because the Republican National Convention originated in Houston. PBS had teamed up with NBC to provide in-depth coverage of events and commentary. A similar arrangement was struck for the Democratic convention in New York City. Channel 8 benefited from the utilization of its staff and facilities and the residual equipment that remained when the convention was over. The convention was generally uneventful, but a plank in the Republican platform, stating "We deplore the blatant political bias of the government-sponsored radio and television networks," gave PBS news anchors like Paul Duke of *Washington Week in Review* something to discuss.[59] "It is especially outrageous that taxpayers are now forced to underwrite this biased broadcasting through the Corporation for Public Broadcasting (CPB)," the plank said.[60] The authors wanted sweeping reform, greater accountability, a one-year funding cycle, and an application of fairness standards for all programming. Ultimately, they sought self-sufficiency for CPB. "That plank, if implemented, would end public broadcasting in the United States," wrote the *Houston Chronicle's* Ann Hodges.[61] Congress had already appropriated $1.1 billion for the next three years. The congressional vote was strongly supported by the National Association of Television Arts and Sciences in a resolution that summarized a widely held view of public television: "Whereas the Public Broadcasting Service (PBS) provides a wide spectrum of educational, public affairs, news, documentary, cultural, and dramatic programming...Whereas PBS programming is viewed and enjoyed by more than 46 million Americans during prime-time each month...Whereas PBS provides employment opportunities for thousands of television professionals including producers, reporters, researchers, craftpersons, technicians, and local station personnel...Whereas PBS has been a a leader in recognizing the multi-racial and multi-cultural nature of our society by producing, supporting and airing programming that promotes understanding of diversity...Whereas PBS has shown coverage by providing a forum for controversial and unpopular subject matter at the risk of criticism...Be it resolved that the National Academy of Television Arts and Sciences and its Board of Trustees applaud the members of the U.S. Congress who renewed their support of this valuable American media resource with an authorization of $1.1 billion over the next three years."[62] Convention ratings indicated that the national networks' averages were between 5.7 and 5.8 points, well below commercial programming, and thus, future network coverage may be less extensive, leaving comprehensive coverage to PBS that ranked fourth, CNN, and other cable networks.[63] The call for an end to federal funding of PBS programming has been mentioned with increasing frequency. Types of programs once exclusive to PBS and KUHT are appearing on other stations and cable channels, such as the Family Channel, Turner Network, Discovery, and American Movie Classics. Thus, the question persists: Why should federal tax dollars pay for similar programs?

LOCALLY ORIGINATED PROGRAMS

An established principle in commercial broadcasting is that the identity of a local station is defined primarily through its local programming. For most commercial stations these programs are newscasts, known for reporting local events, investigative features, and most of all, anchors whose high visibility make them local celebrities. These local celebrities are used by the community for fundraising of many kinds and to lend focus to numerous events, such as inaugurations, parades, and festivals. They carry the station image wherever they go. During the first 15 years of Channel 8's local programming, two instructors became prominent—H. Burr Roney and Richard Evans; two newscasters—John Schwarzwalder and Nick Gearhart; and fine arts anchor William Lee Pryor.

KUHT's main programs centered on these persons. Roney's biology series, Evans' interviews with psychologists, Schwarzwalder's discussions with world leaders, Gearhart's conversations with community leaders and interactive call-in series, and Pryor's interviews with major local and national artists were the best models. Since then, KUHT-TV has had few persons project the image of the station or represent the University of Houston to the viewing public, even for its own fund-raising. KUHT's other local series have not depended on personalities that are remembered over a long period. Yet, television is a personality-driven medium. Even many of the best remembered PBS series depend on the continuity of one personality: Carl Sagan, Julia Child, Alistair Cooke, Big Bird. A distinguished series may depend solely on content—*Doctors in Space, People Are Taught To Be Different.* These programs drew upon expertise from the academic institutions Channel 8 served, and they contributed directly to the development of the region. Unfortunately, few Channel 8 programs have preserved these characteristics during the last 25 years, despite recommendations from KUHT's advisory boards.

Initially, the enthusiasm that motivated ACT members was the notion that they would fund important local productions, as well as PBS. ACT constituted a commitment of production funds for exploration and action toward an entire spectrum of community needs that were mostly rooted in the environment, law enforcement, the disadvantaged, and human relationships. It was quickly pointed out that mobile equipment was necessary to effectively make on-location observations; and in April 1972, KUHT acquired a 27-foot air conditioned, self-generating remote truck that was equipped from an $150,000 HEW grant. Its first assignment, a live pick-up of a teleauction art sale at Sakowitz Post Oak store, was beneficial to the station, but insignificant to the public.[64] University of Houston commencement and 25 hours of the Apollo 17 moon walk, not covered by PBS and hosted by Kent Demaret, were what ACT wanted to pay for, and did.[65] During the 1970s, various community programs appeared; but they continued to verify the conclusion: "University stations will have the lowest costs and the least local programming service; state stations will have the highest costs and greatest local service."[66]

On 16 February 1970 *Talk Point: Houston Reaction* became Channel 8's first colorcast from its own studio. A panel of experts and a moderator answered live call-ins regarding controversial national issues involving the Houston area.[67] *Viewpoint* was a series of special programs that enabled visiting authorities an opportunity to discuss ideas with local leaders concerning national developments and their impact.[68] *Assignment Houston* was a live monthly show featuring print media experts given assignments on such topics as Houston militants, prostitution, Office of Equal Opportunity hearings, and school desegregation.[69] *Youth/70* was an in-depth perspective from those under 30 who were knowledgeable about VISTA, youth activities, the underprivileged in high school, and drugs. *International Magazine* was a local replacement for a NET series that used film provided by foreign distributors. Dr. Charles Peavy, an English professor teaching Afro-American literature and KUHT Film Operations Manager/Director Don Lamkin combined their talents for "El Hajj Malik," by New Orleans playwright N.R. Davidson. The colorcast involved ten actors from the Black Theatre Ensemble, a group of college students organized by University of Houston drama major Willie Calhoun and accompanied by guitarist and singer Thomas Meloncon. Meloncon, a South Texas College student and later a well-known playwright, wrote an original composition, "Revolution Time," for the drama.[70] *The Bayou City and Thereabouts People Show*, a 1973 series underwritten by PBS, focused on local activities. Initial productions included moto cross races at Cloverfield outside Houston, the Austin County fair, Friday night professional wrestling, and a rehearsal of Gilbert and Sullivan's *Patience*.[71] In 1974, KUHT Program *Previews*, its original promotional guide, was replaced with a more attractive schedule, expanded feature articles, and improved photographs. The new publication was called *The Public Times* and was paid for with ACT money. By 1975, local programs included *Women's Advocate* with Poppy Northcutt, *On the Line* with Kent Demaret, *Expressions* with Ken Brantley, *Fresh Water Fishing, Texas Style* with Myrtice Driskell and Denver Watham, and *Noticias con Elma Barrera*. James Blue and KUHT were awarded a PBS/NEA Filmmaker-in-Residence grant that enabled Blue, who was co-director of the Rice University Media Center and known for his films about Africa (*The Olive Trees of Justice*, 1962), to become coordinator of a showcase for new talent, *The Territory*. The experimental film series premiered in January 1976 and was produced by Ann Schachtel.[72] By 1977, Australian Robert S. Cozens, a University of Houston graduate, had become director of Film Operations, gaining recognition with *Galveston: The Gilded Age of the Golden Isle*, 1977, and *Elissa*, 1978, an account of the restoration of a 19th century sailing vessel eventually berthed in Galveston.[73] A local sign language series utilizing the expertise of Cindy Cochran premiered in the mid-1970s, and was on PBS and SECA.[74] A series of lectures on human problems and values, *You Gotta Live*, premiering on 17 September 1968, launched John Bradshaw, chairman of Theology, Strake-Jesuit High School, into a media career, and reports about patient concerns in medicine brought Texas Medical Center trauma surgeon Dr. John H. (Red) Duke (*Lifetime*, 1978) to national attention.[75]

Faced with programming complaints from the black community defined in KUHT's license challenge, the controversy over "Death of a Princess," and to be in compliance with the Public Telecommunications Financing Act of 1978, Public Law 95-567, the University Board of Regents reinstated a Community Advisory Board, which traditionally consisted of distinguished citizens mostly involved with broadcasting.[76] In an effort to embrace broader perspectives, the by-laws were amended to add a seventh member, Rabbi Hyman Judah Schachtel,

Galveston: The Gilded Age of the Golden Isle, 1977, was an award-winning film by Robert S. Cozens.

a distinguished Jewish leader, on 5 May 1980.[77] Within six months the Community Advisory Board had a list of five recommendations for the regents. The members reiterated the widely held belief (1) that KUHT-TV and KUHF-FM

Before appearing nationally, Cindy Cochran's *Signing with Cindy* started locally in the 1970s.

should try to originate programs dealing with the area and avoid the tendency to rely chiefly on east and west coast programs that did not adequately recognize diversity, (2) that budgets should be enhanced to allow origination of high quality programs worthy of national distribution, (3) that greater sections of the community such as education, business, religion, and ethnic groups should be surveyed to define viewer interests, and not just ACT, (4) that allocation of program time should be proportioned over major fields—employment, business, economics, government, taxes, history, science, religion, culture, and entertainment, and (5) that Houston experts provide more direct imput into the program decisions of CPB so as to insure properly balanced programs on complex subjects, inasmuch as it is a primary program provider for Channel 8.[78] "We should devote more attention to expanding the influence of our stations beyond Houston to Texas, the Southwest, and the nation."[79] The major fields the board cited got at least one local live weekly, half-hour series on the air during the 1980s. The programs, using various titles over the years, centered on in-studio discussions between hosts, who were frequently commercial television reporters, with guests,

Jim Bernard interviewed Comedienne Lily Tomlin on the *Greenroom,* produced locally during the 1970s and 1980s.

inserts on film or videotape shot on location, and/or viewer call-ins: the arts (*Greenroom*); news and public affairs (*Houston Weekly, On the Record, Friday Local*); minorities, sometimes separated by race (*Interchange, Porter & Company, City Scene*—black, *La Voz Latina, New Visiones/Neuvas Visiones*—Hispanic, *Camera 8, Images of America, Video Magazine*); business (*Dollars and Sense, For Sale: Houston*); medical and legal matters (*Lawyer To Lawyer,* St. Joseph Hospital specials); and education—sometimes monthly (*Projection 80's, Steps To Learning, Educator's Forum*). Some of the most significant programs appeared as needed. The League of Women Voters questioned all candidates, many of whom could not afford television exposure, in "Meet the Candidates," "Election '80," and again for "Election '85." After University of Houston graduate Kathy Whitmire became mayor, she offered five-minute updates concerning her office, and *Eco-Burnout: Houston* looked at ecology issues in the mid-1980s.

Documentaries presented a wide range of local concerns: "Public Housing: Other End of the Rainbow," 1981; "Where Is Our Parade?" 1981, dealt with Houston Vietnam veterans; "Shoplifting," "Arab Women," "Rhumboogie Retrospective," 1982, was a jazz history; "Nam: Still With Us," "The Chemical People: A Local Look" concerned substance abuse; "River of Innocence" involved pollution; "Tribute To Lee Krasner" revealed a man and his art; "Cheng Kung Means Success" showed the lives of Chinese immigrants in Houston; "Healing Hands" revealed miracle healers, all 1983-4; "Forum Club: Michael Novac" targeted U.S. foreign policy; "AIDS" provided current information from the Texas Medical Center; "Gifted Children" explained child development; "Pas de Deux: A Dance of Two Countries" showed ballet training; "Armand Bayou: An Urban Wilderness" was Robert S. Cozens' history of the 1,800 acre wildlife refuge within the city; "The Big Thicket: A Crossroads in the Texas Forest," produced by Paul Yeager, had Texas humorist John Henry Falk narrating the changes that had taken place over decades; award-winning "In the Name of God," 1984, looked at four controversial religious movements, "Long Journey Home" investigated families caring for impaired and/or financially dependent relatives and "From the Darkest Corner" focused on the profoundly retarded. They were produced by Jim Cirigliano.[80] KUHT received an Emmy award for "Child at Risk," written and produced by Dan Grothaus. It was directed by Mark Schiebl. Originally telecast on 26 February 1985, the program explored the psychic roots of pedophilia, an adult aberration involving abuse and exploitation of young children. Although to this point KUHT claimed about one hundred awards for programming, this recognition from the National Academy of Television Arts and Sciences is its most prestigious.[81]

"Child at Risk" was awarded an Emmy in 1985. The production team included (l to r): Mark Schiebl, Carla Reid, James L. Bauer, Dan Grothaus, and Miriam Korshak.

In the 1980s, the most remarkable program change was the termination of GRETA at the end of the spring term in 1985. Founder/director Dorothy Sinclair had retired the previous August. At that time GRETA was serving 57 school districts, and more than half a million students in Houston and the Gulf coast area. With GRETA's demise, the day schedule was promptly filled with PBS repeats, such as *Sesame Street, Mister Rogers' Neighborhood,* and the CBS series, *Captain Kangaroo.*[82]

By the late 1980s, local programming was in further decline. A comparison of the third week in May—the week the station initially went on the air—for 1988, 1990, and 1992 indicated that about two hours a week were devoted to locally originated programs. In 1988, these programs appeared on Sundays: at 3:00 p.m. was *Video Workshop,* the student laboratory showcase, mentioned earlier, featuring local activities and using KUHT studios; at 6:30 was *The Hispanic Family: Between Cultures* that discussed Hispanic education, and at 7:30 was the *Joyce Gaye Report,* an anthology of events in Houston and Galveston. In 1990, there were only two local programs during the survey week: on Sundays, *Video Workshop* and on Thursdays the *Joyce Gaye Report.* On Wednesdays at 8:00 p.m. was *AIDS Quarterly* with Peter Jennings that used local inserts. In 1992, on Friday afternoons was *Almanac,* on Tuesday evenings was *Community.* Both were repeated later in the week. *Almanac* with Betty Ann Bowser and J.D. Houston was

Betti Maldonado (l) and the KUHT crew visited the home of Mayor Bob and Elyse Lanier (r) for *Community,* 1992. Photo: Bob Thigpen.

produced by Ann-Marie Walko and premiered on 26 May 1989. *Almanac* covered important local topics such as illiteracy and homelessness with experts, had guest editorials, and viewer opinion by mail. Bowser who became a network correspondent and Houston were replaced by Patricia Gras in a less lively 1993 edition.[83] *Community* with Betti Maldonado, aired in 1991. For its second season local artist Cathy Boswell had designed an attractive set. Maldonado, who had hosted Channel 8 programs for more than a decade, visited with people (baseball star Nolan Ryan, artist James Surles, a Chinese folk art group) and revealed places that added dimension to living in the region. The 1993 version of *Community* emphasized local themes concerning heroes, artists, children, pets, music, and history.[84] *Arts Alive*, hosted by Adair Lewis Gockley, began in 1989. It showcased individuals, organizations, and events that promoted Houston as a leader on the national arts scene. In 1992, it featured two original dances for the Houston Ballet and the works of Texas artist Robert Wilson.[85] A work-of-love that has continued since the mid-1970s is *The Territory*, which added short fiction, experimental videos, and social documentaries. Hosted at one point by Ed Hugetz and Marian Luntz of the Southwest Alternative Media Project (SWAMP) and jointly produced by Paul Yeager for Houston Public Television, *The Territory* is one of Channel 8's most enduring and memorable series, a tribute to its originator, James Blue. Another collaboration was *Centerstage*.[86] Beginning in 1991, the University of Houston's School of Theatre and Houston Public Television occasionally presented two 15-minute dramas. New talent, adaptations, and original works brought fresh material to viewers. Once again this series is the work of producer Paul Yeager and theater's chairman, Dr. Sidney Berger. Whereas in the 1960s, a "season" lasted 39 weeks, nowadays a network series runs 23 to 26 weeks before reruns begin. Two and three-part programs and seven to 14-week "mini" series have become commonplace, since the novel-for-television was introduced in the late 1960s. Shorter series of presumably higher quality have become a principal tenet in the increasingly expensive world of television programming.

Recent local productions were *J.D.'s Journal*, 1991, with John Davenport producing features from his yellow Volkswagen. *Alan Bean: Off This Earth* centered on the space art of Astronaut Bean, the fourth man to walk on the moon. "Child Abuse: The Perfect Crime," 1989, was a subject that received frequent attention. Robert Cozens' "Living with AIDS," 1990, was a one-hour documentary distributed by PBS; and "Wetlands," 1991, was a film about the Galveston seashore. In 1992, "Anatomy of a Political Convention" revealed how Houston won the 1992 Republican convention; and "Life Along the Channel," produced by Nancy Nascheke Simonds and Janice Van Dyke Walden, was a vivid account of 24 hours on Houston's ship channel, as photographed by Paul Yeager.

After Jeff Clarke assumed the role of KUHT program director from Stephen Gray, who was departing for Washington, D.C., Clarke said: "We've

For *J.D.'s Journal*, beginning in 1991, John Davenport drove around in a yellow VW "bug" to meet interesting Texans.

gone from 85 to about 160 programs. <u>Town Hall</u> series is the benchmark."[87] Clarke, who holds a master's degree from the University of Wisconsin at Madison, immediately became the heir apparent to Jim Bauer. He was hired for $57,600, effective 29 May 1990, and within two years was promoted to interim general manager. The *Town Hall* format of in-depth discussions between a host, experts, and call-in viewers has been a KUHT mainstay for years. "Voices of the Electorate," "Created Equal?: Politics of Race," "Baby Boomers and Beyond: Growing Old in Texas," all 1992, and "Threads in the Fabric: A Town Meeting on Immigration," 1993, were among the topics. From 1989 to 1993, KUHT's locally produced, but nationally distributed, programs included 34 features for the *MacNeil/Lehrer NewsHour*, three for *The Nightly Business Report*, various stories from *Community*, and 11 longer programs.[88]

Former Astronaut Alan Bean talked about *Art Off This Earth* during the 1990s.

REDEFINING THE ASSOCIATION FOR COMMUNITY TELEVISION

The results of ACT's fund-raising drive, including Festival '80, enabled it to give the station over one million dollars, which tended to offset criticism of the station.[89] ACT's fund-raising activities had always been complicated.

Teleauctions involved hundreds of people who not only raised money but also created community awareness of the station. In earlier years the non-profit corporation managed to get donations, to auction them, and to give the money to the station. After much planning, headed by Exxon's Senior Vice President William T. Slick, Jr., President Hoffman and ACT Board Chairman Marty Levine signed an Agreement on 3 August 1977, discussed previously, that offered employment and integration of the ACT staff into the university, and its consolidation with KUHT-TV. ACT's contribution was to develop short and long term fund-raising plans that would continue to support Channel 8.[90]

Within months of the signing of the first ACT Agreement UHS Board of Regents Chairman Aaron J. Farfel and UHS President Philip Hoffman made a joint announcement that the university would probably suffer a "substantial" net loss from short term investments.[91] The loss was several million dollars. What precise effect the loss, resulting in convictions, had on the university and the stations is difficult to determine.[92] Its rippling effect, for instance, may have dampened any plans to develop a College of Communication or to finish equipping the new School of Communication. Neither goal has thus far been attained. In less than two years Director Harwood was replaced and a stringent budgetary policy descended over the School, resulting in minimal building and studio maintainance and classroom support. Likewise, the effect on the stations is hard to pinpoint. Fortunately, radio found relief by becoming a listener-supported classical music station, and in January 1987 KUHT-TV, financially dependent on ACT, weened itself from noticeable relationship to the university by reinventing itself as "Houston Public Television" primarily through its newly designed *Houston Public Television Guide* and on-air identification.[93]

Each year KUHT envisioned certain goals, and ACT got the money for them. In 1982, the station's budget was $3,558,847. Seventy-one per cent came from ACT, including memberships (41%), auction (18%), and underwriting (12%). The remainder came from federal grants (18%), GRETA (8%), and rentals (3%).[94] That same year the need to expand services and yet consolidate its operation for handling memberships, auctions, volunteers, special events, and staff development required the purchase of a pre-fabricated building constructed behind the main studio complex. The funds were generated from a benefit screening of Columbia Pictures' new movie, *Annie*, and in September 1982, ACT was able to donate the building to the university.[95]

On 10 May 1982, after signing the original Agreement between President Hoffman and Chairman Levine, UHS President Bishop and Levine signed a revised version that redefined the previous provisions. The general functions of the ACT board were:

1.   To bear legal responsibility and authority for all aspects of the ACT organization activities;

2. To represent the membership of ACT and to interpret their positions in the activities of the association;
3. To actively support plans for securing financial support for KUHT, the public cultural and instructional television station of the university;
4. And to participate in setting and attaining major objectives and goals of KUHT.[96]

The details of the Agreement tightened control the UHS insisted upon. For instance, the UHS would determine the benefits ACT employees were entitled to. The UHS would decide the need for and effectiveness of volunteer support within ACT. The UHS retained full control over funds and their investment. All grants, especially those related to programming, were to be managed by the university. Allocation of the $25,000 contingency fund was defined and limited to that amount. The reserve fund guaranteeing the operational continuity of KUHT-TV was raised to $200,000. In return, the university promised to account for and report to ACT the use made of its money, and to avoid integrating University of Houston general fund-raising donor lists with the list of donors ACT had already identified. If ACT decided to suspend all fund-raising activities, the UHS wanted 30 days notice, mainly to work out settlements and to transfer any residual funds.[97] The Agreement suggested that although the UHS appreciated the contribution of the ACT organization the UHS did not absolutely depend upon it: "The University of Houston fully expects to continue the operation of Channel 8. The Board of Regents of the University of Houston is the licensee of KUHT and therefore the University must maintain sole control of the broadcast operation of KUHT. The University will continue to encourage broadly-based community support from the Houston metropolitan area for the continued success of KUHT as a public cultural and instructional service in our city and area."[98] The scope of its prestigious membership tended to threaten the UHS with the idea that ACT deserved more than advisory in-put to programming decisions. Perhaps, inasmuch as UHS gave only modest financial support, the Channel 8 license could more effectively serve the public interest, as a community, rather than a university, station. But the UHS wanted total control, not a partnership.

Concurrently, President Nixon wanted annual funding, President Ford sought matching money, and President Ronald Reagan cut Public Broadcasting's allocation by $35 million.[99] The reduction was felt in the 1983-84 KUHT budget of $4,158,320.[100] Federal support declined by about five per cent, GRETA by two per cent, and auction income by one per cent.[101] Consequently, the FCC relaxed stringencies on advertising. By December 1983, KUHT's program guide offered donors who contributed $3,000 or more in tax deductible funds: a "Video presentation (produced by Channel 8) shown at least six times during auction week;

a write up in Channel 8's *Public Times* (circulation 40,000); and a donor listing in newspaper ads." Channel 8 claimed a potential audience of three million in a 90-mile radius. By contrast, it pointed out, a single 30-second spot produced and aired on a commercial station could cost as much as $5,000. Despite cuts, KUHT's budget was about one-half million dollars higher than previously, and viewers were asked to make up the difference.

By 1986, ACT expressed a position that some members had subdued for many years. "We are concerned about the need for KUHT to remain a public television station and not a purely educational outlet for the University. We feel that ACT is responsible for raising the money to operate the station, to purchase the programming, to produce programming and publicize the programming and should participate in the decision-making process. It would seem that in the past twenty years ACT's contributions should entitle the ACT Board, representing the membership in the Association for Community Television, to become a partner of the University as a joint licensee."[102] This was deja vu, except that when the HISD was a joint licensee, the University put up the money. Now ACT, believing it was providing the principal funds, wanted to be a joint licensee, in part so that it could influence such decisions as to whether Channel 8 should construct a new facility off campus. With this sentiment surfacing and the decision to leave the Monroe position—associate vice president for public service and telecommunications—unfilled after her retirement, yet another revision of the Agreement was signed by Bishop and Levine on 20 August 1986, eleven days before Bishop departed.[103] This Agreement did not address the concerns of ACT. It merely tightened university control over funds and asserted its full authority over every aspect of KUHT-TV. The 1986 Agreement included the notice that while ACT may terminate its association with the university in 30 days, the university may do likewise.[104]

For nearly 20 years ACT had attempted almost every kind of fund-raising technique. Membership drives and teleauctions were the main efforts. The teleauction usually lasted for ten nights by preempting ordinarily scheduled programs. On-air displays of items on tables ranged in value from $100 art objects to video sequences offering lush vacations or a David Weekly home in The Woodlands, valued at about $170,000. By 1989, "Quiet Drives" that did not have live spokespersons proved to be efficient and successful for membership renewals and increased individual contributions.[105] New members, however, were more motivated by live call-in pledge drives, which meant spending time on the air. Increased competition from other non-profit organizations, such as food pantries and medical causes, made obtaining auction items more difficult. By the 1990s, KUHT's membership base grew to 57,000 out of a potential 850,000 homes.

In July 1991, a professional fund-raising company was hired to handle a direct marketing campaign. By 1993, the economically affluent public KUHT was seeking to attract was enticed by numerous expensive gifts and benefits. For example, silent telephone bids were made on luxury trips and items in its "Sweetheart Showcase." With regular membership at $40, KUHT did not honor one as a "friend of ACT" unless the contribution was $1,000 or more. "Channel 8 is depending upon individual memberships for 61.5% of the 1993-94 budget," that according to Houston Public Television amounted to $1,675,213.[106] For a $1,500 donation Channel 8 promised production of a spot featuring the item, airing the spot 20 times over a seven-day period, and showcasing it in various publications with a combined circulation of over 400,000.[107] Competition for corporate contributors to public television intensified. Of course, programs required money to produce, to distribute and to broadcast. But most of the fund-raising was for operation and maintenance, not programming. Still, corporations, foundations, individuals, CPB, and viewers contributed large sums. PBS issued revised guidelines that allowed its program sponsors on-air announcements consisting mostly of company logos and voiced presentations lasting about ten seconds as to what product(s) or service(s) a company provided.[108] By the 1990s, some corporations manufacturing many products produced highly sophisticated spots implying, among other values, that the company was imaginative, important, cutting-edge, high quality, and public dedicated by matching employee donations. Often local executives from these companies further demonstrated the company's community spirit by appearing in ACT's on-air fund-raising task and by encouraging employee volunteers to take call-in pledges during drives. If a company's objective was to reach the upper socio-economic leadership demographics, then KUHT seemed like the perfect choice. In response, it sweetened the benefits of corporate support by often mentioning sponsors on the air; and its *Program Guide* linked companies to the station and programs through features and photographs. In January 1982, KUHT-TV listed 24 corporations or foundations subsidizing the airing of programs; in January 1986, there were 47; in January 1992, the number fell to 32. In July 1995 it was 35.[109]

UPGRADING FACILITIES

When the 1980s began, KUHT-TV facilities were out of date. The changes required millions of dollars in capital investment that was provided largely by ACT funds and various federal grants. Principal technical replacements were digital audio for television and radio enabling them to broadcast off the satellite in stereo, completed in 1979 and 1985; portable cameras, 1979; two temporary buildings for ACT, 1973 and 1985; an in-house computer system, 1980; a powerful new transmitter and tower, 1983; a refurbished truck, state-of-the-art studio cameras and videotape machines, 1985.

KUHT-TV's signal is transmitted from a 2,000-foot "tall tower" near Missouri City, constructed in 1983.

"In the early eighties, I'm embarrassed to say, we still had the original quad videotape machines, so there was about a $2 million purchase made in the 1980s that brought us into the area of one-inch videotape machines and got us into professional quality portable cameras," Bauer recalled.[110] Ikegami 79A ENG cameras, a new Harris transmitter for the Alvin site, and one-inch videotape machines for recording and editing programs were purchased with ACT funds and a $530,000 grant from the U.S. Department of Commerce.[111] These purchases were basic to improving the type and quality of programming recommended by the Community Advisory Board."[112]

According to Bauer, "The most significant thing that happened at KUHT while I've been here [was] getting us over on the tall tower."[113] This major effort began toward the end of the Hoffman/Nicholson administration and was completed during the Bishop/Monroe administration. After a series of hearings with the Federal Aviation Administration, approval was given in fall 1981 for the construction of towers over 2,000 feet tall near Missouri City. Channels 13 and 26 began construction with the agreement that Channel 8 would join them, if the money could be obtained.[114] The basic components of the system consisted of an antenna, transmission lines, microwave receivers, transmitter modification, and a new transmitter building. The estimated cost was $1.2 million. Channel 8, being a "pay as you go operation," was unable to borrow money, and so it had to raise it within a brief period. Application was made to the Public Telecommunications Facilities program that funded the improvement of public broadcasting throughout the nation. While the federal grant was delayed in Washington, D.C., President Bishop, the University of Houston Board of Regents, and the ACT Executive Board authorized the purchase of the antenna so that construction plans could proceed on schedule.[115] Channels 13 and 26 contributed $50,000 each to assure Channel 8's participation in the project. The sale of the Alvin site guaranteed added revenue. By the end of 1981, the Channel 26 tower was completed with the Channel 8 antenna located near the top. The federal grant of over one-half million dollars was approved for less than expected; therefore, engineers modified the existing transmitter instead of purchasing a new one.[116] Nevertheless, full power was achieved, a new transmission line was connected, transmitter components were delivered, and by fall 1982, a transmitter building costing $278,309 was constructed on the site near Missouri City. The benefits of the 2,000-foot "tall" tower that went into operation in 1983 were described by KUHT-TV Chief Engineer Al Leverick: "Our antenna height will be moving from 1,167 feet above average terrain to 1,841 feet about average terrain, a net gain of 674 feet. It is estimated that KUHT will be able to provide service to an additional 2,868 square miles and 98,795 people that are presently without service."[117] Circular polarization would help to fill in around buildings and eliminate ghosts. Sharing a location with other major station transmitters would enhance reception, especially for those who did not have outdoor antennas or used second sets with rabbit ears.

On 26 May 1985, KUHT-TV announced that it was the first Houston station to offer many programs in high fidelity stereo. Claiming that this was the first major change in television broadcasting since color, the "quality and dynamic range of the audio signal significantly improve, equaling and often surpassing existing FM stereo broadcasts."[118] For those without stereo receivers or adapters, the sound remained monaural. That fall Channel 8 started a revitalization agenda for the replacement of vintage videotape and camera equipment, some of which had been in operation since the 1960s. Improved on-air image, ease of operation, reduction in technical interruptions, compatibility with new portable equipment, and a refurbished remote unit was bid at $964,302.[119] At an additional cost of $11,200, the television cameras were fitted with color viewfinders.[120]

With a powerful new transmitter, upgraded portable and studio equipment, a refurbished remote truck, and a $1.5 million in-house revitalization, Dr. Monroe made the ultimate request—for a new physical plant. A planning committee was appointed and various designs were forthcoming. The complex, estimated at about $5 million, was to accommodate KUHT-TV and KUHF-FM. She said it would have a three-fold function: the building would centralize production and broadcast facilities, increase technological service, and decrease crowding.[121] Recent advancements in electronic technology meant expanding facilities to include teleconferencing and cable television. According to Monroe, the overcrowded stations needed to be alleviated as quickly as possible. The influential heads of ACT—Chairman Levine and President Mary Faye Way—endorsed a building, but in order for it to be constructed a concerted fund-raising effort had to be mobilized. On 27 April 1988, the board of regents approved a KUHT Fund for Capital Improvement in the amount of $150,000.[122] Although this initiative seemed as though the regents intended to quickly construct a new building, Vice Chancellor Hugh Walker expressed the prevailing attitude toward KUHT: "It is to manage its operations, and to insure that there is the right kind of integrity there. It is to provide—through its governing board—the right kind of governing body to insure its programming is appropriate for all the citizens of Houston. But I don't think it is necessary to go out and raise money. It is to help other people that want strong public broadcast to provide a management means to make sure that the funds are spent for the purposes intended. But from its own funds, no. I don't think the university is ever going to provide direct support to the station. Too many demands on its funds for that to happen."[123] This has been, and remains, the dominant University of Houston position. It is also a difficult position for the general public to comprehend. The public perception is that the University of Houston is the licensee and owns Channel 8, and therefore should budget sufficient funds for KUHT to carry out its responsibility to broadcast in the public interest. If the university is unable or unwilling to meet this obligation, then why should it retain the license? Why shouldn't the

Houston Public Television's Channel 8 has occupied the same location since 1964.

license be reassigned to, say, a community television authority? "KUHT is one of only three stations in major cities owned and operated by a university. It serves 33 counties and reaches an estimated 2.3 million people in a week, according to Nielsen ratings."[124] Channel 8, meanwhile, consciously distanced itself from the university by minimizing its presence in station identification and logos, and by presenting itself instead as "Houston Public Television."

By the end of the 1980s, Channel 8 added more than $500,000 in technical equipment, some of which extended services to special audiences. Just as closed captioning made television accessible to hearing impaired people, Houston Public Television made its programming more accessible to visually impaired and Hispanic viewers. KUHT-TV was the first Texas Gulf coast station to broadcast in stereo and was the first to make these two services available. By utilizing existing separate audio programs (SAP) technology already on thousands of stereo television sets and stereo videotape recorders, Channel 8 began these services on 23 May 1991. SAP is made possible through an additional channel on some stereo receivers or by adding a converter to older sets. *Mystery!*, *Degrassi High*, and *Wonderworks Family Movie* were immediately aired with Descriptive

Video Service (DVS) for people who are visually impaired. Bilingual services debuted with simultaneous Spanish translations of the *MacNeil/Lehrer NewsHour*.[125] In October 1992, Houston Taping for the Blind Radio (HTBR) began broadcasting to Channel 8 viewers with stereo television or videotape recorders. Local newspapers, some magazines, and some television programs were scheduled each month. HTBR is a division of Taping for the Blind, Incorporated, a nonprofit, tax-exempt organization formed in Texas in 1967. KUHT applied for a low power translator to extend coverage to the Golden Triangle, an east Texas area having 106,000 households in Beaumont, Orange, and Port Arthur. Only half of the homes were served by cable and 40 per cent were minority. This 1992 accomplishment cost $160,000.[126] Memberships raised in the three cities offset the expense. The station anticipated the enhancement of its satellite downlink capabilities so that KUHT would be capable of using Telstar 401 for broadcasting a new PBS National Program Service.

PROJECTIONS

After the departure of President Bishop and Dr. Monroe the University of Houston System experienced rapid turnover of top administrators. Finally, three years later, Dr. Alexander Schilt assumed the position of permanent chancellor on 1 October 1989. He immediately made a pledge to carry out five major commitments:

> Commitment to the *fundamentals* of a first-rate liberal arts education through a vigorous rededication to undergraduate education throughout the system;
>
> Commitment to forge stronger *partnership(s)* with Houston in areas such as energy, space, and health;
>
> Commitment to advance *discovery* through nationally competitive programs in research and scientific innovation;
>
> Commitment to ensure *opportunity* through imaginative minority programs and more productive liaison with public schools and colleges and
>
> A commitment to advance the *celebration* of human creativity and expression through exceptional arts programs."[127]

Reporting to the chancellor was the vice chancellor for academic affairs. Dr. Hugh Walker held this post from 1986 until he was replaced by Dr. B. Dell Felder in 1990. Fortunately, while so many changes were taking place at the highest levels of the University of Houston administration, Jim Bauer remained general manager of KUHT. In the spring of 1992, however, Bauer retired. He had been at Channel 8 since 1957, and its manager since 1969. It could be said of KUHT's former managers that John Schwarzwalder was a dynamic politician who organized the first educational television station operation by carrying out President Kemmerer's vision with Hugh Roy Cullen's money; that John Meaney defined and displayed what quality educational programming ought to be; and that Roy Barthold demonstrated how to survive in financially difficult times, caused in part by the university's transition from private to state control. Building on this legacy, Jim Bauer developed a sense of family within the station and community spirit guided by sound fiscal policy that resulted in a balanced budget during every year of his administration. He realized he was responsible for many people whose welfare depended on KUHT's financial stability, and this became his goal, along with the erection of the tall tower. The regents praised Bauer's achievements: "James L. Bauer has over the years earned a sterling reputation for fairness and open-mindedness, quiet but effective stewardship, foresight and vision regarding the potential for public television, infinite patience, and above all, impeccable integrity in all phases of human relations and station operations."[128]

As the 1990s began, a new set of administrators were in place: Dr. Alexander Schilt, as University of Houston chancellor, Dr. B. Dell Felder, as senior vice chancellor for academic affairs, and Jeff Clarke, as chief executive officer and general manager of KUHT-TV. Optimism reigned. Dr. Felder, familiar with Channel 8's place in education and history, joined the university in 1964, rose to professor and chair of the Department of Curriculum and Instruction in the College of Education, and associate dean for graduate studies and research. In 1983, she assumed the role of chief administrative officer for a branch of the University of Arizona, and later moved to become the president of Eastern Washington University. At the Spokane campus she met Alex Schilt. When the position of senior vice chancellor opened up under Schilt's University of Houston administration, the Port Neches native really wanted it: "I don't think any good Texan likes to be away, particularly if it is north of the Mason Dixon Line."[129] As the principal officer over Channel 8, she had said that because KUHT is located on the central campus "people get confused and think it is the U of H's station and it isn't. It is the community's station. The university's board of regents happen to hold the license. While there is a lot of cooperation and synergistic value that occurs because it had an academic parent at a point in time, the University of Houston doesn't own it. It doesn't operate it solely in the interests of the University of Houston. The community owns it. And we operate it, I hope, in faithful stewardship to the interests and needs of the community."[130]

In the early 1990s, besides Schilt, Felder, and Clarke, a fourth administrator had an impact on the direction of Channel 8. Dr. Marguerite Ross Barnett was appointed president of the university central campus on 1 September 1990. A dominant theme of the black educator's presidency was cultural diversity, and she set an agenda that attempted to recognize the values in all people. Of course, many predecessors had spoken about human equality, but Dr. Barnett campaigned for it in speeches, campus conferences, and employment. After being in office almost a year, Barnett became fatally ill, leaving an outline of her legacy for others to complete. It is, therefore, arguably fair to suggest that the recognition, acceptance, and value of human diversity was passed on to Channel 8. Presumably, an important reason for the University of Houston System's continued trusteeship is to protect diversity and human rights through television. Children, teens, and young adults are among those Channel 8 serves.

Sesame Street teaches a lot of kids a lot of things kids need to know, and I think PBS is doing a remarkably good job."[131] Felder believed Channel 8 had a special niche by attracting young viewers through the *Sesame Street* Preschool Education Program (PEP) Initiative, a 1992 outreach series aimed at enriching the education of at-risk children who may require more motivation. KUHT has made great strides toward the acceptance of women, minorities, and the disabled into society; but embracing diversity by including everyone is a goal, not yet an achievement. Those who think and act differently often cause controversy that may or may not get media attention.

With promising expectations, CEO Jeff Clarke drew up a detailed plan for KUHT-TV, endorsed by the University of Houston System, leading to the year 2000. The principal provisions include: (1) increasing local programming to five per cent by mid-decade, producing more national programs, even a nationally identified series from KUHT by 1998; (2) improving KUHT-TV's technical capability to support additional local, regional, and national productions; (3) raising member households to over 80,000, underwriting revenues to $815,000, and special projects support to $375,000; (4) converting all facilities to High Definition Television (HDTV); and (5) improving station growth, employee morale, and relationships with various publics, enhanced by construction of a new broadcast facility. "When the Creative Partnerships Campaign was launched by the Regents, the highest priority that the Regents gave to the systems administration was raising money for a new facility for KUHT."[132] By spring 1993, the University of Houston System announced it had reached over one-half of its $12 million fund-raising effort, and by 1997-8, a new broadcasting complex, the Center for Public Television, is supposed to be completed on the northeast end of the central campus near Interstate 45, close to the site of the original transmitter.

HIGHWAY HAZARDS

By the mid-1990s, Channel 8 faced rising costs in its effort to get into new quarters with a revised estimate at $20 million, of having an annual budget in excess of $8 million raised mainly by ACT, and of broadcasting over 6,500 hours of programming a year depending upon PBS for about one-third of it, with prime time virtually monopolized by PBS.[133] Channel 8 still produced little local programming, despite recommendations to the contrary from community advisory boards and its own managers. Most of its administrators, including some regents, systems and KUHT officials, were new this decade, and they expressed high hopes for expanding viewership and programming. CEO Jeff Clarke was staunchly sticking to his projected plans for Channel 8, described earlier. By 1995, KUHT-TV ratings continued to suggest that it is watched in about 16,000 homes (one share) during most daytime hours and perhaps in over 30,000 to 75,000 homes (2 to 5 share) in prime time. Increasingly, Channel 8's 24-hour schedule included overnight telecourses. Houston's potential audience in the nation's fourth largest city and eleventh largest television market was estimated at 1,574,300 households, meaning one local rating point equaled 15,743 homes, according to Nielsen Media Research.[134] Practically speaking, these figures suggest that viewers may watch Channel 8 briefly before turning elsewhere, but many may remain. The KUHT-TV staff was a trim 70-plus persons and reflected reasonable diversity in its composition.

Channel 8's future, like in the past, remains precarious. Present and projected competition from commercial broadcasters and cable channels imply that a profusion of alternative media options will leave little programming in genre, quality or content that is the exclusive or primary domain of Channel 8 viewers. The struggle to capture viewers with strong local programming is intensifying; KUHT may have been by-passed already. *Post-Newsweek* ownership of Channel 2 promises increased importance to local news, and recently KNWS, Channel 51, went on the air as Houston's first all-news station. With cablecasting at more than 52 per cent penetration in the greater Houston area, programs for news (CNN), finance (FNN), drama (Arts & Entertainment, Lifetime), children (Nickelodeon), and features like the National Geographic series on the cable compete vigorously with KUHT-TV/PBS.

Simultaneously, the PBS trademark programs, several of which are dominated by personalities, are showing their age. What would the *NewsHour* be without Robert MacNeil/Jim Lehrer (MacNeil departed in 1995), *Wall $treet Week* without Louis Rukeyser for whom substitutes have never been effective, or *Mister Rogers' Neighborhood* without Fred Rogers? The creative loss of Jim Henson, and the retirement of Alistair Cooke from *Masterpiece Theatre* contribute to the decline of PBS product. Furthermore, PBS will experience tougher budgetary battles as the question arises, "Is PBS interconnection needed?" The call to eliminate federal funds for PBS, reiterated at the 1992 Republican Convention in Houston, will get louder. A federal funding source for program production, without interconnection, may still be useful, but only if productions could be protected from political squabbles, such as those surrounding the National Endowment in recent years. Aside from an occasional fresh series, such as *P.O.V.*, and the continuation of a few favorite series, what contribution does PBS make to Channel 8? The future suggests that it will have to take a closer look at what it is getting for the one million dollars or so it pays PBS each year.

Channel 8 has numerous daunting perceptions challenging the value of the station to the University of Houston System and the region it serves. Any of these hazards could create huge ruts in KUHT's information superhighway, and they need to be addressed. Most of these concerns, as history indicates, are not new. Interrelated, they may be grouped into three main categories: programming, funding, and relationships with the university and the community.

In regard to programming, the question is what is KUHT's principal objective? Originally it was instruction for the university and HISD and enrichment programs for the public. Now its purpose is less clear. What audience does Channel 8 really serve? Whom should it serve? Improved research defining its present and probable future audience quantitatively and demographically should be a high priority. Perhaps the expertise of appropriate academic departments should be enlisted to assist in this study. One perception is that Channel 8 programs are selected for the few, the well educated, the wealthy, the leadership groups. If so, do these busy people have time to watch a mini-series lasting several successive nights? In Houston, the much-heralded *Baseball* series registered a low 2.5 rating on its Sunday debut, in a market noted for avid sports fans.[135] To assume that viewers could or would devote nine evenings to watch a single series is debatable. But the persistent programming question is whether Channel 8 produces sufficient local programs of quality and depth. Granted, over the years half-hour formats, evenly allocated along racial lines, have been routinely assigned to local affairs. But where are the programs assessing Houston's quality of life, such as cultural and civic trends, governments projects, and progress in petroleum, medical, and space science, areas in which the region excels? Where are the programs that present the best lectures from educators appearing on local campuses? Where is an exemplary instructional television series, a type of direct learning the university and the HISD pioneered? Where are the programs inviting diverse participation from, for example, the disadvantaged or the growing international communities? Where is the news from the more than 30 counties KUHT serves?

Channel 8's heavy dependence on leasing outside productions allows it to fill airtime and to minimize involvement in the principal problems of the metropolitan area. Where is the forum for controversy? Where are the thoughtful, in-depth discussions that a community of scholars should participate in? Isn't it Channel 8's responsibility to provide some of them? And shouldn't that sponsorship be encouraged and endorsed by fund-raising groups along with the university? Channel 8's memorable programs like the HISD School Board meetings of the 1950s and 60s, some of its documentaries, and local candidate presentations are commendable, but there are too few of them.

The University of Houston System has emphasized community partnerships in recent years. Now more than ever, it needs to rethink Channel 8's relationship to community groups, such as ACT, that raise money for the station. Perhaps the university should extend ACT's participation in fund-raising and in assuming responsibility for what is broadcast. Or, perhaps, the time has come for Channel 8's control to be jointly shared by the university and the city, with the eventual establishment of a community authority that would take over the public station. Why should the university regents continue responsibility for a well established public television station, when they have so much to do regarding their academic trust?[136] The regents have spent nearly 45 years nurturing Channel 8, and they have occasionally come to its financial rescue using private funds, due to the prohibition against using tax dollars, mainly with the expectation that the funds would be returned. The regents have provided land, buildings, maintenance, and utilities for the broadcast stations. By 1995, however, the operational budget for Channel 8 had risen to over $8 million, according to on-air fund solicitation or more than twice what it was less than 15 years earlier. For programming, facilities, and capital improvements, KUHT-TV depended upon the community to finance over 60 per cent of its budget, with the federal government, grants, contracts, and other sources covering the remaining costs.[137] As government funds declined in the mid-1990s, Channel 8 asked its viewers to contribute more: "If you don't support Houston Public Television, who will?" fund-raisers asked. Who then should control such an expensive entity? Channel 8 is one of only five stations in the top 21 television markets, representing more than one million households, still licensed to a university.[138] Should the university continue to provide this public service?

If the university continues to retain the broadcast license(s), perhaps a revised Agreement regarding its relationship to the university's branches and the Gulf region should be written. What does "Houston Public Television" represent? What does it mean? Isn't it a synonym for University of Houston System television? What is the intended relationship of the stations to the community? KUHF radio serves a small audience that appreciates and supports through direct solicitation and other contributions classical music and National Public Radio. In 1995, its Arbitron rating was 1.9, or 20th place among more than 35 Houston area radio stations.[139] It does broadcast some university talk and music programs. By contrast, since the late 1980s Channel 8's "Houston Public Television" concept has often come under attack, in part because of a perception that the television station does not seem as positive a public relations vehicle for the

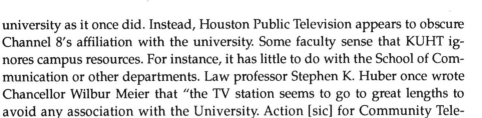

university as it once did. Instead, Houston Public Television appears to obscure Channel 8's affiliation with the university. Some faculty sense that KUHT ignores campus resources. For instance, it has little to do with the School of Communication or other departments. Law professor Stephen K. Huber once wrote Chancellor Wilbur Meier that "the TV station seems to go to great lengths to avoid any association with the University. Action [sic] for Community Television (ACT) has as little as possible to do with the University, and seems to like it that way."[140]

Ironically, instructional television, a sore point historically and excluded from KUHT for nearly a decade, has flourished on the university's closed-circuit Region IV Interact television network. "Ten years after its modest beginning [1984], 215 live classes (103 different classes) have been taught, by 81 professors, to over 9,500 students in the [M.D. Anderson] Library studio/classroom and at remote sites in the metropolitan Houston area."[141] By 1995, once again Channel 8 was telecasting credit courses as an experiment in distant learning. Underfunded, most courses are regressive examples of the telecourses KUHT pioneered. This project has worthwhile potential, but only if it is undertaken seriously. Because telecourses do not have the dynamic benefits of a live presentation, they must take advantage of audio-visual production skills. Poorly produced television classes may even lead viewers to question the quality of teaching at the University of Houston.

By the mid-1990s, the university broadcasting stations and their affiliations with PBS and NPR had reached a turning point. Managements recognize that the nature and requirements of the audience are changing, and the stations must be more responsive to these changes. New relationships will have to be forthcoming. The public will have to take a greater role in paying for the stations' services, in part to balance the increasing support corporations are offering in exchange for more on-air recognition and influence on public stations.

Throughout its history, KUHT-TV has proved that public broadcasting is unique and different from advertisement-supported broadcasting. It has allowed more voices into the media marketplace, has produced and exhibited programs of modest mass appeal for special audiences, and has encouraged controversial subjects. It has been an inspiration in preserving the highest cultural values in society.

In the spring of 1995, the University of Houston System administration under Chancellor Schilt came to a sudden end. Chancellor Schilt, President James H. Pickering, and several other top administrators resigned their posts for various reasons, not the least of which was a challenge by some faculty concerning the place of the system in managing the university campuses and a shift in the political fortunes of the University of Houston relevant to the Texas Legislature and the state's newly elected governor, George W. Bush.

Clearly, at mid-decade, the descendants of a by-gone era had taken over leadership roles at the University of Houston. The new chair of the University of Houston System Board of Regents was Wilhelmina R. (Beth) Morian, Hugh Roy Cullen's granddaughter. Soon thereafter, Elyse Lanier, a former University of Houston student and wife of Mayor Bob Lanier was appointed. They convinced former Lieutenant Governor (1973-91) and Houston resident William P. (Bill) Hobby to assume the post of Interim System Chancellor. Hobby, the son of the late Governor William P. and recently deceased Oveta Culp Hobby, represented another prominent family that has helped to bring the stations into existence and to establish the University of Houston as a dynamic educational institution.

If anything, the future of KUHT-TV promises to be exciting. Regardless of the uncertainties Channel 8 faces, enthusiasm for expanding its community relationships, increasing its funding sources, and improving its programming remains high. If the regents and the new administrators at the University of Houston, and especially, if CEO Jeff Clarke is able to carry out his projected plans that include new facilities, KUHT-TV may claim not only primacy and survival as America's first public television station, but also leadership as the 21st century approaches.

NOTES

PREFACE

1. The pioneer stations are KUHT-TV on the air 25 May 1953; KTHE, Los Angeles, 29 November 1953; WKAR-TV, East Lansing, 15 January 1954; WQED, Pittsburgh, 1 April 1954; also KQED, San Francisco; WHA-TV, Madison; KETC, St. Louis; WCET, Cincinnati. *Educational Television News*, 14 April 1954, 1.

CHAPTER 1

1. U.S. v. Zenith Radio Corporation, 12F.(2d) 614 at 618 (1926).
2. The Radio Act of 1927. Public Law 632, 69th Congress. 23 February 1927. In Frank J. Kahn, ed., *Documents of American Broadcasting*. New York: Appleton-Century-Crofts, 1968, 35.
3. Sydney W. Head, *Broadcasting in America. A Survey of Television and Radio*. Boston, Massachusetts: Houghton Mifflin Company, 1972, 161.
4. Robert W. McChesney, "The Black Hole in U.S. Communications History: The Debate over the Control and Structure of Broadcasting, 1928-1935." Typescript, January 1990, 4.
5. *Ibid.*, 5.
6. Rosel H. Hyde, former chairman, Federal Communications Commission, interview at his residence, Washington, D.C., 22 March 1991.
7. McChesney, *op. cit.*, 19. Published as *Telecommunications, Mass Media, and Democracy*. New York: Oxford University Press, 1993.
8. William P. Hobby (1878-1964) was governor of Texas after James E. (Jim) Ferguson was impeached in 1917 and won the next term. Eventually, he owned *The Houston Post* and KPRC radio and television. Jesse H. Jones (1874-1956) was unparalleled in making Houston a major city. He built 50 commercial buildings, founded Texas Commerce Bank, established Houston Endowment, and published the *Houston Chronicle*. He was head of the Reconstruction Finance Corporation, and later Secretary of Commerce in the Roosevelt Administration. *Houston Chronicle*, Convention '92, Sec. 5, 8-9.
9. McChesney, "The Black Hole in U.S. Communications History: The Debate over the Control and Structure of Broadcasting," *op. cit.*, 19.
10. The Communications Act of 1934. Public Law 416, 73rd Congress. 19 June 1934 (Amended to December 1964). In Kahn, *Documents of American Broadcasting, op. cit.*, 54.
11. *Ibid.*, 69.
12. *Status Report on Public Broadcasting 1973*. Washington, D.C.: Corporation for Public Broadcasting, 1974, 7.
13. Hyde, interview, *op. cit.*
14. Christopher H. Sterling and John M. Kittross, *Stay Tuned. A Concise History of American Broadcasting*. Belmont, California: Wadsworth Publishing Company, 1978, 267-8.
15. *Appointments to the Regulatory Agencies. The Federal Communications Commission and the Federal Trade Commission* (1949-1974). Committee on Commerce, Senator Warren G. Magnuson, chairman. Washington, D.C., April 1976, 18.

16. *Ibid.*

17. Committee on Commerce, *ibid.*, 23. Frieda Hennock succeeded Clifford J. Durr, who declined reappointment. She took office on 6 July 1948 and served one term, to 30 June 1955. *FCC Fourteenth Annual Report*, Fiscal Year ended June 30, 1948. Washington, D.C.: U.S. Government Printing Office, 12.

18. Henry Morgenthau, "Dona Quixote. TheAdventures of Frieda Hennock," *Television Quarterly*, XXVI:2, 1992, 66.

19. Hyde, interview, *op. cit.*

20. Morgenthau, "Dona Quixote," *op. cit.*, 62.

21. Committe on Commerce, *op. cit.*, 25.

22. Sterling and Kittross, *Stay Tuned, op. cit.*, 268-9.

23. Wesley Wallace, "Growth, Organization, and Impact." Chapter in Robert L. Hilliard, ed., *Television Broadcasting. An Introduction*. New York: Hastings House, Publishers, 1978, 13.

24. "Opposition to these reservations was strong but unsuccessful." Dumont and the National Association of Broadcasters were among those opposed. Sterling and Kittross, *Stay Tuned, op. cit.*, 301.

25. Patrick J. Nicholson, *In Time. An Anecdotal History of the First Fifty Years of the University of Houston*. Houston: Pacesetter Press, 1977, 49.

26. At the time Houston's only commercial radio station was KPRC. It was purchased from theater owner Will Horwitz by Governor William P. Hobby and went on the air on 9 May 1925. KTRH, owned by Jesse H. Jones interests, and KXYZ went on the air in 1930. Related activities at HJC included the semi-weekly newspaper, *The Cougar* that started publication before formal courses began and the *Houstonian* yearbook that first appeared in 1934.

27. Walter W. Kemmerer, former president, University of Houston, interview at his residence, La Porte, Texas, 27 July 1991. The bulletin was "Greater Houston Needs the University of Houston," 1938. H.R. Cullen was general chairman of the UH Building Fund.

28. Van Hetherly, "The Signature That Nourished a Baby Giant," *Houston Chronicle*, 1 September 1963, 8.

29. Nicholson, *In Time, op. cit.*, 155.

30. "Last Frontier of Big New Fortunes," *U.S. News & World Report*, 9 March 1951, 17.

31. In 1947 the Houston College for Negroes was ceded back to the State of Texas. It became Texas Southern University.

32. Minutes, UH Board of Regents, Book I, 15 September 1948.

33. In 1947, when Cook took over the Radio department, it had only one faculty member: Evalena Caton. Faculty descriptions from a memo by W.W. Cook, "Meet the New Members of Our Faculty," UH, 1948. Also, Joel Carroll, "Education for Radio," *Houston Chronicle Magazine*, 22 January 1950, 6-7.

34. John C. Schwarzwalder was hired on a nine-month contract as an assistant professor of Radio and Music at a salary of $3,800.

35. Ann Holmes, "Guild Presents Classic Tale of Immortal Love," *Houston Chronicle*, 24 June 1949.

36. *The Houston Post*, 4 December 1949, 3.

37. The technical crew included Walter Coblenz, later a major producer, whose films include *All the President's Men*, 1976.

38. John C. Schwarzwalder, first director, Radio-Television-Film Center, interview at his residence, Austin, Texas, 23 June 1991.

39. Kemmerer, interview, *op. cit.*

40. Ezekiel W. Cullen had been President Mirabeau B. Lamar's floor leader in the Third Congress of the Republic of Texas, 1838-39. As chairman of the Committee on Education, he contributed to an historic report designating a system of free schools. The report became the basis of the Cullen Act, a bill "to appropriate certain lands for the purpose of establishing a general system of education." Nicholson, *In Time, op. cit.*, 157.

41. *The Cougar*, 18 March 1949, 1.

42. Nicholson, *In Time, op. cit.*, 289.

43. *The Ezekiel W. Cullen Building University of Houston*, brochure, 1948.

44. "The U of H Dedicates New FM Radio Station," *The Cougar*, 10 November 1950, 1.

45. This 120-seat studio should not be confused with the main auditorium or the Attic Theatre, a tiny space for experimental plays located elsewhere.

46. Schwarzwalder, interview, *op. cit.*

47. KTRH rebroadcast some KUHF programs. Schwarzwalder was a newscaster for both stations. *Houston Chronicle*, 28 December 1952, 13. One of his students was Tom Jarriel who became a prominent reporter on ABC's *20/20*. Ben Lacy, "Educational TV Grows in Scope," *Houston Chronicle*, 19 November 1954, 12E.

48. *The Cougar*, 10 November 1950.

49. *The Cougar*, 15 December 1950, 1.

50. The Ezekiel W. Cullen Building brochure, *op. cit.*

51. Announcers included Dick Procter, Dan Turner, Lynn Christian, Herman Lensky, Arvil Cochran, Bob Schnarr, Guy Gardner, Bob Gaston, Albert Pavey, James Pinto, Pat Irvine, Ray Lemmon, Phil Zimmerman, W.A. McCaskill, Bill Roller, Jerry Adair, Joe Maranto. *The Cougar*, 10 November 1950.

52. *Houston Chronicle*, 17 April 1953. Following Uray was Raymond T. Yelkin, who died on 31 July 1960, soon after he had won a CBS Foundation News and Public Affairs Fellowship. Accepting the fellowship in his place was his friend, Dan Rather, a graduate of Sam Houston State College, later a distinguished CBS news anchor. Resolution, Raymond T. Yelkin. In minutes, UH Board of Regents Executive Meeting, 27 September 1960, 6.

53. Bob Kingsley, "Departments Furnish Talent, Entertainment for Radio Shows," *The Cougar*, 15 December 1950.

54. William T. Davis, first chief engineer, KUHF-FM/KUHT-TV, interview at the School of Communication, University of Houston, 22 July 1991. Davis, was recognized by alumni and prominent media practitioners John Crow, Lynn Christian, and Charles Whitaker as a Distinguished Alumnus in 1995.

55. *Ibid.*

56. *The Cougar*, 17 April 1953, 3.

CHAPTER 2

1. Minutes, UH Board of Regents, Book II, 17 April 1951, 22.

2. In February 1953, Cook's contract was put on "hold," and he officially resigned as of 1 June 1953. Minutes, UH Board of Regents, Book II, February 1953. "He said he had a Ph.D. from Southern California, which he did not have...and that was that." Schwarzwalder, interview, *op. cit.*

3. Roy M. Hofheinz (1912-1982) was elected Harris County judge at age 24. He became a Texas legislator, and mayor of Houston in the 1950s. He had a principal role in bringing Major League Baseball to Houston and in building the Harris County Domed Stadium, called the "Astrodome."

4. Letter to Mr. and Mrs. John Schwarzwalder ("Ruth & John") from Mayor Roy Hofheinz, 28 November 1955.

5. "This Is Educational Television," a booklet. Washington, D.C.: National Citizens Committee for Educational Television, c. 1954, 15. The conferences at Pennsylvania State College, sponsored by the FAE, began in 1951 and published reports for several years; e.g., "A Milestone in American Education. Preliminary Report. Educational Television Programs Institute," Pennsylvania State College, 20-24 April 1952. Washington, D.C.: American Council on Education;

C.R. Carpenter and L.P. Greenhill, et. al., "Instructional Television Research, Project Number One. An Investigation of Closed-Circuit Television for Teaching University Courses." University Park, Pennsylvania: The Pennsylvania State University, 31 July 1955; "Progress Report. Instructional Television Research Project." University Park, The Pennsylvania State University, Fall 1956-Spring 1957; "Newer Educational Media," University Park: The Pennsylvania State University/HEW Office of Education, 1961. Dr. Kemmerer's attendance is mentioned in John Harris's "Meet Channel Eight," unpublished paper, University of Houston, August 1953, 2.

6. NCCET was formed on 21 October 1952. NCCET and JCET sponsored their first educational television conference on 4 May 1953.

7. "Educational Institutions and Systems Render Public Services through Television," *Higher Education*, Vol. II, No. 15. Washington, D.C.: Federal Security Agency, 1951, 175.

8. Harris, "Meet Channel Eight," *op. cit.*

9. Minutes, UH Board of Regents, Book II, 17 April 1951.

10. W.B. Bates succeeded H.R. Cullen as chairman after his death, a position he held until his retirement on 31 August 1971. Bates was a partner in Fulbright, Crooker, Freeman & Bates (later Fulbright & Jaworski), a prominent law firm. The UH College of Law is named in his honor. "Selfless Servant," *Houston Chronicle*, University of Houston Supplement, 1 September 1963.

11. In October 1951, the HISD filed an application for Channel 8.

12. Sixth Report and Order. 17 Fed. Reg. 3905, 3908. Adopted 14 April 1952, Printed 2 May 1952. In Kahn, *Documents of American Broadcasting, op. cit.*, 554. Also Rosel H. Hyde, interview, *op. cit.* In February 1952, FCC Chairman Wayne Coy resigned leaving a vacancy on the commission. House Speaker Sam Rayburn went directly to the White House seeking the appointment of his nephew, Robert Bartley. In his Senate hearing Bartley promised he would do what he could to thaw the Freeze. Within a month of his appointment, more through coincidence than effort, the Freeze ended. Committee on Commerce, *op. cit.*, 27.

13. *Broadcasting*, 14 April 1953, 23.

14. Committee on Commerce, *op. cit.*, 27.

15. Frieda B. Hennock, "Station KUHT Opens the New Frontier of Educational Television," dedication address, televised on KUHT-TV, Houston, 8 June 1953. Commissioner Hennock had personally delivered the approved application to Kemmerer. Harris, "Meet Channel Eight," *op. cit.*

16. Minutes, UH Board of Regents, Book II, 15 April 1952.

17. John K. Garwell, "School Board Split on TV Station Plan," *The Houston Press*, 23 April 1952, 1; "School TV Plan Hits Obstacle," *The Houston Post*, 23 April 1952.

18. Kemmerer, interview, *op. cit.*

19. *The Cougar*, 18 July 1952, 1.

20. Minutes, UH Board of Regents, Book II, 16 September 1952.

21. "U.H., School Officials Disagree on TV Site," *The Houston Post*, 8 October 1952.

22. Minutes, UH Board of Regents, Book II, 17 March 1953.

23. Maintenance foreman Harvey Wedge was in charge of the reconstruction. Carpentry was done by Sharp Blackman and Elgy Herridge; Johnny Crutcher supervised the painting.

24. *The Cougar*, Special Television Section, 17 April 1953, 1, 5. The control room was the exact floor plan of NBC's Studio 16 in New York.

25. Harold Barron, Guy Ueckert, Richard Albitz, James Page, Joe Sobotik, Gene Sanders, T.D. Shastid, and Gene Rush were on the construction crew. Nancy Watchous, Sara Ewert, Betsy Monday, Shirley Herring, Pat Butler, Loraine Searls, and Martha Cayson gathered props and furniture. Stratton Powell and Donald Blavier worked the special lightboard. Gene Milligan, assisted by students Bill Ham and Jim Culberson, was in charge of art work. Tex Schoffield handled the Line-o-Scribe, a machine that printed title cards. *The Cougar*, 17 April 1953, 6.

26. Davis, interview, *op. cit.*

27. The Associated Press, 8 June 1953.

28. The camera crew, headed by Bob Werbel and Phil Zimmerman, included Paul Kelly, Don Como, Jack Handly, Jim Gardner, Bob Levy, Harold Barron, Rodney Whisenant, Johnie McGaw, Ted Seashore, Morris Adams, Don Merchant, and Glenn Chapman.

29. Billy G. Miller, "Technical Crews Ready For Station Opening," *The Cougar*, 17 April 1953, 6.

30. "Program Schedule of First Week's Programming—May 25 To May 29," KUHT-TV, mimeograph.

31. *The Cougar*, 17 April 1953, 5.

32. Ruthmary Anderson, "First Educational TV Station," *The Texas Outlook*, May 1953, 16. Jim F. Palmer, "School System Prepares for Video Debut," *The Cougar*, 17 April 1953, 1.

33. Proclamation, Mayor Roy Hofheinz, reprinted in *The Cougar*, 17 April 1953, 1.

34. The Associated Press, 1 May 1953.

35. Kemmerer, interview, *op. cit.*

36. *Ibid.*

37. "No Action on Kemmerer Successor," *The Houston Post*, 29 April 1953, 1.

38. *The Extra*, 7 May 1953, 1.

39. Cecil Hodges, "UH Shopping For President," *The Houston Post*, 25 April 1953, 1.

40. *The Houston Press*, 24 May 1953, 28.

41. Paul H. Owen, interviewed by telephone, Antioch, California, 2 November 1991. Director Owen was on a shot of Hennock when she suddenly disappeared from the screen. He panicked. She did not know she was on television; she was looking for her shoes. The incident is also told by Barthold in James Robertson, "An Interview with Roy Barthold," Fort Charlotte, Florida: Robertson Associates, Inc., December 1982. On file: Corporation for Public Broadcasting, Washington, D.C.

42. Hennock, "Station KUHT Opens the New Frontier of Educational Television," *op. cit.*

43. *Ibid.*

44. David Morris, owner, KNUZ, Houston, telephone interview, 7 July 1992.

45. Hennock, "Station KUHT Opens the New Frontier of Educational Television," *op. cit.*

46. William G. Hartley, president, National Association of Educational Broadcasters, letter to the author, 6 March 1968.

47. Karen Childers, "KUHT Begins Telecast In 'Sneak Opening," *Houston Chronicle*, 25 May 1953, 1.

48. *The Houston Press*, 26 May 1953.

49. "Program Schedule of First Week's Programming—May 25 To May 29," *op. cit.*

50. Winston Bode, "KUHT, First Educational TV Station, On the Air," *The Houston Press*, 26 May 1953, 1.

51. "Program Schedule of First Week's Programming—May 25 To May 29," *op. cit.*

52. Schwarzwalder, interview, *op. cit.*

53. At KQED, San Francisco, Dr. Frank Baxter, "The dean of television instructors," hosted a series of Shakespearean plays produced by the BBC. In 1960 broadcasting rights were purchased by NETRC for NET's *The Age of Kings*, which won a Peabody award. A study guide was funded by the Humble Oil and Refining Company. *KUHT Program Previews*, November 1962, 13; *NET News*, Spring 1962, 1.

54. Dr. Richard I. Evans, professor, Department of Psychology, interview in his office, University of Houston, 9 July 1991.

55. "Evans Ready to Start TV Psychology Course, *The Cougar*, 17 April 1953, 6. Evans used a study guide funded by the Humble Oil and Refining Company.

56. Richard I. Evans, H. Burr Roney and Walter J. MacAdams, "An Evaluation of the Effectiveness of Reaction to Programming on an Educational Station," mimeograph, University of Houston, 1953; Richard I. Evans, "Summary of Research Findings Concerning Educational Television at

the University of Houston," 1953. Under the ETRC's first grant for educational television research, Evans formalized his studies: Richard W. Crary, ed., *The Audience for Educational Television*. Ann Arbor, Michigan: Educational Television and Radio Center, October 1957.

57. "Television Without Terror," *The Saturday Evening Post*, reprint, 1955, 4.

58. Schwarzwalder, interview, *op. cit.* In August 1953, Schwarzwalder received a doctoral degree from the University of Houston. His dissertation topic: "An Historical Study of the Legal, Technical and Financial Development of Television."

59. Many journal articles were brief, specific, and varied. These are representative topics from *NAEB Journal*: Peter Carr's "Teaching Mythology and Folklore on Television," *NAEBJ*, November-December 1964; Christopher Kolade's "Hagerstown and Nigeria Cooperate in ETV Project," *NAEBJ*, May-June 1965; Thomas F. Baldwin and Donald G. Wylie, "ITV Rights: Model Policy Statements," *NAEBJ*, May-June 1966; Warren L. Wade's "Let's Program Instructional TV Programs," *NAEBJ*, January-February 1967.

60. In 1953-54, KUHT held workshops for commercial stations in Louisiana, Mississippi, New Mexico, Oklahoma, and Texas. "Welcome To KUHT," a two-week training schedule, mimeograph, 1953-4.

61. "Educational TV Creeps Ahead," *Business Week*, 15 May 1954, 99.

62. "Telecourses KUHT—Channel 8," pamphlet, Fall 1953.

63. *Ibid.*

64. "Factsheet for Educational Journals," Joint Council on Educational Television, 1 January 1955, 1-2.

65. Minutes, UH Board of Governors, 16 June 1958.

66. *Acta Diurna*, University of Houston, 6 February 1957, 2.

67. Minutes, UH Board of Governors, 16 June 1958. Filming for Roney's biology classes was funded by the Educational Television and Radio Center.

68. Reference to *University Forum* in Ann Hodges' column, *Houston Chronicle*, 25 December 1955, Rotogravure; reference to Maxine Mesinger in Hodges' "A UH first: public television," *Houston Chronicle*, reprint, May 1978.

69. *The Houston Press*, 30 April 1956, 15.

70. "School Meetings Going To Be Televised," *The Houston Press*, 15 February 1955.

71. "School Board Meetings on Television a Success," *Better Schools*, 19 May 1955, 1.

72. *Educational Television News*, 15 May 1955. Washington, D.C.: National Citizens Committee for Educational Television, 2.

73. *The Houston Press*, 21 September 1955, 1.

74. "Sound Off: 'Watch the Fights on Channel 8," *The Houston Post*, 20 September 1955.

75. *The Houston Press*, 21 September 1955, 14; *Broadcasting-Telecasting*, 26 July 1955.

76. John W. Meaney, second director, Radio-Television-Film Center, interview at his residence, Austin, Texas, 22 June 1991.

77. *Ibid.*

78. The FAE grant established the KUHT Film Operations unit. "Cameras in the Classroom," *Forum*, 26 September 1958, 5. Minutes, UH Board of Regents, Book III, 20 June 1955.

79. Meaney, interview, *op. cit.*

80. James L. Bauer, station manager, KUHT-TV, interview at KUHT, Houston, 13 November 1991.

81. Minutes, UH Board of Regents, Book IV, 12 June 1956.

82. Meaney, interview, *op. cit.*

83. Schwarzwalder, interview, *op. cit.*

84. *Ibid.*

85. John Meaney, quoted by Vice President and Dean of Faculties Philip G. Hoffman, "Fifth Anniversary Address," KUHT-TV, telecast 23 May 1958, 2.

86. "Cameras in the Classroom," *Forum*, 26 September 1958, 6.

87. *Ibid.*

88. Meaney, interview, *op. cit.*

89. *Educational Television News*, 14 April 1954, 3.

CHAPTER 3

1. *The Houston Post*, 29 March 1953, 1.

2. Morris, interview, *op. cit.*

3. Capital commitments included $175,000 for a building, $310,000 for equipment, and $80,000 for a 749-foot tower that was to be shared with KUHT-TV. Minutes, UH Board of Regents, Special Meeting, 2 September 1953, Book II, 3. In June, KXYZ had been approved for the TV Center.

4. On 17 April 1956, the American Federation of Labor's Education Committee gave KUHT-TV its first fully equipped television remote truck. *The Houston Labor Journal*, 27 April 1956, 3.

5. Minutes, UH Board of Regents, 1 April 1956, Book IV, 84.

6. KPRC-TV, Channel 2, an NBC affiliate, with Jack Harris as vice president and general manager, was already in operation; KGUL-TV, Channel 11, a CBS affiliate, with Paul Taft as president and general manager, went on the air 22 March 1953; KTRK-TV, Channel 13, an ABC affiliate, with Willard Walbridge as general manager, was owned by Mayor Roy Hofheinz and others.

7. Schwarzwalder, interview, *op. cit.*

8. On 13 April 1953, Benjamin Abrams, president of Emerson Radio and Phonograph Corporation, gave KUHT-TV $10,000 for being the first educational television station on the air. He claimed "selfish officials" in many states "are deliberately sabotaging the educational television program." Address and public relations release, Houston, Texas, 13 April 1953. In 1955-56, Channels 2, 11 and 13 gave Channel 8 $10,000 apiece, as reported in *The Journal of the Association for Education by Radio-Television*, February 1956, 23. Within months a Television Advisory Committee was set up, including commercial station heads Jack Harris, Paul Taft, John T. Jones, president of KTRK-TV and the *Houston Chronicle*; John Paul Goodwin, of Goodwin-Dannenbaum, an advertising agency; Roger Jeffery, of Great Southwest Life Insurance Company, representing alumni; Corbin Robertson, of Quintana Petroleum, representing the regents. *Acta Diurna*, University of Houston, 24 May, 1955, 1.

9. "The Cost Structure of Educational Television," mimeograph, University of Houston, 1954, 2-3.

10. *Ibid.*

11. Carl Victor Little, "N.Y. Times Survey Shows KNUT Future Clouded With Doubt," *The Houston Press*, 23 March 1954.

12. Lyndon B. Johnson, letter to John Schwarzwalder, 8 July 1954. The article referred to was "Greater Houston: Its First Million People—And Why," *Newsweek*, 5 July 1954, 38ff.

13. Nicholson, *In Time, op. cit.*, 331-2.

14. Schwarzwalder, interview, *op. cit.*

15. John C. Schwarzwalder, letter to the author, 28 August 1991.

16. Schwarzwalder, interview, *op. cit.*

17. C.F. McElhinney memo to President A.D. Bruce, re: Cost of Radio and Television Operations, 2 October 1956, pp. 1-3.

18. *Ibid.*

19. *Ibid.*, 3.

20. John C. Schwarzwalder, press release, August 1956.

21. *The Houston Labor Journal*, 31 August 1956, 3.

22. Schwarzwalder, interview, *op. cit.*

23. A.D. Bruce, press release, August 1956.

24. KTCA-TV, Channel 2, licensed to Twin Cities Public Television, Inc., Minneapolis-St. Paul, Minnesota, went on the air 3 September 1957.

25. Robertson, "An Interview with Roy Barthold," *op. cit.*

26. KETC, owned and operated by the St. Louis Educational TV Commission, a non-profit corporation, went on the air 20 September 1954.

27. Owen, interview, *op. cit.*

28. Minutes, UH Board of Regents, 10 December 1956, Book IV, 103.

29. *Acta Diurna*, University of Houston, 6 February 1957, 6.

30. John Meaney, letter to the author, 23 June 1991.

31. *Ibid.*

32. Minutes, UH Board of Governors, 20 April 1959.

33. *Extra*, UH Alumni Association, May 1959, 12.

34. *Ibid.*

35. *The Houston Post*, 9 June 1953.

36. John W. Meaney, letter to the author, 8 October 1991.

37. Minutes, UH Board of Governors, executive committee meeting, 26 October 1959.

38. Meaney, interview, *op. cit.*

39. Schwarzwalder, interview, *op. cit.*

40. Minutes, UH Board of Governors, 1 December 1960.

41. During the Kennedy Administration, the 87th Congress, 1961-62, made a number of significant contributions to the development of educational television nationally: The all-channel television receiver legislation covered the more than two-thirds of educational television channels allocated in the UHF range; the Educational Television Facilities Act (PL 87-447) provided matching grants for the construction of educational television facilities; the Surplus Property Law (PL 87-786) enabled educational television stations to receive U.S. surplus property; National Defense Education Act encouraged more effective use of television for instruction. In addition, the FCC established a Division of Research and Education, and its Educational Broadcasting Branch, under Dr. Robert L. Hilliard, promoted and expanded ITFS. "Current Developments in Educational Television." Washington, D.C.: National Educational Television and Radio Center, January 1963, 10-11. By 1977, these FCC activities were dissolved or downgraded. *ETV Newsletter*, 12 April 1976, 2.

42. Minutes, UH Board of Governors, 27 September 1960.

43. *Ibid.*

44. General Chemistry never became a television course; Biology continued to 1965; American Government was aired 1962-65.

45. In *General and Special Laws of the State of Texas*, passed by the Regular Session of the Fifty-Fifth Legislature, H.B.No. 133, Appropriation-General, Article V, Sec. 13, p. 1139. In 1991 this law was reaffirmed by Texas Attorney General Dan Morales, after it was challenged by UHS Chancellor Alexander Schilt. Todd Ackerman, "UH seeks state money to fine-tune Channel 8," *Houston Chronicle*, 26 April 1991, 1. Also, Philip G. Hoffman, former UHS president, interview at the School of Communication, 18 June 1992.

46. "Join Now in the Support of KUHT, Channel 8," the first solicitation of funds, in *KUHT Program Previews*, November 1962. *Program Previews* was first published in March 1962.

47. "Address by Dr. Philip G. Hoffman, vice president, dean of faculties, at KUHT's Fifth Anniversary telecast, Friday, May 23, 1958." This address included a description of The Houston Plan.

48. *Ibid.*, 5-6, and "The Houston Plan," a mimeograph, KUHT Educational TV—Channel 8, UH, c. 1958.

49. *Ibid.*, 8.

50. *Ibid.*

51. In a letter of 19 April 1961 to Colonel Bates and the regents, Chancellor Bruce sought retirement on 31 August, and recommended that the title of chancellor be eliminated.

52. KUHF-FM was assigned a small suite in the Humanities Building, consisting of a reception area, two offices, music storage, news room, two production studios, and master control.

53. Hoffman, interview, *op. cit.*

54. Roy E. Barthold, handwritten notes to the author, 1967.

55. Roy E. Barthold letter to Dr. Patrick J. Nicholson, re: Radio-TV Operations under state support, 22 November 1961, 1.

56. *Ibid.* The exchange of memoranda throughout 1968-69 was extensive.

57. *Ibid.*

58. Roy E. Barthold, memo to Patrick J. Nicholson, c. 1962.

59. Roy E. Barthold, memo to Scott Red, Spring 1962.

60. Solicitation, in *KUHT Program Previews, op. cit.*, November 1962.

61. Paul Owen was rehired as a television consultant for special projects, 1 May 1962.

62. In 1960, KUHT-TV monthly salaries based on 12 months were Roy E. Barthold, $680; James R. Bennett, $450; James J. Byrd, $605; Arvil A. Cochran, $555; George L. Collins, $745; O.C. Crossland, $655; Kenneth K. Edwards, $400; Joseph G. Harrison, $580; Alfred L. Haubold, $530; Bruce Alan Monical, $380; James M. Page, Jr., $500; Frederick W. Smith, $450; Jackie Bo Veres, $320; Frank B. Wood, $495; Raymond T. Yelkin, $665; Charles P. Zimmerman, $465. John W. Meaney was on leave and Ainslie A. Bricker, $595, was on 9 months contract. In the Radio-Television Department Dr. Patrick E. Welch, $800, and Dr. Tom C. Battin, $750, were on 12 months, also. In 1962, KUHT Film Operations listed only Jim Bauer, $720, and Arnold Bergene, chief editor, at $500 per month. Personnel Recommendations, UH Board of Governors, 1960-62.

63. "Informal statistical analysis of KUHT/Channel 8 schedule for 'typical' composite week," mimeograph, February 1963.

64. During 1953-54, faculty taught 15 hours a week and ran KUHT and KUHF; 50 to 75 students volunteered.

65. Patrick E. Welch, "Why Communication Arts?" *Communication Arts Magazine*, Communication Arts Department, Spring 1963, 3.

66. Minutes, UH Board of Regents, 20 June 1955, Book III, 96.

67. Tom C. Battin (1905-87), "A Survey of the Televiewing Habits of School Children," unpublished doctoral dissertation. Ann Arbor, Michigan: University of Michigan, 1951.

68. "KUHF Plans to Broadcast UH Home Baseball Games," *The Daily Cougar*, 12 March 1968, 5; "KUHF-FM airs rock, editorials," *Houstonian*, 1968, 229; Russell Murphy, "KUHF-FM to Air 'Hippie' Series," *The Daily Cougar*, 11 October 1967, 3; ""KUHF Plans To Increase News Coverage," *The Daily Cougar*, 14 February 1968, 3." Several radio students became prominent; e.g., Bill Worrell, sports anchor; Ron Selden, disk jockey; Luis DeLlano, Mexican television; Clement Diei, NBC/Nigerian television; Robert Ritchey, station owner; Lyn Salerno, television administrator.

69. The author's annual reports on KUHF-FM, forwarded to Dr. Patrick Welch, 1966-69. In a memo to Nicholson, Barthold claimed FCC and legal responsibility for FM; but "KUHF is at present 100 percent student operated, through the Communications department.... "Under the present student operation, Dr. Hawes is responsible. He is an experienced broadcaster and is quite competent to make judgments related to overall University policy and to FCC rules....In fact, my considered opinion is that student involvement in radio (or TV) broadcasting at the University of Houston is peripheral on all counts.... Gentlemen, the question is not who is going

to run it—the question is whether there will be an FM station next year." Roy E. Barthold, memo to Patrick J. Nicholson, 5 December 1968.

70. Author's report to Dr. Wilbur Schramm, as requested by Roy Barthold, 10 March, 1966, 1-4.

71. Patrick J. Nicholson, memo to Dean Alfred R. Neumann, Subject: Laboratory Facilities and Personnel for Department of Communications, 23 August 1968; President Philip G. Hoffman, memorandum to Patrick J. Nicholson, Subject: Laboratory Instruction for Students in Communications Department, 18 September 1968; Roy Barthold, memorandum to Dr. Patrick J. Nicholson, Subject: Committee on Communications Laboratories, 24 October 1968; Patrick J. Nicholson, memorandum to President Hoffman, Subject: Separation of Radio-Television-Film Center Production and Broadcasting from Laboratory Instruction for Students in Department of Communications, 15 January 1969. In a Nicholson to Hoffman memorandum dated 27 January 1969, Nicholson concluded that the ad hoc committee Hoffman asked for recommended that KUHT-TV be separated from departmental laboratory responsibilities and that "KUHF-FM should be looked upon as a minimal operation, retained primarily for possible expansion of overall RTFC operations...."

72. Robert F. Ritchey, letter to Ben Waple, 24 February 1969; "Phi Chi Alpha, Lanyard Serve," *Houstonian*, 1968, 230. George L. Collins, memo to Patrick J. Nicholson, re: KUHF Application to FCC for Frequency Change, 17 February 1969. Marvin Rosenberg, letter to Ben Waple, FCC secretary, with application for frequency change, 5 February 1969.

73. Patrick J. Nicholson, memo to Dr. John C. Allred, 6 March 1968.

74. Patrick J. Nicholson, memorandum to President Hoffman, Subject: Separation of Radio-Television-Film Center Production and Broadcasting from Laboratory Instruction for Students in Department of Communications, 27 January 1969, *op. cit.*

75. Carol Hames, "Channel 8 denies time to UH labs," *The Daily Cougar*, 9 March 1973, 9; *The Daily Cougar*, 21 September 1972.

76. "We are one of 11 universities in the country with an American Council on Education for Journalism—accredited sequence in radio and television, and we have the only such accreditation in Texas. Most colleges and universities do not attempt technical television courses with broadcast-grade equipment; our ability to provide such equipment for laboratory instruction had undoubtedly been a major factor in ACEJ accreditation and in the wide acceptance of our graduates." Nicholson memorandum to Hoffman, Subject: Separation of Radio-Television-Film Center Production and Broadcasting from Laboratory Instruction for Students in Department of Communications, 27 January 1969, *op. cit.*, 2. "Journalism Accreditation Report: Accrediting Committee on American Council on Education for Journalism," mimeograph, 11-12 December 1972. Radio-Television (General) is recommended for accreditation by meeting minimal standards only.

77. *Effort Toward Excellence: The University of Houston Self-Study*, prepared for The Commission on Colleges of the Southern Association of Colleges and Schools, March 1966, 319.

78. *Ibid.*

79. *The Cougar*, 8 September 1965, 1.

80. Hoffman, interview, *op. cit.*

81. Joyce Weedman, "College Course Teaching by TV May Return Here," *Houston Chronicle*, 18 June 1967, 3:3.

82. *Ibid.*

83. "KUHT Film Productions," a list of productions to 1972, typeset; *The Houston Post*, November 1968.

84. "On April 4, 1969, Dr. Denton Cooley made medical history when he implanted an artificial heart in the chest of Haskell Karp at St. Lukes Episcopal Hospital in Houston." The heart Cooley used was developed by a research team headed by Dr. Michael DeBakey, president of Baylor College of Medicine. "The Heartmakers," *KUHT Program Previews*, November 1969, 3.

85. Quoted in "Critical Issue," a KUHT press release, 11 August 1969.

86. "The Arts in Houston," *KUHT Program Previews*, March 1962, 1-2. The author produced the series briefly in 1967.

87. "KUHT—its future," *EXTRA*, UH Alumni Association, 1963, 4.

88. *KUHT Program Previews*, May 1964, 2.

89. KUHT's first transmitter mounted on the oil derrick tower located at the northeast end of the campus was removed at no charge to the university in exchange for the value of the steel.

90. Willard E. Walbridge, letter to the author, 15 February 1968.

91. James C. Richdale, letter to the author, 18 January 1968.

92. *Ibid.*

93. The regents approved the university's FCC application for a full-power (316 kilowatt) transmitter for KUHT-TV in conjunction with its application to HEW (under Public Law 87-477) for expanded coverage at its regular meeting on 16 March 1964. HEW approved the grant in August: Nicholson, *In Time, op. cit.*, 438-9.

94. Minutes, UH Board of Regents, 18 January 1965.

95. Patrick J. Nicholson, letter to viewers, 11 September 1964.

96. Minutes, UH Board of Regents, 7 February 1967.

97. In January 1967, when KHTV, Channel 39, went on the air, it asked the author to produce a student oriented series like one he had originated for sister station KTVT, Fort Worth-Dallas. The result was the University of Houston Television Workshop series, for which the author was executive producer and Dr. Tom C. Battin was executive director. The original colorcast, *College News Conference*, 1967-69, featured students talking to celebrities such as Houston Symphony Conductor Andre Previn and Television Sitcom Director Bud Yorkin. *News on Campus*, 1969-75, aired on both Channels 39 and 8, gave students more opportunity to develop their skills on and off camera.

98. As early as 5 April 1966, the regents approved an application to HEW for a $300,000 grant for color; the UH was expected to have to put up $50,000. Carolyn Perroni, "Regents Approve Bid for Color on KUHT-TV," *The Daily Cougar*, 6 April 1966, 1.

99. The grant took longer than expected. KUHT was unable to produce its own color programs until 1970.

100. In 1963, the FCC opened 31 channels in the 2,500-2,690 megahertz frequency range for use by educational institutions and organizations. This system called Instructional Television Fixed Service (ITFS) combined aspects of on-air and closed circuit television by allowing buildings in a school district to be linked by cable and microwave. "Notable among the districts is the Spring Branch Independent School District, which was awarded two private channels in 1965. The station, KRZ-68, transmits its signal from a control sending tower to receiving towers located in 27 different school sites within the district. Instructional television is received in all classrooms on channels 7 and 9. Programs are repeated seven times a day according to a pre-determined schedule. The studio complex with vidicon cameras, videotape recorders and a 16 mm film chain is $70,000." "Magic Carpet Media," *Houston*, May 1969, 22.

101. "In-School Television," *KUHT Program Previews*, November 1963. This issue is devoted to HISD television and describes classes in Spanish and physics, among others.

102. "Background Material on KUHT," news release, KUHT-TV, c. 1966.

103. "GRETA Forms To Provide ITV On Coop Basis," *GRETA Progress Report*, March 1966, 1. In 1964, the UH provided $20,000 in initial support.

104. Robertson, "An Interview with Roy Barthold," *op. cit.*

105. "GRETA Forms To Provide ITV On Coop Basis," *GRETA Progress Report, op. cit.*, 1, 6.

106. "A Bill To Be Entitled," S.B. 149, Texas Legislative Service. Introduced by Senator Richter and Representative Hale, 1 February 1965.

107. "GRETA Projected Budget 1965-66," GRETA *Progress Report*, March 1966, 5.

108. *Teacher's Manual for Instructional Television Classes*, GRETA, 1966, title page.

109. Minutes, UH Board of Regents, 7 February 1967.

110. Vice President Nicholson notified the regents that the administration was readying a proposal seeking Channel 14. *Ibid.*

111. "Advantages of Instructional Television," GRETA *Progress Report*, March 1966, 2.

112. *Teacher's Television Manual for Instructional Television Classes, 1966-67.* Houston: GRETA, 1966, i.

113. Various guides were printed each year; e.g., *Teacher's Manual for Instructional Television Classes—Primary Grades*, another manual for Elementary Grades.

114. Robert F. Ritchey, "The Preparation of the Classroom Teacher's Guide for the Gulf Region Educational Television Affiliates," unpublished paper, 15 May 1968, 5.

115. "1967-1968 GRETA Schedule," booklet. Houston: GRETA, May 1967, 14.

116. Course descriptions based on "Summary and Annotation of GRETA Television Series," 1967-68.

117. Minutes, UH Board of Regents, 29 October 1969.

118. *KUHT Program Previews*, January 1968, 6.

119. Minutes, UH Board of Regents, 7 February 1977.

120. SETINA's charter members were Lamar State College of Technology, Texas Southern University, Sam Houston State College, Prairie View A&M University, Texas A&M University, Stephen F. Austin State College, University of Houston, Alvin Junior College, Blinn College, Lee College, San Jacinto College, Wharton Junior College, Brazos Junior College, College of the Mainland, Galveston Community College. In October 1968, the regents were told that the Texas Coordinating Board of Higher Education would look with favor upon a request from the university to form SETINA and that "such an association would not involve any expenditures on the part of the University." Minutes, UH Board of Regents, 1 October 1968. An application was prepared on 16 October 1970.

121. *Ibid.*

CHAPTER 4

1. Jim Robertson, *TeleVisionaries*, Charlotte Harbor, Florida: Tabby House Books, 1993, 90.

2. John F. White, president, National Educational Television, letter to the author, 8 March 1968. George L. Apply, NET's vice president for network affairs, cited KUHT "as the oldest member of our family...." in a letter to Roy Barthold, 21 May 1968.

3. Shelley Brandes, letter to the author, 31 January 1968.

4. Sterling and Kittross, *Stay Tuned, op. cit.*, 332.

5. Frederick Jauch, "A True Fourth Network: Why and How," New York: National Educational Television and Radio Center, 1962, 10.

6. Richard B. Hull, "A Note on the History Behind ETV," in *Educational Television The Next Ten Years*. Stanford, California: The Institute for Communication Research, 1962, 335.

7. Brandes letter, *op. cit.*; *KUHT Program Previews*, November 1967, 1; *KUHT Program Previews*, September 1966, 2.

8. In spring 1968, insufficient funds cut *Mister Rogers' Neighborhood* (a.k.a. *Misterogers' Neighborhood*) to twice weekly. The Junior League funded one season with a plea for the public to support it in the future. *KUHT Program Previews*, September 1968, 1.

9. *Public Television: A Program for Action*. Report of the Carnegie Commission. New York: Harper & Row, 1967, vii.

10. *Ibid.*, 1.

11. "The Carnegie Commission's Public Television Proposal," in *Documents of American Broadcasting, op. cit.*, 576.

12. "President Johnson's Message to Congress," in *Documents of American Broadcasting, Ibid.,* 582.

13. Frank Stanton, statement to James R. Killian, Jr., CBS press release, 25 January 1967.

14. Hyde, interview, *op. cit.*

15. Hartford N. Gunn, Jr., "Public Television Program Financing," *Educational Broadcasting Review,* October 1972, 283-308.

16. Marilyn A. Lashner, "The Role of Foundations in Public Broadcasting, Part I: Development and Trends," *Journal of Broadcasting,* Fall 1976, 537 & 546.

17. "Welcome to the Chicago Educational Television Center—(Home of WTTW/Channel 11 and WXXW/Channel 20)," pamphlet, c. 1965, 2.

18. James L. Bauer, Grant Proposal, Section III, Exhibit 4A(b), University of Houston, 16 October 1970.

19. Arthur L. Singer, Jr., "The Carnegie Report Revisited," *Educational Broadcasting Review,* August 1971., 10.

20. Richard K. Doan, "Bring on the Sons of Sesame Street," *Educational Broadcasting Review,* August 1970, 6.

21. Dr. John C. Schwarzwalder, "Public Broadcasting Must Clean House," *TV Guide,* 20:40, 30 September 1972, 6.

22. *Ibid.,* 8-9.

23. Association for Community Television/Channel 8, "A Brief History," information summary, 1977, 1.

24. *Ibid.*

25. Lashner, "The Role of Foundations in Public Broadcasting, Part I: Development and Trends," *op. cit.,* 532-533.

26. Julia Child's cooking series first appeared in 1963 as *The French Chef.* "Julia Child & Company," *The Public Times,* November 1978, 5.

27. "Sesame Street," *KUHT Program Previews,* November 1969, 2; "It's so good that commercial stations want it; and they are getting it in various locations," according to George E. Blair, "The Haunted House of Public Television. Reconceptionalizing ETV's Self Image," *Educational Broadcasting Review,* October 1970, 6. "Mister Rogers' Neighborhood," *February on Channel 8,* February 1975, 2.

28. Vincent Terrace, *Complete Encyclopedia of Television Programs 1947-1979.* South Brunswick, New Jersey: A.S. Barnes and Company, 1979, 160.

29. Kenneth Clark, *Civilisation, A Personal View.* New York and Evanston, Illinois: Harper & Row, Publishers, 1969. This illustrated book is based on scripts from his television series.

30. Alistair Cooke hosted *Masterpiece Theatre,* PBS's most popular anthology, for 21 years. His last appearance was 29 November 1992. *Houston Chronicle,* 22 July 1992, 1D.

31. *PBS News,* Special Edition, Fact Sheet, October 1977, 1.

32. *Ibid.*

33. *Ibid.*

34. Michael G. Reeves and Tom W. Hoffer, "The Safe, Cheap and Known: A Content Analysis of the First (1974) PBS Program Cooperative," *Journal of Broadcasting,* Fall 1976, 549.

35. *PBS News,* Special Edition, *op. cit.,* 3.

36. "Happy 25th Birthday," press release, University of Houston, 1978.

37. *PBS News,* Special Edition, *op. cit.,* 3.

38. Laurence A. Jarvik, "Masterpiece Theatre and the Politics of Quality: A Case Study," unpublished doctoral dissertation. Los Angeles, California, University of California at Los Angeles, 1991, 471.

39. "Great Performances," *November on Channel 8,* November 1976, 4.

40. "News in Depth on The Robert MacNeil Report," *August on Channel 8,* August 1976, 3.

41. On 3 March 1974, *Nova* debuted with "The Making of a Natural History Film." It featured the life cycle of fish. "NOVA," *March on Channel 8*, March 1974, 5.

42. *The Public Times*, November 1981, 6.

43. John Bustin, "The Schedule," (*Austin City Limits*), program schedule, Southwest Texas Public Broadcasting Council, reprinted in *January on Channel 8*, January 1976, 3.

44. "American Indian Artists," *August on Channel 8*, August 1976, 2.

45. "Wall $treet Week," *The Baltimore Sun*, 25 November 1973, reprint.

46. "Join Now in the Support of KUHT, Channel 8," envelope enclosure, in *KUHT Program Previews*, March 1962. Classification ran from $10 for "subscribers" to $100 for "sponsors."

47. *KUHT Program Previews*, September 1966, 1-2.

48. Robertson, "An Interview with Roy Barthold," *op. cit.*, 17-18.

49. Roy E. Barthold died on 8 March 1982, as director emeritus, RTFC. "In Memoriam—Roy E. Barthold," UHS Board of Regents, 12 July 1982, 123.

50. James L. Bauer, general manager, KUHT-TV, interview at KUHT-TV, 3 November 1991.

51. Bauer, *ibid*.

52. Bauer, *ibid*.

53. After Philip Hoffman became University of Houston president, the RTFC was administered under the Office of Development headed by Vice President Nicholson. Since Meaney's departure, no one was named director, RTFC, until 1967. Then, Barthold held the title until his retirement in 1969. Nicholson "assumed the post of acting director of the Radio-Television-Film Center in addition to his other responsibilities...." "Bauer Appointed KUHT-TV Manager," *Acta Diurna*, 13 November 1969, 4. Throughout the 1970s, Nicholson was frequently listed as director, RTFC, in *The Public Times*. When the University of Houston System was formed, Nicholson became vice president for Public Information and Television. Minutes, UHS Board of Regents, 2 April 1978.

54. Patrick J. Nicholson was hired on 16 April 1956, as executive director of development, for $725 a month. In 1957, he was made vice president for development at $920 a month. In September 1960, as vice president, University Development, he was paid $1,125 per month.

55. *KUHT Program Previews*, December 1969, 1.

56. *Ibid.*, 2.

57. *KUHT Program Previews*, January 1970, 1.

58. *KUHT Program Previews*, March 1970, 1.

59. James L. Bauer, Grant Proposal, "Anticipated First Year Operating Costs," Section III, Exhibit 6C, 12 October 1970.

60. "Important Events in KUHT-TV History," typeset, Association for Community Television/ Channel 8, revised 13 May 1983; Minutes, UHS Board of Regents, May 1983.

61. According to Barthold, he had $10,000 to $20,000 that Vice President McElhinney knew about when Nicholson asked for seed money from President Hoffman.

62. Nicholson, *In Time*, *op. cit.*, 464.

63. Bauer, interview, *op. cit.*

64. "Important Events in KUHT-TV History," *op. cit.*

65. "Background of the Association for Community Television," statement, typeset, c. 1986, 1.

66. *Ibid.*

67. Bauer, interview, *op. cit.*, 3 November 1991.

68. *Ibid.*

69. Robert U. Haslanger, president, United Gas Pipe Line, was ACT president.

70. Minutes, UH Board of Regents, 1 May 1973.

71. "The PBS Convention in Houston," *March on Channel 8*, March 1975, 2. PBS held its first mem-

bership meeting outside of Washington, D.C. in Houston in January 1975. ACT membership was frequently reported to the regents: Minutes, UH Board of Regents, 7 February 1977.

72. "Important Events in KUHT-TV History," *op. cit.*

73. "The University of Houston/The Association for Community Television/KUHT Reorganization Agreement," 3 August 1977.

74. *Ibid.*

75. Minutes, UHS Board of Regents, 9 February 1977.

76. Minutes, UHS Board of Regents, 21 August 1978.

77. Minutes, UHS Board of Regents, 12 September 1977.

78. John J. O'Connor, "Public Television Highlights Its 25 Years," *The New York Times*, 19 March 1978, D:33.

79. On the occasion of the 150th *News on Campus* program, President Hoffman presented a plaque to KHTV Vice President and General Manager Crawford Rice for "Distinguished Contribution to Broadcasting Education," *Houston Chronicle*, 20 March 1971, 6:1. From 1975-84 the series was retitled *Campus Workshop*. Since its move to Channel 8 in 1984, the magazine format is called *Video Workshop*.

80. "Regents OK reorganization plan," *Acta Diurna*, 7 February 1974, 1. On 15-17 March 1974, the National Association of Broadcasters and Broadcast Educators Association held their conventions in Houston. The appearance of President Nixon, educator access to several FCC commissioners, conversations with celebrities like Rod Serling, and tours of NASA and the central campus drew favorable attention to the Communications Department.

81. "Preliminary Report of the Steering Committee," *Mission Self Study*. University of Houston Central Campus, September 1975, 14.

82. *Ibid.*

83. Minutes, UHS Board of Regents, 6 June 1977, 3.

84. *Ibid.*

85. Dr. Harwood had a 12-month appointment. Minutes, UHS, Board of Regents, 3 August 1979.

86. *Acta Diurna*, 6 November 1975, 1. By the time the complex was equipped, it cost about $6 million.

87. In 1978 Gus S. Wortham, founder of American General Insurance Corporation, gave an unrestricted gift of one million dollars to the University of Houston "to express his wife's appreciation for the privilege of serving on the Board of Regents...." Minutes, UHS Board of Regents, 2 February 1976.

88. In 1967 Jack Valenti initiated a series of central campus visits with distinguished directors, the first being Norman Jewison who had just completed *In the Heat of the Night*.

89. "Ella Fitzgerald and Dick Cavett Celebrating the Twenty-Fifth Anniversary of Channel Eight," at the Museum of Fine Arts, Houston, program, 25 May 1978. "Channel 8 Celebrates 25th Anniversary with Special Programming," *News from 8*, news release, 25 May 1978, 2. Betty Ewing, "Ella and Dick and strawberry mousse at Ch. 8 party," *Houston Chronicle*, 28 May 1978, 10:8; Susan Linner, "Houston's KUHT, public TV now 25 years old," *The Dallas Morning News*, 22 May 1978, reprint; Janis Parks, "8 + 25 = 1. Houston public TV silver anniversary saluted," *The Houston Post*, 29 May 1978, 1B.

90. "KUHT Archival Roll," log of film segments, 1978, 1-7.

91. "A Proposal for Commercial Underwriting of Channel 8's 25th Anniversary Celebration," solicitation, KUHT, 1978; "Budget for the 25th Anniversary Celebration," typeset, KUHT, Spring 1978.

92. Patrons financing the evening's dinner were Exxon Company USA, Fayez Sarofim & Company, First City National Bank, Galveston-Houston Company, Highland Resources, Incorporated, Houston Natural Gas Corporation, Edward J. Hudson, Shell Oil Company, Lloyd H. Smith, Southern National Bank, Transco Companies, Incorporated, Vinson & Elkins.

93.   Minutes, UHS Board of Regents, 21 August 1978, 14.

94.   UH Office of Information, release, 10 July 1978.

95.   Ann Holmes, "Channel 8's tribute on 25th birthday," *Houston Chronicle*, 24 May 1978, 8:11.

96.   Minutes, UHS Board of Regents, 21 August 1978, 14.

97.   Minutes, UHS Board of Regents, 5 February 1979.

98.   Unexpectedly, President Hoffman retired sooner than he intended, because for the first time the regents failed to support a Hoffman appointment—Dr. Joseph Champagne as interim Chancellor UHD. In executive session, the regents appointed Hoffman senior advisor, UHS Educational Planning. Dr. Robert Maxsom was appointed interim president, UHS. Minutes, UHS Board of Regents, executive session, 26 September 1979. Also Hoffman interview, *op. cit.*

99.   "Expansion of Television and Radio Operations Planned by UH System," UH Office of Public Information, 10 July 1978, 1-4.

100. Dr. Nicholson retired as special assistant to the president on 31 August 1981.

CHAPTER 5

1.   Nicholson, *In Time, op. cit.*, 436.

2.   *Ibid.*, 457.

3.   UHS vice presidents for academic affairs: Dr. Joseph E. Champagne, 1978-1980; Dr. Martha Piper, 1980-1981 (both interim); Dr. Robert C. Maxson, 1981-1984; Dr. Hugh Walker, 1984-1990; Dr. B. Dell Felder, 1990–1995.

4.   KUHF-FM was administered by the Radio-Television-Film Center, but after 1978 it was housed in the Communication Building. The UHS continued to provide legal and engineering services, especially at the transmitter site.

5.   Philip G. Hoffman, interview, *op. cit.*

6.   *Ibid.*

7.   "UH Appoints New Administrator. Will Oversee KUHT," *The Public Times*, April 1980, 2.

8.   Dr. Florence Monroe, associate vice president for public service and telecommunications (retired), interview, River Cafe, Houston, 30 January 1992. Also William Carlyle Holland, "KUHF-Houston's Newest 100,000 Watt FM Station, *The Public Times*, April 1980, 13.

9.   KUHF ordered a new transmitter, with $50,000 in special purpose funds and $68,000 in CPB funds for full power and official affiliation with National Public Radio. Memo to Hoffman from Nicholson, in Minutes, UH Board of Regents, 10 September 1979, 23. Also, Holland, *ibid.*

10.   Arvil Cochran was terminated, effective 31 August 1981. Minutes, UHS Board of Regents, personnel recommendations, September 1981.

11.   Florence Monroe, interview, *op. cit.*

12.   Arvil Cochran told the author the law suit was settled in 1994.

13.   *The Public Times*, September 1982, 4.

14.   KLEF(FM) went on the air 1 November 1964. In the 1980s the 100 kilowatt station was owned by Entertainment Communications, a group owner, and had a classical music format. John Proffitt was operations manager.

15.   Florence Monroe, interview, *op. cit.*

16.   John Proffitt, station manager, KUHF-FM, interview, at KUHF-FM, 25 July 1992.

17.   Florence Monroe, interview, *op. cit.*

18.   Minutes, UHS Board of Regents, 23 August 1989, 157.

19.   *Ibid.*

20.   *Ibid.*

21. In the late 1980s, KUHF usurped office/hall space adjacent to the instructional television studio, ruining the approach, and in 1994, took over one of two rooms used for teaching film production.

22. "'Roots' author to lecture," *Acta Diurna*, 17 February 1977, 1.

23. Petition to Deny Renewal of Broadcast Licenses, before the Federal Communications Commission, Washington, D.C., in re: Application of the University of Houston Licensee KUHT-TV and KUHF-FM, Houston, Texas, filed 30 June 1977.

24. *Ibid.*, 4.

25. *Ibid.*

26. Opposition to Petition to Deny Renewal of Broadcast Licensees, before the Federal Communications Commission, Washington, D.C., in re: Application of University of Houston, Houston, Texas, for Renewal of Licenses of KUHT(TV) and KUHF(FM), Houston, Texas. File Nos. BRET-6, BRED-69. Attachment 1-8.

27. *Ibid.*, 19-20.

28. Affidavit of Granville M. Sawyer, 9 September 1977.

29. Petition to Deny Renewal of Broadcast Licenses, *op. cit.*, 7.

30. Opposition to Petition to Deny Renewal of Broadcast Licenses, *op. cit.*, 16.

31. Richard D. Marks, letter with FCC Memorandum Opinion to James L. Bauer, 25 April 1978; Minutes, UH Board of Regents, 22 May 1978.

32. Pluria Marshall, letter to Office of the President, 17 April 1979, 2.

33. Cause #75H644, filed by Jeannine Wilkins and related to EEOC proceedings filed on 19 June 1974; EEOC Charge Number 064813228, filed by Yvonne C. Johnson, 16 September 1981.

34. *Houston Chronicle*, 31 March 1978, 16:1.

35. Minutes, UH Board of Regents, 7 May 1979. Quarterly reports were submitted for two years beginning with: "Quarterly Report of KUHT-TV for April-June, 1979, to the Board of Regents," submitted by James L. Bauer, station manager. Approved in Minutes, UHS Board of Regents, 10 September 1979, and regularly thereafter.

36. Florence Monroe, interview, *op. cit.*

37. James L. Bauer, general manager, KUHT-TV, interview at KUHT, 4 February 1992.

38. Florence Monroe, interview, *op. cit.*

39. James L. Bauer, interview, *op. cit.* Yvonne Menuet became development director in March 1979. *The Public Times*, March 1979, 16.

40. "Public Television Announces Reorganization," UHS Creative Partnerships *Newsletter*, Summer 1994, 4; Rich Levy, "KUHT/KUHF receive funding boost from UH System campaign," *UHouston*, 5 March 1993, 1.

41. "World Special. Death Of a Princess," *WORLD*, PBS Press Kit. Boston, Massachusetts: WGBH-TV, 12 May 1980.

42. *The Houston Post*, 12 May 1980, 2A.

43. Ann Hodges, "Ch. 8 did the right thing in refusing to air 'Princess'," *Houston Chronicle*, 5 May 1980, 1:23.

44. *Houston Chronicle*, 20 August 1980, 7.

45. *The Houston Post*, 21 August 1980, 27A.

46. KUHT, news release, typeset, 1 May 1980.

47. Fred Barbash, "Court Orders Airing Of Protested TV Show," *The Washington Post*, 10 May 1980, 20:1.

48. Pat Bailey was university counsel, Richard D. Marks of Dow, Lohnes & Albertson, a Washington, D.C. law firm, was special counsel.

49. *The Houston Post*, 13 May 1980, 1.

50.	Compiled from *KUHT Quarterly Reports* to the UH Board of Regents, 1980-1981. KUHT received 1,272 calls: 539 supported the station, 733 opposed it, 5 wanted their membership money back, but the station refused. *The Houston Post*, 16 May 1980.

51.	"High court lets stand ruling in UH case," *The Houston Post*, 8 March 1983, 4B. Attorney David Berg said that the decision was typical of this Supreme Court involving Civil liberties. "We are disappointed, but not surprised." *Ibid*.

52.	Jill Pickett, "Channel 8 Opts to Air Controversial DEATH OF A PRINCESS," KUHT news release, March 1983.

53.	*The New Voice*, 5-11 July 1991, 28; Dwight Silverman, "8 of 12 Texas stations bar film on black gays," *Houston Chronicle*, 17 July 1991, 11A.

54.	*Houston Chronicle*, 20 June 1992, 6D; "Don't Silence PBS's Voice," *Electronic News*, 24 June 1992, 14.

55.	*Nielsen Station Index, Houston, TX.* Metered Market Service, February, May, and July 1990.

56.	*Houston Metropolitan*, Channel 8 Guide, October 1991, 112.

57.	Ann Hodges, "Good Stereotypes," *Houston Chronicle*, 30 May 1992, 4D.

58.	By the time Ken Burns' nine-part series, *Baseball*, premiered on 18 September 1994, he was also producing documentaries on how he made his documentaries. *Program Guild*, Houston Public Television, September 1994, 22.

59.	*Houston Chronicle*, 18 August 1992, 6E.

60.	Ann Hodges, "GOP blasts public TV," *Houston Chronicle*, 18 August 1992, 6E.

61.	*Ibid*.

62.	*NATAS* [National Association of Television Arts and Sciences] *News*, 16:2, Summer 1992, 3.

63.	The four night average rating was 3.3 for PBS/NBC and 1.9 for CNN. Ann Hodges, "PBS scores political victory," *Houston Chronicle*, 24 July 92, 1:6E.

64.	"The $16,000 donation which paid for the truck was contributed to ACT in part by the Moody Foundation, The Foley Foundation and individual gifts of local leaders." The truck cost $13,000; lighting, $12,000; installation, $1,000. Remote equipment on the truck was $150,000 paid for by an HEW grant. Sandra Meineke, UH news release, 26 April 1972.

65.	From 1967-72, the author hosted the University of Houston commencements on KUHT-TV. Ann Hodges, "Specials Galore, But Ch. 8's Moon Coverage Tops 'Em All," reprinted from the *Houston Chronicle, January on KUHT*, 1973, 4.

66.	James A. Anderson, "Public Television in 1976: A Projection of Station Operations and Costs," *Journal of Broadcasting*, 18:2, Spring 1974, 242.

67.	*Program Previews*, May 1970, 8.

68.	Grant Application, Section III, Exhibit 4D, University of Houston, 12 October 1970.

69.	*Program Previews*, October 1970, 3.

70.	*Program Previews*, April 1970, 4.

71.	"Houston: TV Looks at Houstonians," *February on KUHT*, February 1973, 4.

72.	"Channel 8 Awarded Grant," *July on Channel 8*, July 1975, 3.

73.	"The Gilded Age of the Golden Isle," *June on Channel 8*, June 1977, 2.

74.	"Signing with Cindy," *October on Channel 8*, October 1975, 2. Cindy Cochran did the news in sign language for KTRK-TV, Channel 13.

75.	"Houston's Own Stars," *KUHT Program Previews*, September 1978, 2.

76.	Letter to Dr. Patrick J. Nicholson, from Pat Bailey, university counsel, re: By-Laws Amendment to Community Advisory Board, 9 April 1980.

77.	Minutes, UH Board of Regents, 5 May 1980.

78.	"Report of Community Advisory Board of KUHT & KUHF," Minutes, UH Board of Regents, 3 November 1980.

79. *Ibid.*

80. *Public Times*, December 1984, 13.

81. The 100 awards are mentioned in Houston Public Television and the Association for Community Television invitation to James L. Bauer's retirement reception at KUHT, 30 March 1992. Between 1981-91 KUHT received 67 awards and recognitions by actual count: "KUHT Production Awards and Honors," list, c. 1991, 1-9.

82. *Public Times*, September 1984, 2. GRETA was classified as a UH public service. Its funds were restricted to the purchasing of airtime on KUHT-TV. GRETA's only income source was the pro-rata share each school district owed. Minutes, UHS Board of Regents, 2 March 1981.

83. In 1993, Jeff Clarke claimed 50 to 75 faculty appeared on *Almanac*. A year later the program was cancelled. Ericka Schiche, "KUHT, KUHF more than call letters to UH," *The Daily Cougar*, 9 June 1992, 1.

84. *Program Guide*, Houston Public Television, October 1991, 104.

85. John M. Moore, "Arts Alive '89," *Program Guide*, Houston Public Television, June 1989, 96.

86. Ann Hodges, "Local drama lights up Channel 8 stage," *Houston Chronicle*, 2 October 1991, 3D.

87. Jeff Clarke, interim general manager, KUHT-TV, currently CEO and general manager, interview at KUHT, 29 June 1992.

88. "National Distribution of KUHT Local Productions," list, c. 1992, 1-3.

89. Between 1 September 1979 and 7 April 1980, ACT raised $1,091,000. Minutes, UHS Board of Regents, 5 May 1980.

90. "The University of Houston/The Association for Community Television/KUHT Reorganization Agreement," 3 August 1977. The ACT staff was transferred to the university and functioned under KUHT's Development Department as of 1 September 1977. In Opposition to Petition to Deny Renewal of Broadcast Licensees, before the FCC, Washington, D.C., *op. cit.*, Attachment 1, 3-4.

91. "University experiences loss on investments," *Acta Diurna*, 12 January 1978, 1, 4.

92. "Safe Investments," *Houston Chronicle*, 10 August 1994, 20A.

93. Since 1987 the widely distributed *Program Guide* carries the cover reference Houston Public Television, but no mention of the University of Houston System. It was delivered as a supplement of *Houston Metropolitan Magazine*.

94. *The Public Times*, May 1982, 5.

95. For $250 a Daddy Warbucks guest could attend a cocktail party, dinner at the Waldo Mansion, and see the premiere. *The Public Times*, May 1982, 2-3.

96. "Agreement between the University of Houston and the Association for Community Television," signed by Charles E. Bishop, UHS president, and Marcella L. Levine, chairman, Board of ACT, 10 May 1982, 4.

97. *Ibid.*

98. *Ibid.*

99. "Introducing his administration's proposal for long-range financing of public broadcasting in 1975, President Gerald R. Ford stated: 'To assure that Federal support does not dominate public broadcasting, and to encourage continued non-Federal contributions, the Federal funds would be provided on a matching basis.' Subsequent legislative authorizations of funds for public broadcasting all have featured matching provisions. In 1982-83, the Reagan administration cut public broadcasting funding from $172 to $137 million. *Final Report*. Temporary Commission on Alternative Financing for Public Telecommunications, 1 October 1983, 2, 4.

100. *The Public Times*, December 1983, 3-4.

101. *Ibid.*, 7

102. "Background of the Association for Community Television," ACT statement, c. 1986, 2.

103. "Resolution in Appreciation. Charles E. Bishop," Minutes, UHS Board of Regents, 12 August 1986, 34.

104. "Agreement between the University of Houston and the Association for Community Television," signed by Charles E. Bishop, UHS president, and Marcella L. Levine, chairman, Board of Directors, ACT, 20 August 1986.

105. Fund-raising took on many forms: on-air and silent auctions, membership drives, contests, sports tournaments, "dream" packages, gifts and mail solicitation. Money from these sources was conveyed to UH as grants: 1975, $259,475; 1976, $400,000; 1977, $600,000; 1978, $1,667,566; 1979, $1,529,982; 1980, $1,926,344; 1981, $2,225,110; 1982, $2,644,937; 1983, $2,927,330; 1984, $3,400,484; 1985, $4,100,910; 1986, $3,571,385; 1987, $4,149,113; 1988, $4,028,761; 1989, $4,157,941; 1990, $4,118,126. Source: Price Waterhouse for Association for Community Television.

106. "You Make It Happen," *Program Guide*, Houston Public Television, March 1994, 21.

107. *Ibid.*, 24.

108. Jeannine Aversa, "PBS might air shows at same time," *Houston Chronicle*, 5 June 1994, 12F.

109. *The Public Times*, January 1982, 17; *Public Times*, January 1986, 6; *Program Guide*, January 1992, 71. "As the new PBS fall season approaches, a number of series and specials lack corporate underwriters. Companies that associate with public television enhance their image and reach an educated and influential group of viewers." *Program Guide*, Houston Public Television, September 1990, 105.

110. Bauer, interview, *op. cit.*, 4 February 1992.

111. "Important Events in KUHT-TV History," ACT chronology, revised 13 May 1983.

112. "Report of theAdvisory Board of KUHT & KUHF," Minutes, UHS Board of Regents, 3 November 1980, 35.

113. Bauer, interview, *op. cit.*, 4 February 1992.

114. James Bauer, "New Antenna Scheduled," *The Public Times*, September 1981, 2.

115. *Ibid.*

116. Minutes, UHS Board of Regents, 28 June 1987.

117. Al Leverick, "A Report from the Chief Engineer," *The Public Times*, November 1981, 5.

118. *The Public Times*, June 1985, 7.

119. Minutes, UHS Board of Regents, 13 August 1985, 61.

120. *Ibid*, 62.

121. *Public Times*, June 1984, 6.

122. Minutes, UHS Board of Regents, 27 April 1988, 17.

123. R. Hugh Walker, former UHS senior vice chancellor, interview at the Conrad N. Hilton College of Hotel and Restaurant Management, University of Houston, 20 July 1992.

124. Todd Ackerman, "Fund-raising campaign set to make waves at Channel 8," *Houston Chronicle*, 6 January 1993, 16A.

125. "New Channels of Communication. Channel 8 First Texas Gulf Coast Station to Offer SAP Audio Services For Visually Impaired and Hispanic Viewers," news release, Houston Public Television, May 1991.

126. Application for low power translator to extend service to 106,000 households in the Golden Triangle. Minutes, UHS Board of Regents, 24 April 1991.

127. Minutes, UHS Board of Regents, 24 October 1990.

128. "Resolution of Appreciation for James L. Bauer," UHS Board of Regents, 19 February 1992.

129. B. Dell Felder, UHS senior vice chancellor for academic affairs, interview, UHS office, 30 July 1992.

130. *Ibid.*

131. *Ibid.*

132. "KUHT Television, University of Houston System, Mission Statement," 1992.

133. Jeff Clarke, CEO and general manager, KUHT-TV, telephone conversations, 12 & 14 September 1994.

134.   Mike McDaniel, "Channel 2 again home for MDA telethon," *Houston Chronicle*, 31 August 1995, 6D.

135.   Mike McDaniel, "'Baseball' scores nationally but not in Houston," *Houston Chronicle*, 21 September 1994, 8D.

136.   "Members Opportunities," *Program Guide*, Houston Public Television, October 1994, 15.

137.   "KUHT-Houston Public Television," Quarterly Report for 1 March 31 May 1992. Minutes, UHS Board of Regents, 24 June 1992, 77.

138.   The other universities are: WABU, Boston (6th largest market), licensed to Boston University; WHMM, Washington, D.C. (7th), Howard University; WUSF-TV, Tampa-St. Petersburg (16th), University of South Florida; KAET, Phoenix (21st), Arizona State University. *Broadcasting&Cable Yearbook*, 1994. New Providence, New Jersey: R.R. Bowker, 1993.

139.   "The figures represent the percentage of all Houston listeners turned in to their radios during an average daytime period." *Houston Chronicle*, 7 August 1995, 2D.

140.   Stephen K. Huber, professor of law, letter to Wilbur Meier, UHS chancellor, 16 June 1987, 1. Also mentioned was the possibility of selling KUHT's VHS allocation for a large sum and then continuing service on a less expensive channel. The profit would be applied to Channel 8's benefit. No dialogue of consequence resulted from this idea.

141.   "The View from Beneath the Park," newsletter, University Media Services, University of Houston, fall 1994.

INDEX